Focus-Group Research for School Improvement

What Are They Thinking?

Joseph D. Latess

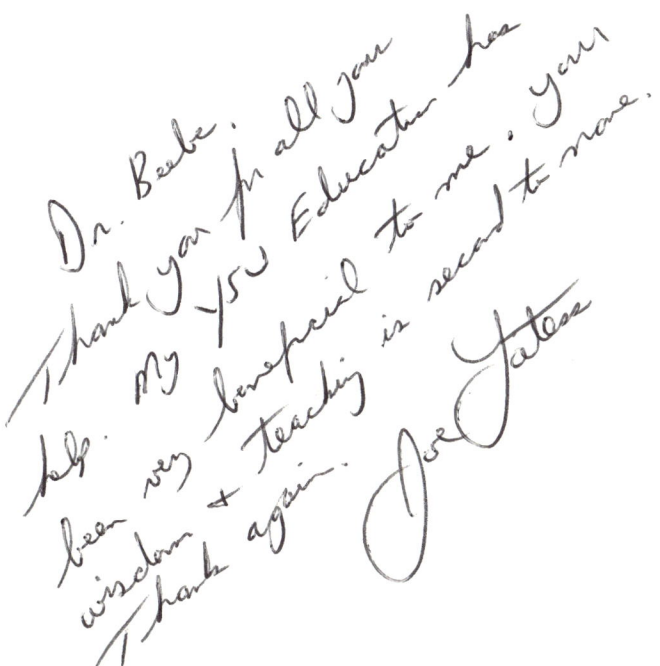

Rowman & Littlefield Education
Lanham • New York • Toronto • Plymouth, UK

Published in the United States of America
by Rowman & Littlefield Education
A division of Rowman & Littlefield Publishers, Inc.
A wholly owned subsidiary of The Rowman & Littlefield Publishing Group, Inc.
4501 Forbes Boulevard, Suite 200, Lanham, Maryland 20706
www.rowmaneducation.com

Estover Road, Plymouth PL6 7PY, United Kingdom

Copyright © 2008 by Joseph D. Latess

All rights reserved. No part of this publication may be reproduced, stored in a retrieval system, or transmitted in any form or by any means, electronic, mechanical, photocopying, recording, or otherwise, without the prior permission of the publisher.

British Library Cataloguing in Publication Information Available

Library of Congress Cataloging-in-Publication Data

Latess, Joseph D., 1956–
  Focus-group research for school improvement : what are they thinking? / Joseph D. Latess.
      p. cm.
  Includes bibliographical references.
  ISBN-13: 978-1-57886-780-6 (cloth : alk. paper)
  ISBN-10: 1-57886-780-0 (cloth : alk. paper)
  ISBN-13: 978-1-57886-781-3 (pbk. : alk. paper)
  ISBN-10: 1-57886-781-9 (pbk. : alk. paper)
  1. Education—Research—Methodology. 2. Focused group interviewing. I. Title.
  LB1028.L287 2008
  370.7'2—dc22
                                                                    2007049629

∞™ The paper used in this publication meets the minimum requirements of American National Standard for Information Sciences—Permanence of Paper for Printed Library Materials, ANSI/NISO Z39.48-1992.
Manufactured in the United States of America.

Contents

Acknowledgments		v
Introduction		1
1	Schools as Organizations	5
2	A Brief History of Focus-Group Research	7
3	Silenced Voices	9
4	Causes for Silence	11
5	Efforts to Hear the Voices	16
6	The Focus-Group Process: An Ideal Method for Breaking the Silence	21
7	Focus-Group Design	24
8	Procedures for Conducting Focus Groups	29
9	Social Constructions and Context Underlying the Focus-Group Process	34
10	Data Presentation and Action-Plan Development	42
	Focus-Group Case Study #1	44
	Focus-Group Case Study #2	120

11	Application of the Process: The Focus-Group Process Tool	227
12	Other Tools of the Trade	231
	Participation Request Letter	232
	Statement of Participation	233
	Sample Interview Guide	234
	Sample Focus-Group Questions	235
13	Reflections	238
References		241
About the Author		242

Acknowledgments

This book is the product of some special people who have helped me to persevere in many aspects of my life. I express my deepest appreciation to:

My parents, Anthony and Rosemary Latess, for guiding me from childhood through adulthood, teaching me the morals and values that have permeated my life and have made me one with a desire to help people and to love others for who they are.

My brothers, Anthony, Dennis, and Robert Latess, who through their actions have always served to give me inspiration and ambition to give my best.

My loving wife, Carleen, who has been the support I needed to continue with this book and has provided the opportunity to discuss and discover what is truly important in life.

My children, Vinnie, Arianna, Anthony, and Zane. Your inspiration provides my motivation.

Dr. Glorianne Leck, my colleague and friend. She has provided me with inspiration to pursue conducting focus-group research and is one who surely listens to the voices of others.

Introduction

In April 1983, the report of the National Commission on Excellence in Education declared the United States a "nation at risk" in regard to student academic performance, particularly in the areas of math and science. Concerns for raising academic standards continued and were fueled by national and international reports of the failure of American students. In addition, the current educational accountability movement grew out of the national education goals of 1989 and the publication of national standards by various professional organizations such as the National Council for Teachers of Mathematics, National Science Teachers Association, and the National Council for Teachers of English. Today, forty-nine states either have in place or are developing content standards in at least three of the four core subject areas of mathematics, science, English language arts, and social studies. In order to be accountable, school systems as recipients of public funds have an obligation to demonstrate that they are doing their jobs and that their students are in fact learning. If they fail to do so, it is reasonable for the public, parents, and legislators in particular to demand change.

Administrators need to be careful in assuming that the reasons for increases in achievement or successes with other school programs are a direct result of their efforts. Leaders should be cautious and check viewpoints of others. There is a tendency of school officials to think they are the leaders in setting standards and the pressure they bring to bear on their staff is the impetus for school improvement. It would be an error to continue to hear only the voices of school leaders when we may be missing critical feedback and new descriptive data about student performance in our school districts. As we evaluate the effectiveness of programs using quantitative information, we must also use qualitative methods to examine viewpoints of those involved in disseminating the value of the program. If not, the groups experience a phenomenon referred to as *discourse of silence*. That refers to the exclusion of voices from certain groups, including stakeholders, in an educational organization. The discourse of silence may affect decisions in the organization that in turn influence the performance of students.

I wish to suggest that by using carefully developed focus groups, we can gain meaningful input from any stakeholder or group of stakeholders in the organization. The input we gain can be valuable in assisting with improving any change process, and may also be important in allowing those who are often silenced a voice in that process.

In your professional and personal life, have you ever wondered what other people were thinking? During the time I was writing this introduction, the 2007 National Football League draft was taking place. Being a lifelong Pittsburgh Steelers fan, I was quite interested in this event. In my opinion, and that of many others, it was assumed that the Steelers would select at least one running back because they were very thin in that area. As it turned out, they did not select a running back. Instead, they chose two linebackers, a tight end, and a punter among their selections. The question everyone was asking was: "What were they thinking?"

After listening to all the fallout from the sports talk radio shows and the *expert* draft analysts on television, I continued to wonder what the organization was thinking. Sometime later, I read an interview with the Steelers Director of Football Operations in the local newspaper. The reporter asked some very well-constructed questions aimed at getting at the controversy. It was determined that after conferring with the coaches and other front office personnel, the feedback showed that, counter to popular opinion, the positions in need of a critical infusion of talent did not include running backs. After reading this dialogue, I had a much better understanding of why they selected who they did, and why they did not select a running back as everyone said they should.

In schools, leaders often make decisions that leave many wondering: what were they thinking? As an administrator, I try to get as much information as I can that will help me or a committee make a better decision. The Steelers had a wealth of information on each player that allowed them to make the appropriate decisions on who to draft in the best interest of the organization. How do you determine what is best for your school organization? How can you get information from stakeholders that will help you, or a committee, make the best decisions possible?

The primary way you can investigate an organization is through the experiences of the people who make up the organization, or are involved in carrying out some facet of processes in the organization. Social abstractions, like education, are best understood through the experiences of those individuals who are the stakeholders. So much research has been done on schooling in the United States, yet so little of it is based on studies involving the perspectives of students, teachers, administrators, counselors, special subject teachers, nurses, psychologists, cafeteria workers, secretaries, school crossing guards, bus drivers, parents, and school committee members whose individual and collective experiences constitute schooling. Focus-group interviewing is investigative in nature and attempts to learn from the experiences of the individuals and the group as a whole.

Our society's cultural industry, in many instances, tends to socialize our minds and teaches us how to act, live, and dream. Children often experience this when relating to adults in their lives. Adults may listen to what children have to say, but dismiss their thoughts or ideas as inconsequential because children are not considered wise enough or experienced enough to know about anything. Therefore, children are not heard.

Parents often experience similar silencing. They tend to rely on the school to handle decisions because school officials are perceived as the experts in this kind of decision-making. I sense teachers often feel the same way. They will implement a program or change because the research says it is good, or because a school official directs the program to be implemented on the premise that it must be good enough. In each instance, those directly involved in implementing the new program are often not asked about their viewpoints regarding any facet of the school organization.

Focus-group research produces data that occur in indigenous form, in the group participants' own words using their own categorizations, perceptions, and interpretations. The focus-group process attempts to bring out the voices not normally heard. When implementing any kind of reform effort, it is important to hear the voices of those who will ultimately be affected by the change.

One of the strengths of focus-group research is that it will allow you to gain a better perspective of thoughts and ideas that others are able to share. In addition, the process used to gain that perspective can be valuable and will give you the experience to examine other school programs in the future.

My goal in writing this book was to provide a practical guide that school leaders can use to help develop their own focus-group studies. I want it to be useful and most of all *user-friendly*. My hope is that I have accomplished this goal. Chapters 1 through 5 cover information that will provide you with an understanding of the process and how it can be used to gain valuable information. Chapters 6 through 8, and 10 through 12 provide practical information that can help you conduct your own research. I chose to insert chapter 9 to discuss the philosophical and epistemological basis upon which focus groups are established. And finally, chapter 13 includes some of my reflections on the previous twelve chapters and the process as a whole.

As administrators and school leaders, I feel that our job is to be instructional leaders and agents for change. Changes that need to be made in any facet of an organization must be based on current research and appropriate data. I also feel that our job is to hear the voices of stakeholders and to utilize ideas that could be beneficial to the academic programs and other processes that affect the organization. We must listen to the voices, because in those voices we will find valuable information that can benefit us as we do our jobs. Those voices will also affect the entire school community with the focus on academic achievement in the interest of continuing to increase student performance. Enjoy reading this book and applying the process as you conduct your own research. Undoubtedly, incorporating the dynamics of focus-group research in decision-making will provide persuasive answers to the proverbial query, "What were they thinking?"

CHAPTER 1

Schools as Organizations

In order to understand the benefits of using focus-group research in a school organization and to realize what may cause people in the organization to remain silent on various issues, it is important to first understand the workings and dynamics of such an entity. While many administrators (particularly those who have been administrators for a long time) feel they have a pretty good understanding of how a school system works, it is essential in this context that the complexities are identified that may lead to "silenced voices" in the decision-making process.

A school system cannot be looked at in a linear fashion. It is a bureaucratic, open, and loosely coupled organization. Institutional environments, such as schools, use mechanisms such as rules, regulations, and inspections to produce organizational effects. The survival of the organization is dependent upon conformity by most of the personnel within the organization to the institutional norms and procedures. School systems commonly exhibit the bureaucratic characteristics of a high degree of role specialization, including centralization of authority in a vertical hierarchical structure where control is achieved through formal policies, rules and role prescriptions, and functionally specialized units. Using this description, it is no wonder that this type of system leads to silenced voices inside and outside of the hierarchical structure.

Schools are also open systems that must interact with the environment to survive. It consumes resources and exports resources to the environment. The school cannot seal itself off. It must continually change and adapt to the environment. The organization has to find and obtain needed resources, interpret and act on environmental changes, dispose of outdated equipment, and control and coordinate internal activities in the face of environmental disturbances and uncertainty.

If school districts were isolated from external influences, it might be assumed that there exists a logical progression from mission statement to goal development, to development of implementation strategies, to evaluation and revision of goals and strategies. However, due to the uncertainty brought on by external environmental dynamics, there often exists a loose coupling. In reality, action often precedes planning, and policies and practices are adapted later to reflect previous actions. Hence, we often react to situations as opposed to being proactive.

We must not forget the political framework of school organizations. School systems are influenced by formal and informal power groups both within and external to the system. An educational system can be assumed to have interest groups and conflicts similar to those found in cities, states, and other political entities. What is called "public relations" because of *occupational taboos* is actually politics: trying to establish coalitions of groups and individuals who will support the mission of the schools and minimize any damage done by critics. As a result, those employed in school systems must work diligently to provide a framework that would allow voices of all stakeholders to be heard.

This is not an easy task to accomplish. Have you ever made a decision that you thought was a *no-brainer* only to find out later that you had upset someone or a particular group of people over it? Often, because of the complexities involved in a school organization, it is sometimes difficult to predict if a particular decision will trigger a chain of events that might end in someone or a group of people becoming upset because a decision was made that you thought was perfectly justified.

School administrators deal with the developing brain from kindergarten to adulthood. Everyone sees and interprets ideas and situations differently. As a result, this bureaucratic, open, and loosely coupled organization by its very nature is cause for misunderstandings, communication breakdowns, and problematic decision-making that may lead to lack of progress and productivity. Implementing a method for gathering perspectives from individuals inside and outside the organization can be extremely beneficial in breaking down some of the barriers that impede progress in the organization. This can be accomplished through the use of focus groups.

CHAPTER 2

A Brief History of Focus-Group Research

In many organizations outside the educational arena, focus-group research is used for a variety of initiatives to develop action plans aimed at increasing productivity, or to determine what the public or organization wants in regard to marketing strategies. I have used focus-group research as a means of determining a variety of educational initiatives from curriculum reform efforts to increasing parent involvement and communication in schools. I have found it to be an extremely useful tool to determine why a particular phenomenon has occurred, and to then develop an action plan on how to better serve the organization and its constituents. In addition, it allows stakeholders in the organization to provide input and to know that their voices are being heard.

In school districts in which I have worked, we often have issues to deal with and in many cases we are not aware of what it is that causes these issues to occur. Our principals have used focus-group research in their buildings to determine what has caused certain issues to occur, and then have developed action plans to address these issues. We have also used focus groups at the Central Office level to address various issues that face us district-wide, such as grade level reconfiguration initiatives, student transitions between buildings, employee morale, and public satisfaction.

When I mention using this process to colleagues in other districts, they often are not aware of the process and how it can help to improve their school organization. It is my belief that many school organizations across the country, and even the world, do not employ this opportunity for school improvement. On a daily basis, school organizations experience issues that often are not resolved simply because no one has the ability to get the information needed to determine the genesis of the issue, the impact it has on the organization as a whole, and the stakeholders who would be instrumental in determining a program improvement or process to achieve success. For officials in education, knowing how to conduct focus-group research can be an essential element for school improvement. This is an untapped opportunity and resource in the educational arena.

My first encounter with focus-group research came in a qualitative research class I was required to take in my doctoral program. Prior to that, I had no experience with or training in the process. During my undergraduate studies (in the 1970s) I was required to take a research class which was composed entirely of learning quantitative research methods. Although focus-group research has been used for some time, until fairly recently it was seldom addressed in teacher and administrator training.

The first use of focus-group research began with social science literature in the late 1920s. Focus-group research was also used during World War II, and its use continued for many years after. Marketing research has employed the use of the focus-group interview since 1941, when Paul Lazarsfeld of the Office of Radio Research at Columbia University invited Robert Merton to assist him in the evaluation of audience response to radio programs. During World War II, Merton was commissioned by the U.S. Army Information and Education Division to use focus-group research to investigate Army training and morale films.

In the 1940s, focus groups were the most popular means of evaluating television commercials for the thirty-seven largest users of television advertisers. However, in the 1950s, 1960s, and 1970s, focus-group research was limited because of a societal preoccupation with quantitative methodologies. Focus-group research made a comeback in the United States in 1990 mostly in the area of marketing and in the business sector. Using the focus-group interview continues today to be a viable methodology in qualitative research. Not often, though, is focus-group research used in educational organizations as a means to investigate a phenomenon, and as an aid in the decision-making process.

CHAPTER 3

Silenced Voices

In order to create an understanding of how voices can be silenced, let us examine an area of school improvement that we can all relate to: the implementation of academic standards and curriculum reform with the aim of improving test scores and meeting compliance with No Child Left Behind (NCLB) federal legislation. School leaders often develop the philosophy that setting standards and the pressure imposed on the teachers, as well as the accountability rhetoric disseminated to parents, are the impetus for improved test scores. It is erroneous to continue to hear only the voices of school leaders when critical feedback is missing from other stakeholders regarding data about student performance in our school districts.

As we evaluate the effectiveness of standards implementation using quantitative information, we must also use qualitative methods to examine viewpoints of those involved in disseminating the standards—the teachers as well as the parents, who are, in most cases, closest to the child. These two populations, and more specifically the parents, are generally unheard when it comes to large-scale curricular change. Teachers are most often involved in the process of curricular reform, but are often led into theory and practice by school officials (e.g., principals) who must disseminate mandates handed down from state and federal bureaucracies (e.g., the Department of Education), which use their own research to justify such changes.

Parents are rarely involved in the process at the secondary level, often because they are not invited to participate, or because they are intimidated by the prospect of not possessing a knowledge base in curricular change. As a result, the two groups experience a phenomenon I refer to as *discourse of silence*. That refers to the exclusion of the voices of certain groups, including stakeholders, in an educational organization. The discourse of silence may affect decisions in the organization that in turn influence the performance of students.

Standards continue to force educators to move from naïve, comfortable assumptions about what is and what has been happening in American classrooms, to a more honest and productive reckoning with what and how well children are actually learning. Hence, the role of teachers and parents is often defined by the programming and curricular reform decided by school administrators. It would certainly seem unjust if their voices were not heard in this process.

One school district I worked for as an administrator had parents and teachers included on the curriculum review teams. I must say, the parents were there only to satisfy administrative guidelines, which specified parent participation during a curriculum review cycle. At least one parent was required to be involved in the process. What I observed was the parent sitting at the meetings essentially uninvolved while everyone else was discussing the curriculum and what changes needed to be made. Once the process was completed, the parent signed her name on the document indicating her inclusion in the process. Now, is this really including the parents and hearing their voices?

As it happened, it became increasingly more difficult to get parents to serve on the committees because they heard from others who had served that they were not really involved other than to provide a physical presence. Now, because people are generally more comfortable when they are placed with those from similar backgrounds, a parent focus group on a particular facet of curricular reform would most certainly provide more information than a parent sitting alone on a committee unable to offer a meaningful voice in the process. The inclusion of a parent focus group can then be useful in the planning process for curriculum review and reform. The point is, there is a way to hear the voices of others in processes that will be beneficial to the school organization.

CHAPTER 4

Causes for Silence

As you read this chapter, keep in mind the need to understand some of the reasons that voices are silenced. This is not something we consciously think about as administrators and school leaders. Know that there are people out there in your school districts either internally or externally who really want to be heard on some issue that is important to them. But for some reason, they are not able to have a voice. What are some of the reasons this occurs? Let us examine some of the causes for silenced voices.

STATUS DISTANCE LEADING TO SILENCED VOICES

Even in a democracy, elected or appointed officials are necessary to the functioning of the local, state, or national unit. Although their role is to represent their constituents, leaders come to hold elite status dimensions, which often result in decreased contact with those in lower status dimensions. Teachers and parents surrounding a school organization are often insulated from social and professional contacts with administrators and board members. The administrators and board members on the elite status dimension constitute a small fraction of the total school population, thus leading to little face-to-face contact with staff members and constituents. The tendency of higher positions in a status hierarchy to have fewer representatives than lower ones is not confined to elite positions. The elite status dimension is merely an example of the comparatively small size of higher strata. Status distributions are by nature positively skewed, with a majority of the population occupying lower status, and relatively few occupying status levels of power.

With increasing status in a school organization, be it prestige, income, or power, frequency of contact is widely distributed at the lower status levels, but decreases in proportion to the fewer representatives occupying the higher levels. As a result, status structures may resemble pyramids. Principals, central office personnel (e.g., the Assistant Superintendent, Superintendent, and/or Curriculum Director) and members of the districts' Boards of Education, are at the top of the pyramid possessing greater status than teachers and parents at the bottom. This organizational structure, prevalent in all schools, leads to a power structure that silences the voices of those at the lower level of the pyramid.

POWER AND DOMINATION LEADING TO SILENCED VOICES

Weber (1947) defines power as "the probability that an actor within a social relationship will be in a position to carry out his own will despite resistance, regardless of the basis on which this probability rests." This concept includes imposing one's will on a single associate in direct social interaction and imposing one's will on an entire unit collectively, whether or not doing so involves direct social interaction. In a school organization, decision-making power is imposed both in direct interaction with constituents, as well as executed void of direct contact with the stakeholders.

Domination, according to Weber (1968), comes in two forms. One is domination by virtue of constellation of interests; the other is domination by virtue of authority. The former rests mainly on superior economic resources that make it possible to influence people by controlling the conditions of their existence so that their self-interests constrain them to act in certain ways. The pure case of this is a monopoly. Authority, on the other hand, rests on social positions in which are vested the legitimate right of command, backed by sanctioning power and complemented by the duty to obey. The pure case in modern society is a bureaucratic hierarchy (Weber, 1968). This social structure is one that seems most prevalent in school organizations.

Lasswell and Kaplan (1950) distinguish *power* from the broader concept of *influence* on the basis of its deterrent effect. Command over any resources that are valued by people bestows sanctioning power and, therefore, is a base of power. There are three quantitative dimensions of power: its weight is the extent to which certain decisions are influenced; its scope is the number of different value spheres in which decisions are influenced, such as economic, political, and religious; and its domain is the number of persons whose conduct is influenced or controlled. In school organizations, these three quantitative dimensions reflect the basis on which many decisions are made.

Young (1990) discusses insurgent social movements that seek to limit state and corporate powers, to push back the bounds of their commodifying and bureaucratizing influence. They seek to release social life from the colonizing influence of welfare state and corporate bureaucracy, to create alternative institutional forms and independent discussion. Most focus on issues of oppression and domination, and seek democratization of institutions and their practices for more direct popular control.

These campaigns and movements fall into three categories. The first are those that challenge decision-making structures and the right of the powerful to exert their will. The environmental movement, antinuclear power movement, and urban social movements are examples of groups that question the authority of political and social agencies to make policy issues without considering public sentiment. The second are those that organize autonomous services. The women's movement has established health services, rape crisis services, and shelters for battered women. Many of these services later become part of the bureaucratic establishment. Third are movements of culture and identity. Cultural politics serve a critical function: to identify which practices, habits, attitudes, compartments, images, symbols, and so on contribute to social domination and group oppression, and to call for a collective transformation of such practices.

OPPRESSION LEADING TO SILENCED VOICES

In its traditional usage, oppression means the exercise of tyranny by a ruling group. Oppression also traditionally carries a strong connotation of conquest and colonial domination (Young, 1990). Freire (2000) describes organizations where the oppressed realize the extent of their oppression and, through conscious effort, commit themselves to the action of transforming the world. Paradoxically, when persons free themselves from oppression, they tend to replicate oppressive actions that have been done to them, and therefore become oppressors themselves. As this concept implies then, a person can never be free; one is either an oppressor or one who is oppressed. Those who oppress others dehumanize themselves and engender the process that blinds them from seeing how their dominating, manipulative behavior is self-destructive. Oppression, in its many guises, has effectively silenced voices in the modern world.

Young (1990) discusses what she refers to as the five faces of oppression. These five faces of oppression include exploitation, marginalization, powerlessness, cultural imperialism, and violence. The first, exploitation, occurs through a steady process of the transfer of the results of labor of one social group to benefit another. Exploitation enacts a structural relation between social groups. Marginalization refers to people the system of labor cannot or will not use. Most affected by marginalization are minorities.

Powerlessness is evident when many people in society do not have the means to participate in decisions that might affect them. Relatively few who are not in power positions have the opportunity to participate in policy decisions. Therefore, many are affected by the decisions of a few. Frequently, who one is or the position one holds gives him/her a certain degree of power. In a sense, others are more inclined to listen to someone who is in a respected position or one associated with power. This form of oppression is most closely related to the phenomenon of the discourse of silence I described in chapter 3.

Cultural imperialism involves the paradox of imagining one's self as invisible at the same time that one is imposing a visibly different identity on the oppressed. And finally, violence, the fifth face of oppression, refers to members of some groups that live with the knowledge that they must fear random, unprovoked attacks on their persons or property, which have no motive but to damage, humiliate, or destroy the person. This form of oppression effectively serves to discourage people from voicing dissent.

DEMOCRATIC PROCESSES LEADING TO SILENCED VOICES

Democracy is also a condition for a public's arriving at decisions whose substance and implications best promote substantively just outcomes, including distributive justice or establishing parity and fairness for all. Democratic processes occur only in institutions that make laws and state policies, while other institutions, such as private corporations or the bureaucracies that administer state policies, remain undemocratic. The leverage of inequality in bureaucracies that permits participatory processes to favor the will of the powerful is often traceable to the authority inherent in these institutions. If constitutional democracy restructures all institutional forms, and not merely institutions now falling under public policy decisions, then people are less likely to feel powerless to express their voice.

Hopefully you can envision why voices in your educational organization are silenced. The reasons I have just described are complex, and in many cases occur unconsciously. We as school leaders do not sit around in a room trying to decide how we can best keep people from providing input into our decision-making. I have never even thought about silencing others in my district. But it happens, far more than we would like to admit. What is important, though, is that we are able to recognize when it is happening and how we can include stakeholders in providing input into decisions that affect the organization.

CHAPTER 5

Efforts to Hear the Voices

You no doubt have heard the story about Rip Van Winkle. Critics of education say if he woke up today, he would not recognize the world because so much has changed, but if he entered a school, he would know exactly where he was. Schools have not changed in years. I dislike when someone tells that story, because I think schools have changed significantly over the years. One area that has not changed, however, is that administrators still monopolize control over policy reform and allow little outside input into decision-making. So far I am guilty of painting a fairly dismal picture of our schools in regard to hearing the voices of our stakeholders. If Rip Van Winkle had something to say about our schools and wanted to provide any input, would we listen? Before responding, let's consider two processes utilized in school organizations that have provided efforts to hear the voices of others.

DEMOCRATIC STRUCTURES AND PROCESSES: AN EFFORT TO HEAR THE VOICES

Although not all school systems adhere to a true democratic form of decision-making at all levels of the organization, there are some that do. To say that democracy rests on the consent of the governed is not simply a platitude. In a democratic school it is true that all of those directly involved in the school, including young people, have the right to participate in the process of decision-making. Democratic schools are marked by widespread participation in issues of governance and policy making. Committees, councils, and other school-wide decision-making groups not only include professional educators, but also young people, their parents, and other members of the school community. In classrooms, young people and teachers engage in collaborative planning, reaching decisions that respond to the concerns, aspirations, and interests of both. This kind of democratic planning, at both the school and the classroom levels, is not the engineering of consent toward predetermined decisions that have too often created the illusion of democracy, but a genuine attempt to honor the right of people to participate in making decisions that affect their lives.

The focus on improving schools and revitalizing the teaching profession has led to many proposals for changing the governance of schools. These proposals examine new structures for empowering teachers and giving them decision-making responsibilities over such issues as hiring, curriculum options, teacher evaluation, and school policies. When decisions are made through a shared distribution of power, they are viewed as legitimate. People feel appropriately involved and can therefore accept decisions, even those that are contrary to their personal views. Conversely, when a school or district has low morale or poor cohesiveness, decision-making processes are usually ailing. Often, this inadequacy is at the root of the school's problems and needs to be addressed before commitment to school goals, collegiality among staff, or strength in any other form of healthy school culture can be expected.

Since democracy involves the informed consent of people, a democratic curriculum emphasizes access to a wide range of information and the right of those of varied opinion to have their viewpoints heard. Educators in a democratic society have an obligation to help young people seek out a range of ideas and to voice their own. Unfortunately, many schools persistently shirk this obligation in several ways. First, they narrow the focus of knowledge to what we might call *official* or high-status knowledge that is endorsed by the dominant culture and necessary to its perpetuation. Second, they silence the voices of those outside the dominant culture, particularly people of color, women, and, of course, the young.

What is most disturbing is that all too many schools have taught this official, high-status knowledge as though it were truth arisen from some immutable, infallible source. Those committed to a more participatory curriculum understand that knowledge is socially constructed and that it is produced and disseminated by people who have particular values, interests, biases, and agendas.

SITE-BASED MANAGEMENT: AN EFFORT TO HEAR THE VOICES

Criticisms of public education during the 1980s and early 1990s resulted in a number of conclusions about elementary and secondary schools. Among the more prevalent were the following:

1. In many school systems, authority remained centralized and these conditions served to block meaningful change.
2. Schools could not improve significantly by simply doing more of what they were already doing.
3. Teachers and schools needed fewer, not more, controls to become effective.
4. Meaningful improvement was more likely to occur at the school rather than at school district levels.

Collectively, these findings increased interest in concepts of decentralization, and none became more popular than site-based management (Kowalski, 1995).

Despite its popularity, not all educators readily embraced site-based management as a positive concept. In part, this is evidenced by the fact that many school districts have made no attempt to move in this direction. Some critics believe that resistance to decentralization within school districts is simply a product of power-hungry superintendents refusing to relinquish bureaucratic control. But more enlightened observers realize that centralization, especially in the past forty or fifty years, has been prompted by increased concerns over litigation. For example, laws governing equal protection and equal rights led superintendents to insist on uniform and proper employment practices. When decision-making is shared within schools, it can be argued that the potential for legal problems increases significantly (Kowalski, 1995).

Over the past fifty years, school systems have often restricted freedoms for individual schools to develop their own policies, even in the areas of curriculum and instruction. Interventions of the federal government and the courts are largely responsible for creating a compliance orientation that made superintendents and school boards fearful of not applying uniform policy across all units of the organization. In large part, the current interest in decentralization is sparked by several beliefs:

1. Teachers will become more effective if they are treated more like true professionals.
2. Decisions about student instruction will be improved if teachers are empowered to truly individualize their teaching strategies.
3. The overall governance of the schools will improve if individual schools are not shackled by school districts' policies and rules.
4. Schools will improve if all those who are a part of the school community are allowed to participate in critical decisions. (Kowalski, 1995)

Clearly, giving individual schools more authority to chart their own courses increases flexibility. The lingering question is whether or not having more authority increases accountability and productivity. Critics note, for example, that having more people involved in decisions does not necessarily result in better decisions. Many also realize that site-based management is dependent on school boards, administrators, and communities being willing to treat teachers as true professionals, a condition that has not been widely practiced.

One area of special interest in school administration is the leadership role of principals in schools that have decentralized governance. On the one hand, the principal ought to be trusting of individuals, especially of those who are given the power and authority to make critical decisions. On the other hand, principals are usually expected to maintain some degree of control to assure that decisions are made in a timely fashion. Principals are typically expected to provide direction to assure that democratically derived decisions are not counterproductive to the goals of the school. In this regard, principals working with school councils must walk a fine line between allowing others to make key decisions and maintaining responsibility for those decisions.

More than just a strong instructional leader, principals in a site-based management system must be seen by others as real change agents and as true facilitators of any reform process. They must possess a strong personality as well as a clear set of ideas about the direction they want the school to take. But they must work hard to accomplish their objectives through other people as well by seeking out their input, getting them committed to new ideas, and delegating to them the responsibility for implementing the changes needed to improve the school.

Principals must also be effective managers in the sense that they recognize the need to design and operate the school as an organizational system in such a way that reform is encouraged and allowed to take place. They must give a lot of attention to the appropriate design of the school structure necessary to generate active involvement in decision-making. Effective communication with all constituent groups is necessary to keep them informed of what the school is doing, as well as solicit their input and reactions to changes. By delegating tasks and encouraging others to take initiative, the principal helps to create a leadership coalition at the school. In this way, a sense of collective responsibility for success of any reform effort can emerge, and people will feel empowered to design and implement new practices needed to achieve the school's vision.

Conversely, principals at struggling schools believe it is expedient to consolidate their power in order to impose regulatory controls. As a result, they fail to exert true leadership at all, and instead trap themselves in a style of micromanagement that undermines staff motivation, causes internal power struggles among administrators and staff, and suffocates the reform process. Hence, effective curriculum reform efforts must include all stakeholders in the process and welcome voices not normally heard.

To the extent that school districts are given local control over the governance of their organization, democratic process and site-based management are two examples of how we have attempted to gain input from those not normally included in any decision-making process. For a moment, Rip Van Winkle might have to stop for a reality check when he enters a school governed by democratic process or through site-based management.

CHAPTER 6

The Focus-Group Process: An Ideal Method for Breaking the Silence

DEVELOPING AN EFFECTIVE FOCUS-GROUP PROJECT

The focus-group process is a useful method to use in an effort to break the silence of stakeholders in an educational organization. Developing a focus-group project is much like what many of us have done in conducting other research projects in our undergraduate, graduate, and educational leadership programs. You usually begin with a question to help determine the phenomenon you wish to investigate. Why has, or is, something occurring in your district or school that you wish to find out about? For example, why are parents expressing concerns over their lack of involvement in the school? Or, why do teachers feel that morale is low in the school? These are two simplistic examples. Chapter 10 contains two specific focus-group research projects that I have conducted, and chapter 11 presents what I call my focus-group process tool, which takes you step by step through the process.

Arranging the participants according to their constituent groups appears to create an atmosphere conducive to the discussion of information that normally would not be shared in mixed group settings. I believe participants grouped in this manner are usually comfortable enough with one another that they are able to speak candidly, and are appreciative of having the opportunity to express their views about programs and procedures in their school. Incidentally, the participants gain a better understanding of the focus-group process, how it is designed to hear their voices, and they gain perspectives not normally obtained in discussions about the phenomenon under investigation. In the following section are essential elements to be considered prior to conducting a focus-group study.

The Group Moderator

The group moderator serves to facilitate the groups. He/she will read the questions to the group and essentially keep the group moving in terms of staying on track. In a school organization, this person might be a secretary or an aide. This prevents the situations whereby the data become suspect. If the researcher (a school official) is seen as holding authority over the population samples, the subjects may say what they think the researcher wants to hear. In order to minimize this possibility of data contamination, a facilitator may also be chosen who is not affiliated with the school district or is from another education agency.

Elements of Questions That Will Generate Discussion

Once you determine the phenomenon under investigation, you must develop questions that pinpoint what it is you want to find out about. You should develop ten to twelve open-ended questions that will lead the group to discussion. You want to avoid asking a question that will result in a yes-or-no answer. This will result in the group coming to a halt and gives you very little data to analyze. Remember, you want to generate discussion and dialogue within the group, so open-ended questions will get you the data you need. See chapter 11 for examples of open-ended questions.

Keeping the Group on Task

Keeping the group on task is the job of the group moderator. If appropriate questions were developed, the group will engage in discussion and dialogue pertinent to the question. Sometimes, however, members of the group will veer off course and begin discussing a topic that might be near and dear to them, but not in line with the question asked. At this time the group moderator must recognize that the participants are off task and he/she must guide them back on track. This may be done simply by asking that the group remain on task with the question asked, and/or the moderator may restate the question to encourage on-task behavior.

Eliminating Personal Bias

It is important to remember that even though focus groups are an extremely effective research methodology, they, like other research tools, are not a panacea. Concern exists that involvement in a group discussion may influence a participant's contribution. This may limit generalizability and therefore confidence that the data are representative of stakeholders across the school or district. In addition, the group moderator may knowingly or unknowingly bias the data by providing verbal and/or nonverbal cues to the participants. To minimize the second concern, the group moderator should be instructed on how to ask the questions and told not to engage in any dialogue with the focus-group participants. It should also be explained that nonverbal cues could affect the participants' responses. Therefore the group moderator should be cautioned to refrain from exhibiting body language that might encourage consensus at the expense of debate.

Bringing the Focus Group to Closure

After the group moderator asks each question, he/she should sit back and listen to the dialogue. If the group gets off track, he/she should redirect them. Once the dialogue is exhausted, there will be a period of time where there is complete silence. At this point, the group moderator will move on to the next question. In the event a question elicits very little response, the group moderator should ask if anyone else has anything to add. If there is continued silence, then he/she should move to the next question. At the end of the dialogue following the final question, the group moderator should ask if anyone has anything else related to the topic they would like to add. If so, the moderator should let them add their thoughts. At the conclusion of the session, the group moderator should thank the participants, shut off the audio recorder and video recorder, and dismiss the group.

CHAPTER 7

Focus-Group Design

The purpose of using focus-group research is ultimately to assist administrators and other school leaders in making better decisions about any phenomenon under investigation that will improve their school or district. Qualitative studies using focus groups are critically important means for gathering information from participants to investigate different viewpoints they may hold regarding the phenomenon. The design is an essential element in conducting a successful focus-group study.

At minimum, two focus groups would be used in a small study. Ideally, a researcher would use more than two focus groups to ensure representativeness depending on the size and complexity of the study. As an example, the following are the representative focus groups tapped in a previous study I conducted. The purpose of the study was to gain viewpoints from parents and teachers regarding the connection between the implementation of state curriculum standards and student assessment performance at a suburban high school in which I was the principal. The focus groups were composed of teachers and parents.

Teacher Population

Focus group 1: English language arts teachers
Focus group 2: Mathematics teachers
Focus group 3: Teachers randomly selected from disciplines other than English language arts and mathematics.

Parent Population

Focus group 1: Parents of students in grade 12. Students must have had at least three years of standards instruction at the high school and have met proficiency on the state exam.

Focus group 2: Parents of students in grade 11. Students must have had at least two years of standards instruction at the high school and have met proficiency on the state exam.

Focus group 3: Parents of students in grades 9–10. Students must have had at least one year of standards instruction at the high school and have met proficiency on the state exam. This group will have had no prior education or experience in regard to standards and their implementation. These were parents who never attended any meetings held by the district regarding the state exam and curriculum standards. They indicated they knew nothing about the exam (only that their child had to take it) or curriculum standards.

Teachers and parents were selected according to the following criteria:

Sampling Criteria for the Selection of Teachers

1. Must be a high school teacher (grades 9–12).
2. Must have taught the standards since their initial year of implementation.
3. Must be a teacher of English language arts (focus group 1), mathematics (focus group 2), or from any other discipline (focus group 3).

Sampling Criteria for the Selection of Parents

1. Must be a parent of a high school student (grades 9–12).
2. Parent must be a biological, nonbiological legal guardian, or foster parent.
3. Student must have lived with the parent for at least one full school year.
4. Parent's child must have been a student in the district long enough to have met the time requirement of being taught the standards as described for each separate focus group.

5. One group was composed of parents who have had no prior education or experience in regard to standards and their implementation.
6. Parents' children must have met proficiency on the state assessment.

I had to be careful that data would not become suspect. I may have been seen as holding authority over the two population samples, causing the subjects to say what they thought I wanted to hear. In order to minimize this possibility of data contamination, a facilitator not affiliated with the school district was chosen to lead the focus-group questioning process. Focus-group research is not intended to be generalized to other settings, and the interactive and context-specific nature of the research should be disclosed as part of the study.

Names of teachers were selected from the English language arts and mathematics departments. There were thirteen members of the English language arts department and eleven members of the mathematics department. I asked for six to nine volunteers from each group. Six to nine volunteers from the remainder of the staff (from a total of eighty teachers minus the twenty-four from the English language arts and mathematics departments) were also assigned to the third focus group. Teachers were sent a letter describing the research to be conducted and returned a form to me indicating their desire to participate or not.

Parent volunteers were selected from members of the school "Key Communicator" parent support group. Parents who were members of the group were sent a letter describing the research to be conducted and were asked to return a form back to me indicating their desire to participate or not. The Key Communicator parent group was an active high school–parent organization that worked together to support and assist with many academic programs as well as extra and cocurricular activities. Many members of the group were actively involved in the school and had a good grasp of standards implementation. There were, however, members of the group who were not as active in the school and represented an uneducated sample in regard to standards implementation. These volunteers were divided into the three focus groups of six to nine participants that met the criteria for parent selection.

The actual data collection took place in focus groups composed of six to nine participants in each group who met the sampling criteria. The interviews were conducted in a conference room at the suburban high school, utilizing an independent facilitator. In addition, each focus-group session was audio and videotaped.

Using the administrative conference room presented some advantages. It was of the optimum size and contained excellent lighting, comfortable furniture, and a bright décor. Focus-group participants were seated in comfortable chairs around a large rectangular table. The video camera was set up at one end of the table behind the facilitator and at an angle to assure that all participants were clearly visible. This allowed the camera to pick up nonverbal feedback as well as verbal feedback. Although all focus-group participants were visible while being audio- and videotaped, anonymity was maintained. Subjects were identified by initials. Once the tapes were viewed and transcribed, they were stored in a locked cabinet in my office.

Transcribing the data consisted of typing of the audiotapes verbatim. Transcription of the audiotapes is usually done by a secretary or administrative assistant. Caveat: the transcriber must be knowledgeable about the coding procedure you wish to use. I would advise that the participants' initials be used followed by the group designation (e.g., JL for Joe Latess and A for Administrator, hence JLA). Remember, the dialogue that is created among the group is the data you will analyze. Once the data are transcribed, you, as the researcher, will read then organize the data into common themes. This is the most time-consuming phase of the process. In addition, you must view the videotapes and make notes of the participants' body language and demeanor throughout the dialogue. Often, nonverbal cues will indicate a participant's feelings about a topic, even though he/she did not verbalize it.

At the end of the set of responses from each question, you should write a summary or discussion section encompassing the highlights of the data combined from that question. I always try to retain much of the original wording of the participants in this section as I summarize their responses. Generally, I then review the summary or discussion sections and begin to develop common themes. Once these themes have been identified, you can create what I refer to as "assertions derived from the data." The assertions are a compilation of all the emerging themes evident in the data. The assertions are used to create further discussion and develop action plans that will address the phenomenon under investigation.

CHAPTER 8

Procedures for Conducting Focus Groups

This chapter will outline the procedures for conducting focus-group research. During my earlier years as a teacher, I also coached football at the high school level. I remember when I got my first head coaching job. The first thing I did was contact my own high school football coach (who was still coaching at the time) to discuss his offensive and defensive strategies. These strategies made him a very successful football coach, so I assumed they would work for me. As I gained experience as a football coach, I added to and subtracted from these strategies to eventually develop my own strategies based upon my offensive and defensive philosophies. As you gain experience in conducting your own focus-group research, you will find certain intricacies that work best for you and will develop them into your own set of procedures. The following elements and basic procedures provide the foundation you will need to conduct focus-group research. You will no doubt build on these as you develop experience in conducting your own focus-group research.

POPULATION AND SAMPLE

Determining the population you will use and how you will select participants is an important step. Purposive sampling is one you can employ in selecting participants for your study. Purposive sampling involves selecting participants not because they represent a given population, but because they represent a portion of the population that is likely to be knowledgeable about the issue under investigation. The decision to use purposive sampling arises when specific groups are targeted for investigation (e.g., a select group of administrators, teachers, or parents).

Random sampling techniques can be used when a large population is targeted for investigation. Perhaps you want to investigate an issue that affects an entire district parent population. In this scenario, it is impossible to conduct focus groups with thousands of participants (remember six to nine per group is recommended). As a result, you may randomly select participants from the given population. In doing this, you can be confident that the data collected are fairly representative of data you would collect from the thousands of that population, and certainly it is a more manageable technique.

DATA COLLECTION

The primary way a researcher can investigate an organization is through the experiences of the people who make up the organization or are involved in carrying out some facet of the process. Social abstractions, like education, are best understood through the experiences of those individuals who are the stakeholders. So much research has been done on schooling in the United States, yet so little of it is based on studies involving the perspectives of students, teachers, administrators, counselors, special subject teachers, nurses, psychologists, cafeteria workers, secretaries, school crossing guards, bus drivers, parents, and school committee members whose individual and collective experience constitutes schooling. Focus-group interviewing is investigative in nature and attempts to *get at* the experiences of the individuals and the group as a whole.

Focus-group research produces data that occur in indigenous form, in the group participants' own words using their own categorizations, perceptions, and interpretations. It is important to note that respondents can give meaningful responses only to questions they comprehend. It is essential then to pretest potential questions to determine if they are contextually appropriate and comprehensible to group members.

Four pilot-testing techniques can be used in developing and refining the questions for a study:

1. Colleagues in the field can review potential questions.
2. Potential questions can be reviewed by lay people who fit the criteria as focus-group participants.
3. A pilot focus-group interview can be conducted to test the questions.
4. A preview of the questions can be used with participants of the pilot study.

Utilizing audio- and videotape in focus-group research is widely documented. Focus groups should be audio- and videotaped to create verbatim transcripts of discussions that are used to identify emergent themes, to determine individual reactions to emergent themes, and to examine nonverbal cues (body language) of the participants.

DATA INVESTIGATION

Once the focus-group interviews are completed, the facilitator should conduct peer debriefing and "member checks" to verify the accuracy of the data. The data from the audio- and videotapes need to be transcribed, coded, and investigated for emergent isomorphic themes.

Peer debriefing entails the process of verifying the accuracy of the study's analysis with a key informant (the facilitator in this case) who can help the researcher understand the context-specific data that will have been collected in the focus-group interviews. Member checking is the process of verifying the accuracy of research descriptions with members of the group from which data were collected.

Peer debriefing and member checks should be done following the focus-group interviews to verify the accuracy of the data, and to allow the facilitator and group members a chance to correct errors of translation. The data are then presented to reveal participants' viewpoints on the issue under investigation.

METHODOLOGY

The word *interviewing* covers a wide range of practices. There are tightly structured survey interviews with preset, standardized, normally closed questions. At the other end of the continuum are open-ended, apparently unstructured, anthropological interviews that might be seen almost as friendly conversations. The focus-group process involves in-depth, careful interviewing informed by assumptions drawn from phenomenology—the careful description of phenomena in all domains of experience. Interviewers use primarily open-ended questions. Their major task is to build upon and explore their participants' responses to those questions. The goal is to have the participant reconstruct details of his or her experience within the topic under study. The focus-group process attempts to bring out the voices not normally heard.

When implementing any kind of reform effort, it is important to hear the voices of those whom the change will ultimately affect. In many cases certain groups traditionally are not heard in any kind of change process the school may be considering. This takes us back to the phenomenon that I refer to as *discourse of silence*, which is the exclusion of voices from certain groups, including stakeholders, in an educational organization. The discourse of silence may affect decisions in the organization that in turn influence the performance of individuals who are intimate with the groups that are silenced. In many cases, this is the voice of the students.

It is my intention to promote the recognition and the hearing of these voices, and allow them to be included in any reform effort you may be undertaking. Each and every human being possesses a brain and the capabilities to think and learn. Using the thoughts and ideas presented from some of the traditionally silenced groups prepares for the continuous growth, development, and improvement of academic programs.

CONCERNS ABOUT FOCUS-GROUP RESEARCH

It is important to remember that although focus groups are an extremely effective research methodology, they, like other research tools, are not a panacea. The first concern is the restriction of participants to small homogeneous groups relative to the research criteria. This significantly limits the generalizability of the data. The second concern is that involvement in a group discussion may influence a participant's contribution, which may again limit generalizability. The third concern is that the facilitator may knowingly or unknowingly bias the data by providing verbal and/or nonverbal cues to the participants. To minimize the second and third concern, the facilitator should be given instruction on questioning techniques and told not to engage in any dialogue with the focus-group participants. It should also be explained that nonverbal cues could affect the participants' responses and, therefore, the facilitator should refrain from exhibiting body language that would influence responses.

CHAPTER 9

Social Constructions and Context Underlying the Focus-Group Process

For those of you who enjoy the epistemological basis of any discussion, I offer this chapter. Under any process in which humans are involved lies some philosophical discussion for why we do what we do. It may be important for you to understand the basis of organizations and their development, human interactions, and the premise behind the silencing of voices. My hope is that an explanation of the social constructions and context underlying the focus-group process will assist you in your school improvement efforts.

In the context of organizations, social order is a human product and exists only as an outcome of human activity. For human beings, everyday life is an interpreted reality subjectively meaningful to them in a coherent worldview. In other words, we interpret our world based on our own background, experiences, self-image, self-concept, and a host of other factors. In an organization, habitualization provides direction and specialization of activity. It reduces the accumulation of tensions that result from unspecified responses by giving a standard way to address and interpret issues.

People act in habitual patterns that become organized. Organizations reach the status of institution when people in an organization move in the same larger pattern, not in just separate organized roles or tasks. In short, an institutional organization arises when people conduct activities in a like fashion in an effort to achieve common goals. Schools tend to fall somewhere midway between an organization and an institution. To say that a segment of human activity has been institutionalized is to suggest that this segment of human activity has been subsumed under social control. Using that description, schools can be deemed institutions subsumed under social control, with the controlling facet—the administration and school board—determining what is good for the institution to maintain social order. Part of that ordering is evident, for example, in the way we determine what changes are best for the students.

An organization becomes rigid when members conduct themselves in the same manner over and over because that is the way it has always been. The members become sedimentary because they believe the only way to achieve a desired result is to continue to act just as those before them did. These experiences become ingrained as they gather a sense of legitimacy through repetition. This occurs when the modus operandi has been cultivated as some kind of a sign system, that is, a system enabling an understanding of shared experiences. Only then is it likely that these experiences will be transmitted as the "successful" organizational structure from one generation to the next. This rigid operational structure is then readily transmittable to all who share, or may share in the future of, the sign system.

The most common of these sign systems is linguistic or language exchange. Disenfranchisement of certain groups (e.g., parents) in a school organization usually occurs as a result of their past educational experiences. In some parent populations this seems to lead to a silencing of their voices. It is assumed that most parents have attended high school in their past. Unfortunately, some parents have had negative school experiences that may cause them to refrain from getting too involved in their own child's education. Some have gone through school assuming that the teacher was always right and their responsibility was to listen, learn, and not open their mouths. These experiences contribute to the marginalization of these parents, which in turn seems to prohibit them from assertiveness and communication with regard to their own child's education. At many schools, the traditions ingrained in the culture over the years have caused a unidirectional decision-making process that involves, most commonly, the administration and school board. As a result, the voices of parents and teachers, for example, are often not heard in any discussions related to school reform.

In conducting focus-group research, it is important to hear the voices not normally heard in discussions about the phenomenon under investigation. As noted earlier, the phenomenon of *discourse of silence* refers to the exclusion of voices from certain groups, including stakeholders, in an educational organization. The discourse of silence may affect decisions in the organization that in turn influence the performance of students. This phenomenon is born out of the social constructions and contextual understandings that underlie the investigative methodology inherent in focus-group research. Much of the influence on groups comes from the construction of their own knowledge. Knowledge is a human construction, and individuals build their own understanding of the world as they reflect on their experiences.

It is assumed that all knowledge is contextual and constructed. It is based on the amount of the individual's attention to and the quality of information each individual gathers in his or her situation. In addition, it is influenced by the quantity and quality of attention the individual applies to the information. Thus, understanding of facts is integral to the processing of information, as is the level of sophistication at which each person processes that information.

From the realist's point of view, a real world consists of facts that exist independently of human agreement. Facts fall into two categories. In one category are *brute facts*, which exist independently of what we humans think about them. In the other category are *social facts*, which depend on human thought for their existence. In order to state these facts, we need a common language, which itself is a social fact. Even a realist posits the existence of language as a social fact. Moreover, certain types of school reform depend upon language to convey information relevant to the reform. To become integrated, silenced voices must be able to navigate the language of the organization. Voices are silenced because they lack the ability or opportunity to access and use the necessary language. In order to exist in a coherent sense, and to utilize the social facts integrated with human thought to produce the necessary language, humans must be free from feeling disaffected. This freedom from the oppression of disengagement is important in allowing people to express themselves honestly and openly without fear of some type of embarrassment or retribution.

In its traditional usage, oppression means the exercise of tyranny by a ruling group. In the field of education, school reform efforts should reflect an effort to diffuse oppressive actions, either real or perceived, so that all facets of the learning process can be addressed. A part of that learning process, from the perspective of parents and teachers, for example, is that students should not only be taught facts, but should learn how to think, to reflect on their lives, experiences, and the activities of others around them. Students are not passive learners, nor are they passive in their community. Involved and active parents of these students are aware of their stake in their children and they believe their voices deserve to be heard, that they will help produce school reform. Parents need to feel that they are valued and listened to by school leaders in producing reform that will meet their own children's contemporary needs. For parents to remain silent is, in a sense, an oppression of a vitally important resource for change. Oppression has taken many forms over time in the realm of silencing voices, an example being the domestic realm of the family unit.

The family unit has experienced oppression that has impacted divorced men with children. This most catastrophic phenomenon in today's society continues to rear its ugly head and silences the voices not only of divorced fathers, but of their children as well. As with the silencing of voices of parents and teachers in the educational arena, the traditions of the past have deeply carved a barrier between men and the family court system, silencing their voices in the legal arena.

Because of the patriarchal traditions and the oppression of women before the onset of feminism and the feminist movement, divorced men today face nearly insurmountable odds in the bureaucracy of the family court system that imposes authority when it comes to custody and financial arrangements. This, like silenced parents in an educational organization, is a typification of the traditions and sedimentation that has permeated a system. The sign system is reflective of linguistics tied with feminist rendering of unfairness in a patriarchal system that brings about thought processes in the family court system that oppress men in this divorcing situation.

In short, the family court system has in many instances catered to angry women who may or may not have been unfairly treated (in regard to financial and custodial arrangements) in the aftermath of divorce. Before the feminist movement, women's voices were silenced in the family court system and in other arenas. Since the feminist movement, however, the legal backlash that has produced the silencing of fathers' voices has contributed greatly to this new configuration of injustice.

There is no question that the intense suffering and toxic trauma inflicted on fathers and children by judicial bias and incompetence is serious, widespread, and shameful. Hence, the voices that become silenced are the fathers themselves and their children, whom they so desperately wish to have as an active part of their lives. Although some fathers persevere, many are silenced to the extent that they drop out of society and become entrenched in a painful existence without meaningful interaction with their children.

If we assume that such a system is unjust, then we should argue for a redistribution of power. This redistribution might serve to disperse and decentralize power so that it is not in the hands of only a few individuals or special interest groups. The contemporary philosophy in today's corporate world is one of teamwork and shared decision-making that includes all stakeholders in the organization. This philosophy is not in agreement with frequent examples of the domination and oppression present in many institutional organizations. The question I ask myself is, "Does education today reflect this contemporary corporate model?" The answer may lie in the focus-group process, the descriptive data of which, when dissected, may produce themes reflective of the school's ideal organizational structure.

Young (1990) discusses what she refers to as the five faces of oppression, which I discussed in chapter 4. These consist of exploitation, marginalization, powerlessness, cultural imperialism, and violence. Most affected by oppression are minorities. However, other groups are affected, such as the elderly, people laid off from jobs, young people, single parents and their children, the mentally and physically disabled, and Native Americans, especially those on reservations. Among Young's five faces of oppression, marginalization and powerlessness are perhaps the faces that have the most relevance to voices that are silenced in school reform efforts.

Powerlessness refers to the idea that many people in society do not have the means to participate in decisions that might affect them. Relatively few are in power positions where they have the opportunity to participate in policy decisions. Therefore, many are affected by the decisions of a few. Many times, who one is or the position one holds gives a certain degree of power. In a sense, others are more inclined to listen to someone who is in a position that is respected and associated with power. The phenomenon I am calling *discourse of silence* seems to center on this sense of marginalization and powerlessness of many stakeholders in educational reform.

Many discussions of social justice not only ignore the institutional contexts within which the distribution of decision-making occurs, but often the discussions presuppose specific institutional structures that are assumed to defend and support a just representation. Some political theories tend to assume centralized legislative and executive institutions separated from the day-to-day lives of most people in the society and those state officials with the authority to make and enforce policy decisions (Young, 1990). In the arena of school organizations, decisions made without hearing the voices of those affected by the decisions will invariably promote social injustice.

Inequality refers to the distinctions drawn among people in terms of how widely they differ in power, wealth, education, or income. In the context of an organization, social status assumes a variety of forms, as does inequality, since every analytical dimension of status is also an analysis of inequality. Thus, the concentration of power in a school organization, more specifically in the hands of administrators and board members, may constitute a dimension of inequality for teachers, parents, and other stakeholders in the decision-making process. This refutes a philosophy of leadership that alludes, "The more power you give away, the more you have." This simple statement has overwhelming ramifications in the realm of organizational leadership and policy development in the educational arena. Administrators should relinquish some of the power structure in decision-making and policy development in order to hear the voices of others, empower the stakeholders, and gain widely accepted policy change.

Another factor that may affect the silencing of certain groups is the prevalence of cultural diversity. In many schools, there are students who may feel like they are in an alien environment with rules that are unfamiliar to them. Both teachers and students end up feeling frustrated, but the students are the real losers if this frustration causes them to perform poorly and/or drop out altogether. In the context of teachers' and parents' input into the educational system, they may often feel powerless as a result not only of the unequal distribution of power and social justice, but because of the presence of possible cultural differences as well. Obviously, determining who should make school reform decisions can be a complex process.

The ground rules for decision-making rarely are neatly demarcated, whatever the political arena. In state legislatures, the stakes are high because of the dollars and public constituency involved. The role of power is accepted and refined to a high level of sophistication. In academia, where the public stakes are considerably lower, the power game often is conducted with such subtlety that it is scarcely observable to the outsider. Nevertheless, one's status is usually understood and often relished by players on the inside. Since much of school reform efforts are a political activity, the various players usually prefer to keep their options open. Consequently, one resorts to monopolizing power when one has assumed it, or when the prospects for all parties playing by the rules of inquiry appear remote. Almost inevitably, then, the decisions seen as most important are made by the dominant power holders. The result is that the rhetoric of empowering teachers (and parents) essentially leaves teaching to teachers (and parenting to parents). These stakeholders are anything but empowered with respect to decision-making, for example, with regard to content and materials.

Persons and groups at the state and national level believe it is their responsibility to make decisions about what is necessary for the local institution. Some educators, particularly in their school's organizations, believe their power is abdicated as well. Are there any levels and domains where educators and their organizations may play, with impunity and good conscience, according to an epistemology and with local tools of power? In other words, are educators enacting school reform with integrity and ethical standards, possessing the knowledge necessary to enhance certain educational programs in the best interest of all students in their schools? The significance of this question rises out of the nature of public education itself.

The public educational process functions at its best when decisions are kept open at the point of local application and addressed with the unique blend of stakeholder voices appropriate to its nature. The process of inquiry to be brought into play is complex and must be learned. It is corrupted by the infusion of rigid rules and tools of power. The self-interests inevitably brought into play in the inescapably political domains of decision-making must not run counter to the perceived common good.

CHAPTER 10

Data Presentation and Action-Plan Development

FOCUS-GROUP CASE STUDIES

You are in the process of completing your own focus-group research. You have followed the entire process from defining the phenomenon you are investigating to receiving the completed audio and video transcripts of the participants and everything in between. You have all these data at your fingertips to improve your school organization. In this chapter, I would like to take you step by step through the entire focus-group process, from defining the topic of your study to developing and implementing your action plan. I will do this by first discussing the steps involved. Then you will have the opportunity to view two complete focus-group studies that I have conducted.

The first focus-group study involved the incorporation of students from grade 3 at five K–3 elementary schools into a new grade 4 at an upper elementary school containing grades 4, 5, and 6. The second study explored the viewpoints of parents regarding their involvement in the schools and home/school communication. I am hopeful a review of these studies will give you an accurate depiction of how to proceed with the process. Let us begin with data analysis.

DATA ANALYSIS

As you read through the transcripts, you will notice common themes. In addition, as you view the videotapes, you will observe nonverbal cues (body language) from the participants from which inferences can be drawn. Take the data from the dialogue generated from each question, and cut and paste these common themes in a separate document, or at the end of the transcripts. I recommend reading through the transcripts several times, continuing to combine common themes. Extraneous information or dialogue that has nothing to do with the question that was asked should be removed to avoid confounding the pertinent information that can be useful.

Once you feel you have exhausted the possibilities of combining the common themes generated from the dialogue, develop a two- or three-paragraph discussion section from the common themes. Place this discussion section following each question and common theme section in your document. Continue this process until you have completed combining common themes and developing a discussion section for each question. Depending on how fast you tend to work, you can accomplish this task in anywhere from one full day to about one week. I prefer spreading this process over about a one-week period. As you reread the data each time, you may find more common themes than you realized in the previous reading.

Next, from the data you will develop what I call assertions that will directly guide your action plan. These assertions are statements derived from the common themes you determined and the discussion sections following each question. Each assertion should contain information that affirms, refutes, or has potential to develop a given practice within the organization. The focus-group case studies presented in this chapter give you a visual of how the process looks as it is developed into a complete study. These are actual studies that I completed in a school district. The first study was conducted as a result of some controversial issues regarding a grade configuration change in the school district. The second study was one I initiated because of my commitment to communication and parent involvement in schools. Some of the information is stated in a general sense so as to protect confidentiality. Also, keep in mind that the transcripts are verbatim so grammar, and so on, were not edited.

FOCUS-GROUP CASE STUDY #1

The Transition of Grade 3 Elementary Students to Grade 4 in an Upper Elementary School

Abstract

This investigation encompassed the viewpoints of administrators, parents, and teachers regarding the future transition of students in grade 3, at their respective elementary school building, to grade 4 at a future upper elementary school. Three focus groups of six to nine participants were formed with members from each of these sample populations:

Focus group 1: Administrators
Focus group 2: Parents
Focus group 3: Teachers

Administrators, parents, and teachers were sent a letter describing the research to be conducted and were instructed to return a form indicating whether or not they desired to participate. Focus-group interviews occurred during the month of November. Interviews were conducted in a conference room in the school district, utilizing an independent facilitator.

Participants' responses were audio- and videotaped. To protect their identity, all participants' names were coded. In addition, only the researcher viewed the transcripts. Once the tapes were transcribed, they were locked in a storage cabinet. Forty-three common assertions were discovered that relate to the future transition of students in grade 3, at their respective elementary school building, to grade 4 at the future upper elementary school. From these assertions, planning committees were developed and strategies implemented for a smooth transition for the students and their parents.

The Purpose of This Study

The purpose of this research was to assist planning committees in developing and implementing strategies to conduct a smooth transition for students in grade 3, at their respective elementary schools, to grade 4 at the newly configured upper elementary school.

This study was limited to the following:

1. The research for this study took place in one suburban school district.
2. This study was limited to the responses of a purposive sample of six to nine administrators from focus-group interviews conducted by one facilitator.
3. This study was limited to the responses of a random sample of six to nine parents from focus-group interviews conducted by one facilitator.
4. This study was limited to the responses of a random sample of six to nine teachers from focus-group interviews conducted by one facilitator.

This study was limited by the following:

1. This study was limited by a fixed population in one suburban school district, which prevents the results, but not the process, from being generalized to other suburban school districts.
2. This study was limited by the effectiveness of the researcher's ability to gather data through focus-group interviews.
3. This study was limited by the capabilities and consistency of the facilitator in asking questions and in prompting group members in order to elicit responses.
4. This study was limited by the purpose of exploring administrator, parent, and teacher viewpoints regarding the transition of students in grade 3, at their respective elementary schools, to grade 4 at a newly configured upper elementary school. It is not the intention of this researcher to provide normative data or master narratives for the purposes of prediction and control.
5. This study was limited by the conditions under which the focus-group interviews were conducted, and the limitations of the facilities, setting, and the setup for audio- and videotaping.

Focus-Group Interviews and Discussion

Data from each of the three focus groups were compiled into similar categories. Participants' initials are indicated along with the designation of their group as a coding procedure (e.g., A-Administrator, P-Parent,

T-Teacher). The first letter or letters are the participants' initials. The last letter is the group designation (A-Administrator, P-Parent, or T-Teacher). A number at the end indicates that there were two participants with the same initials. Material included in this summary was information that was directly related to each specific question. Information that was extraneous or, in this researcher's opinion, not related to answering the specific question was not included. This summary encompasses group participants' similar responses to each question, with a discussion specific to each question following each set of responses. This investigation encompassed the viewpoints of administrators, parents, and teachers regarding the future transition of students in grade 3, at their respective elementary school building, to grade 4 at a future upper elementary school.

Question #1

How do you envision the elementary school program in a K–3 model?

BA1   We need to have interventions set up for the incoming kindergarten kids. One thing that we need to incorporate in our schedules for both the K–3 building and the 4-5-6 building is a period for intervention time. At the current middle school we're trying to steal time from social studies—that period needs to be scheduled. When I get together with you about this Response to Intervention model, that will be the time for the research-based interventions, so kids can have their reading and during intervention time they'll have a research-based intervention. Children are coming into kindergarten at great disadvantage in terms of the amount of words that they have been exposed to—there can be as much as a three-million-word deficit in kids who come from poverty environments versus nonpoverty environments. We need to right away do an assessment for the incoming kindergarten kids and then in that afternoon period begin our interventions with those kids in the area of language.

RA   I do agree. One thing I really want to take a look at and consider, we're going to view it as we're losing kids because fourth grade is moving up and the numbers are decreasing so maybe we don't need as much staff, but I think it's very important to continue the level of interventions that we currently have. Now we have kindergarten all day and it's not in a split amount, and we'll have slightly less kids. I think the services we have currently are very successful and I would hope that they don't become watered-down so they're not as useful as they have been.

MA I think that as a district we need to seize the opportunity to take a real close look at primary education in our district over the next two years because our elementaries will be K–3. We made great inroads the last few years with supports for our students through the reading coaches, through AmeriCorps volunteers, through an elementary guidance program. We need to continue to look at all of our programs in elementary because what our goals should be in the elementary schools, because third grade is a benchmark year and it will be an exit grade from our elementary school, we need to do everything we can to ensure that we have students who are 100 percent proficient in reading and mathematics by the time they leave our building; that's the overall vision. I think this is the perfect opportunity to look at our reading program, Title I, and take a look at how we're delivering those services and how that might look a little bit different in more of a primary setting. Also consider taking a look at elementary guidance and their role in the K–3 building, as well as the curriculum and what we're doing in our buildings to meet the developmental needs of the younger children.

RA I tend to agree. We talk about looking at the full-day kindergarten program, maybe we need to look at primary programs. Now that we're going to be K–3 I think we need to look at what the primary model may look like and what changes need to be made.

LA I agree that we need to provide support for those young kindergartners coming in and look to explore some Head Start for some of our students here in the district. Currently the closest one is in ____; we don't always have the resources to get children there. Parents don't get children identified for DART [Discovery Assessment Referral Tracking] perhaps as regularly as they could. Having said that, I know you can house a Head Start program within public schools, I think it would be of great support to have those children with us. We could provide them with good, rich experiences prior to coming to kindergarten.

MA The other thing that I think is important is that we seize the opportunity with the reconfiguration of grades to take a closer look at diversity. Our community's changing and I think it needs to start in the elementary schools. We need to be working with our students and our parents around the whole issue of diversity. That's an area in terms of education that we're a little bit lacking.

BA2 I agree with what's been said to this point. In the area of Head Start, twenty years ago in the district that I was with we had Head Start within the school. It was a school within a school. In addition to the Head Start maybe we need to look at running our own day care. I know that's out on a limb, but I'm just wondering how that would be worked into the program. I will say the Head Start school within a school and being treated as part of the school worked together and jelled and it makes a beautiful program for students.

BA1 I agree. We should be looking at that. A lot of those families that the counselors and social workers deal with—they need that kind of support. They need to have the day care there; they need to have the Head Start there. Some of these folks are having a very difficult time taking care of themselves. In terms of services, and diversity, it made me think of those Second Step lessons that we're doing, we have to have at least three elementary guidance counselors even though we're going to K–3 buildings, the only one who's going to have a lighter load would be ____, the other ones have to travel. I know that one ninth grade counselor has to go to the high school, so if we keep the three counselors in elementary we're going to need to add one in the 4-5-6 building. I'd like to see those lessons delivered in grades 4-5-6. These lessons focus on three areas: impulse control, anger management, and empathy. It's all the things that get kids sent to your office. There's a kit for each grade. The younger kids have a little puppet that talks for the

DATA PRESENTATION AND ACTION-PLAN DEVELOPMENT   49

little kids, and the older ones do have more age-appropriate. Each grade gets seventeen to eighteen lessons. But I guess my point is that we're going to need another counselor.

KSP   I guess I wouldn't expect it to change much from what it is now.

KAP   Other than the full-day kindergarten, there wouldn't be much of a change. The middle school would be having more changes happening.

ARP   I thought it would stay the same—that it would be more affecting those kids moving from the elementary now to the upper elementary.

DBT   I envision it very much the way it is right now. I don't see too much of a change. We'll have the same amount of students. Kindergarten will have specials, I believe, and they'll have their academics in the morning and their specials in the afternoon, they'll eat lunch. I don't see too much of a change at that level.

MOT   It was brought up at a meeting recently that the music and art departments do not have a kindergarten curriculum, so they don't know what they're supposed to do when they have them, so that's something that needs to be addressed.

Discussion

Participants were much in agreement that we should incorporate time in our schedules at all levels for interventions. We currently pull kids out for interventions, or as in the case at the current middle school, we developed Personal Learning Plans and use our social studies classes as a means to provide interventions for students not reaching proficiency on the state test. Participants also expressed an interest in looking at early interventions (which we currently have such as the Reading Achievement Center [RAC] program, Sonday, and Intervention Coaches), and including a Head Start program within our existing framework.

Primary education seems to be an area to be explored according to the participants. Parents and teachers envisioned the K–3 model much as it is currently with some emphasis on preparing appropriately for the full-day kindergarten program. In short, it seems we should look at adjusting our schedules at all levels to include time, specifically, for interventions.

Question #2

How do you envision the upper elementary school program in a 4–6 model?

MA   I've been thinking a lot about this because my youngest child is going to be affected by this. The 4-5-6 school that will be forming needs to be an elementary school. It needs to look like an elementary school, feel like an elementary school, needs to have a curriculum that meets the needs of elementary students. I know that there's been talk about having fourth grade do the same thing they're doing now only in another location and have fifth and sixth grade doing the same thing they're doing now, and I commend the staff up there for realizing that there's a need to have a little bit more closer connection with the students in fifth and sixth grade and having that longer communication arts period in the middle school. I think that's critical, that school needs to look like an elementary school, not a middle school. Fourth, fifth, and sixth grades need to look a lot more similar in terms of their schedule, the way that instruction is delivered, in terms of the way the teachers are grouped and the students are grouped—it needs to look like an elementary school—not a middle school. The 7–8 building should be our new middle school.

EA   I concur with that. Philosophically and instructionally it's an elementary school. Actually I don't think there's any resistance out there. The current middle school staff has not come to me and said "Let's keep it a middle school." I think it's pretty clear that it's going to be an elementary school. But semantics are everything to the public. I think we have to not worry about how confused they get on names. I think we have to name it and let them get used to it. A great example would be the intermediate school needs to become a middle school—it needs to be a 7–8 accredited, national middle school. I think if they do not follow the middle school philosophy, it would be a mistake. Junior highs do not work. There's a lot of research on that. I think with this program in grades 4–6 there are some key elements that are going to make it successful. There needs to be a lot of time spent on how we're going to get them off the buses, how we're going to put them on the buses, are we going to line them up, what are we going to do with the walkers. There needs to be some time taken into the layout of the building, how parents can pick kids up, and the safety issues. They're younger kids and there's probably going to be about 1,100 kids there so they really need to be thinking about logistics. Part of that is creating smaller learning communities—that's what we tried to do this year with smaller teams. Last year in fifth grade there were about 130 kids on a team, this year they have about 70. Teachers have more time to work on communication arts with their kids. This schedule change had a huge impact on the building, and those are the kinds of things we need to be looking at. Smaller learning communities—schools within the school—teams within the school, elementary teams. We need to have the whole building on the same schedule. I don't think one grade should be a six-day rotation, the other two different. All that will cause is some divide between staff, divide between parents, and divide within the school. It needs to be a unified school and all grades need to be on the same schedule. If you try to run two schedules you will cause traveling problems, staff problems. It should be an elementary-type schedule. We also need to have high expectations for academics. We shouldn't decrease programs to save money. Typically in changes like this programs and staff are eliminated. I think there needs to be some transition for programs too. Some of the current programs K–4 that are operating and working need to be transitioned appropriately into the 4–6 building. I don't want to see us eliminate staff just because they have to move up to another building. One program that works at the middle school is that the counselors follow the students through. It's probably one of the best things that have ever happened at ____. I have a pretty serious vision for this building and have been thinking about it for a year. I see the students in fourth grade coming in with not a lot of independence. I think we're going to create something called progressive independence. As the kids get through the building, they get more and more independence so that by the time they get to sixth grade they're able to walk themselves to the bus.

ARP   One concern is with recess. Those fourth graders are used to having recess and are they going to have that opportunity now, and how will that fit into the schedule, where would they have it.

KSP   I agree and I also think that it's OK that the fifth and sixth would be included in the recess and I'd like to see them have a playground.

JP   I also agree with that and I think that the older kids are still elementary and so they really have not had recess in the last couple years and I think it's very important for their age.

PP   So I guess I'm envisioning that too. There may be even more changes to what the fifth and sixth graders are experiencing—make them more like elementary. I think the biggest change for the fourth graders—new building, lots of kids, I guess that's one of my questions is do they have a homeroom, how much switching of classes would there be. I would like it to be more like an elementary school. They just happen to be in a different building.

ASP   I agree with that. My main concern is the class size. Now it's small—nineteen kids—even the three second grades at our school my daughter knows every single kid. I'm worried that over there it's going to be huge and how much changing will they do. They change a little bit now and that's good, but how much more will there be.

AS   I had wondered if there's a possibility of getting kids that come in from a very small school—my kids came from a small school—into this huge environment and I think a lot of success can depend on how many of your friends are in your classes, not for socializing, but just comfort level. That there's some way that the smaller schools can be on the same team and still

DATA PRESENTATION AND ACTION-PLAN DEVELOPMENT   53

KDP   meet new kids. I know from talking to other parents in my school that's one of the hardest adjustments for them. In bigger schools you know more kids.

KDP   My daughter came from ____, which is one of the bigger schools and she's in fifth grade right now at the middle school. She's having problems even with kids being in her class. Talking with guidance counselors it sounded like it was something that does happen more often than you think whether they're from a big school or small school, it depends on the kid. I know she would always talk about that in fifth grade it seems all you do is schoolwork; there wasn't a chance to get to know other kids in your class. Maybe if there was more of an opportunity early on in the year to get to know the other kids—icebreaker types of things—that might have helped her in fifth grade. If you did something like that in fourth grade when you're intermixing the schools that might help the younger kids who are not as socially savvy.

ARP   Which is another point for them having recess and how important that is. There are issues that come with that also, but there's a lot of socialization that goes on there that would help them get to know each other better than just passing in the hallways.

ASP   Another thing that I've been thinking about that isn't really academic are the parties. The kids in elementary school love those parties. I just wonder if they're going to keep those for the upper elementary kids.

KSP   I agree. I think that these days our kids are growing up too fast, and we need to have parties and field trips incorporated as long as we can. Just because the fourth grade is moving in with the older kids I'd hate to see them lose that.

JWT   I see it more as an elementary setting as the elementary setting is now—definitely geared more toward elementary as they are only eight and nine years old coming up through the middle school.

SDT   I teach at the middle school now and I see it being more as an elementary building. I would think that we would possibly provide recess, which is not happening now. I think the children would need some type of recess, and I think that as far as our

	activities that we do now, we need to look more toward elementary activities—get away from school dances and have more elementary-related activities. I just hope we do not go on a six-day rotation—we're used to the five-day rotation in our building, and I think as far as the current teachers that are there we would prefer to stay with a five-day rotation and not go to the elementary six-day rotation. Another concern that our staff has is not going to elementary hours. The current staff would like to stay on middle school hours.
OT	What are middle school hours?
MKT	It's 7:43 a.m. to 3:08 p.m.
JWT	Are those teachers' hours or kids' hours?
MPT	The kids get off the bus and go into the auditorium and then they dismiss at 3:00.
MOT	As a fourth grade teacher in an elementary building, we would really be excited about those hours. So that's not a concern of the people in the elementary buildings.
JWT	I wonder about PE and right now they get it twice in a six-day rotation. Are we going to be elementary really—I'm worried that when we get there they're going to try to conform us to a middle school feel. That shouldn't be the case. They keep saying that fourth grade will stay like it is, but fifth and sixth grade will stay like they are, that's not possible. We need to go either one way or another and I think that since this is fourth grade it really needs to be elementary.
CT	I think that what we're going to need to do is to make sure that, except for maybe the hours, that K, 1, 2, 3 is very similar to 4, 5, 6; otherwise we're not being truthful when we say it's an elementary school; we're not a middle school. So I think that things like recess need to be in place.
SPT	It would be interesting also to see other districts that have implemented this—how they worked out some of those problems and issues along the way.
JWT	I have concerns about special ed. in that at the elementary buildings now, special ed. teachers have their own classrooms and are able to meet the needs of the students better in that type of a setting than at the middle school being on a cart. I would

	hope that because it's not going to be a middle school, special ed. teachers would be afforded their own classrooms.
MPT	There are plans to build something like sixteen new classrooms.
DBT	Let's make sure we have enough space for the special people that come in. You're probably going to end up with two speech clinicians if not more there full time. You're going to need room for occupational therapy, physical therapy, gifted, and ESL [English as a second language]. You do share rooms at the secondary level, but the need isn't as great as when you bring that fourth grade in—you're gonna have a lot more need for those kinds of specials.
MPT	We do have two speech clinicians full time now and I assume that will just stay. From the gifted perspective, I hear that question too. We have two full-time now, but there are two that travel between five elementary schools and I'm not sure how that will change—if there will be one and a half with somebody traveling to some, maybe one elementary school and the middle school—I think we need to look at that entire thing from top down and reevaluate how many people are where.
CT	I teach gifted children and differentiated education as part of my time. What my feeling about what is going to happen since there's going to be a full-day kindergarten that's going to increase the enrollment in each elementary school enough so that elementary gifted education would not to be changed. I think you'll still have about the same number of children you were servicing. We would just have to make sure that the children were identified from the younger grades in a timely manner.
SDT	Along the lines of special education, the way the elementary schools run their special education classes are different than how we run them in the middle school and there has to be some consistency there. We have a full inclusion program at our middle school which I believe is a thriving program and I would like to see that extended into the fourth grade, I do not believe the fourth grade special ed. children have that advantage. We do need to look at the different levels of intervention that we're going to offer and we need to be more consistent with that.

MOT Right now gifted is a couple hours one day in a six-day rotation, I'm wondering how that will be addressed in the future. Are we going to the middle school schedule or is the middle school going to be like us? They're trying to conform fourth grade to be like fifth and sixth and I'm afraid of that.

MPT We've had this conversation many times—we'd like to change the way we do it at the middle school anyway. Right now they come for a nine-week period every day and then we don't see them every day again until the next year, so we could randomly see them at the beginning of one year, at the end of another, and not really see them much in between. But we do an awful lot of activities in between. One way we did propose doing it, is possibly having the kids on one or two teams and then possibly teaching a gifted reading and maybe compact it into three days and then we have them the other two days for gifted things. Or depending on the certification of the gifted teacher, actually teach the reading class and incorporate the gifted into the class. I don't know the answer to your question, but we'd like to change the way we do it.

MOT Another concern about the locks—that's everyone's big concern coming to the middle school—we don't have locks on our lockers now, why would we need them when we came there? If it's going to be 4-5-6 do we need to have locks, is that something we need to address? That's our biggest problem when kids come to the middle school so why are we having them if we don't have them in the elementary.

MPT The building's so big—we have the swimming pool and we have the gymnasium that is used constantly. The building could be partitioned off so the fourth grade could be relatively isolated from the rest of the school, particularly in the new fifth grade wing.

SPT The only problem with that is there are so many kids in that building that are moving, if something is missing from somebody's locker, there's no way to track it down.

MOT I would feel safer with my own child having a lock on their locker, it's just a big nightmare—they're already talking about it.

SDT I understand what you're saying, but their anxiety is gone within the first two days. Even for the most involved child. However, we could look at purchasing different types of locks. Our combination lockers are old and ancient, there are new locks out there today that are so much easier, and if we continue to use locks I think we need to get away from the combination locks and go to another type of lock.

JWT If we're set up as an elementary setting, they really wouldn't have much in their lockers to begin with, because it would be in their desks. They don't need to go to their lockers in between each class, because there's not going to be in-between classes. I agree the lock situation is crazy the first few days and that is what the fourth grade talks about, but it could be easier for them to get over that.

MOT I'm hoping we keep the desks that we use now, so there's a place where they can put their books. My biggest concern is that they're going to try to pigeonhole fourth grade and make us like fifth and sixth.

JWT If they are going to utilize the swimming pool then they would need to use the lockers. If I can teach life skills kids to use a combination lock, we can teach fourth graders.

DPT The other point is that our building is utilized almost every night. There are groups that come in and even though gates are drawn, people are always walking by lockers in addition to kids just yanking on lockers and seeing if something opens or not, there are people in our building constantly. That's probably the biggest issue more so than kids.

CT A lot of us are concerned about how the fourth grade will do in the middle school which is going to be an upper elementary school, but what I'm thinking of is, if I'm correct, most of us had those concerns when the fifth grade went to the middle school—how would the fifth grade do in a middle school setting—and as far as I know they've done fine. I really just wonder how much of this is their anxiety about change, and they'll be fine.

NT We were concerned about orientation—more visits to the middle school—or even getting all the third graders together before they get to fourth grade. I worked in a school district where we did that before, and by the time they did go over to the middle school, their concerns were very minimal.

OT I see that fourth grade already goes in May to the middle school. I would see that fourth grade going at one time and then third grade going another time. Fourth grade also has orientation with their parents over the summer and there's a parent night in May so there are three times that are offered to fourth grade.

NT Even with the one time with the fourth grade now and then they go with their parents, but something more to get the students throughout the whole school year.

MPT This is a different topic. Do we know who's going to be the administrator for the building? That might make a huge difference on whether it's perceived as making the fourth grade conform to a middle school even though it's not a middle school, or if you have a current elementary administrator running it, then it's an elementary school.

JWT I think we also need to remember that the fourth graders coming into fourth grade are only eight years old, they're very young, very immature and they do mature a lot in fourth grade, I have concerns trying to make them conform to a middle school–type setting.

SDT I was on the committee when the fifth grade moved over to the middle school and everything you're saying is exactly what we said about our fifth grade babies, and the parents' anxiety the first year was very high, the second year it diminished significantly and by the third year there was no anxiety anymore. So I think we all understand, and I think you need to understand we are in a middle school building but our fifth graders—we're elementary teachers, and our fifth graders are operating on basically very much an elementary environment. They are secluded in the building and they are protected and nurtured and I don't think there's anybody on our fifth grade staff that isn't an elementary teacher. I wish you teachers could spend some time in the building and that could reduce some of your anxiety. I think you would be pleasantly surprised at how elementary we really are.

JCT I completely agree with that. I'm actually looking forward to the fourth grade coming up so that we can get back to the elementary mind-set. It has helped tremendously going to three-person teams this year—I already feel we've made a big step in the right direction for the ten-year-olds.

MPT I think it will be a bigger transition problem for the sixth grade teachers, than there will be for the fourth grade teachers, because they've been basically secondary for fourteen years.

DBT Remember developmentally too they can't make predictions and inferences and figure out where to go if they're lost. They'll have to have more supervision.

Discussion

Participants agree that the 4-5-6 school will need to be an elementary school. It needs to look like an elementary school, feel like an elementary school, and needs to have a curriculum that meets the needs of elementary students. This seems to be the viewpoint of all three groups. Fourth, fifth, and sixth grades need to look a lot more similar in terms of their schedule, the way that instruction is delivered, in terms of the way the teachers are grouped and the students are grouped—it needs to look like an elementary school—not a middle school. The 7–8 building should be our new middle school. We need to have the whole building on the same schedule. If we have one grade on a six-day rotation and the other two on a five-day schedule, we will experience problems. That type of schedule will cause some divide between staff and parents, and within the school. It needs to be a unified school and all grades need to be on the same schedule. If you try to run two schedules you will cause traveling problems and staff problems. It should be an elementary-type schedule.

There is some consensus on having grades 4, 5, and 6 on a five-day schedule. We also need to have high expectations for academics. We shouldn't decrease programs to save money. Typically in changes like this, programs and staff are eliminated. There needs to be some transition for programs too. Some of the current programs in K–4 that are operating and working need to be transitioned appropriately into the 4–6 building. We should not eliminate staff just because they have to move up to another building. There is a belief that we should keep recess for at least grade 4 and even extend it to grades 5 and 6. This will also impact the physical education program. We seem to experience similar anxieties now with fourth graders coming over to fifth grade, but once they are at the school for a while, it all disappears. One concern is "Who will be the administrators for the new building?" This is something that needs to be decided soon. There was also some discussion about locks and if the students should have locks on their lockers.

Question #3

What do you see as prevalent issues affecting a student who transitions from grade 3 to grade 4?

MA   I think anytime there's a transition there is some anxiety on the part of the students and the parents. Some of the issues that we're going to see are orienting students and parents to the programs and to the physical layout of the building so that they know where they're going to be, they know what their program's going to look like, and that they're oriented to the staff. Creating smaller learning communities is crucial to addressing that. I envision in an elementary school we're going to see two- or three-person teams—people working together with a group of two to three classes of students to make those learning communities even smaller. We need to be prepared to answer questions, we need to be prepared to answer the questions and show that we've done our homework, stick together to make sure this new concept of an upper elementary school work. I think that students need to feel when they come into a new setting they feel a sense of belonging and a sense of security in their new group. The teams need to develop some activities where the students can socialize and get to know each other and really get to know their teachers as well.

RA   One issue that fourth graders now have is that they go from smaller elementaries to one large group of students at a grade level. That will be the same issue. We have third graders going

	into fourth grade now who are coming from five buildings all funneling into one building. There're a lot of new people they'll end up meeting. It's a new environment and so many things are going to be changing.
BA1	One of the huge changes that the kids experience now is instead of being walked to music or walked to gym the bell rings and 1,300 kids are in the hall. We can do a lot to ease the transition by having things be similar from the K–3 buildings to the 4-5-6 building. With your idea of progressive independence, maybe the sixth graders could walk themselves, but in fourth grade and fifth grade the class should go as a whole, so that when the bell rings kids aren't just scattering. The closer we can make it to what they're used to at the elementary the better the transition will be.
SA	I think another means of transitioning students from third to fourth grade relatively smoothly is to beef up the summer program. Develop a program at the upper elementary school that would get them comfortable with coming to the school and meeting some different kids from all the elementaries and looking at different programs that would give them some time in the building before they become students there.
MA	One last thing on the 4-5-6 school, let's not forget that in the course of transitioning from third grade to fourth grade there are going to be some students who experience difficulty academically, behaviorally, and socially. We need to have programs in place. We're not going to eradicate all the problems and all of the academic issues in K–3, there will still be students who struggle to achieve. We need to make sure that we provide the resources necessary in 4-5-6 grade for those students to be successful.
BA2	We should hold informational sessions for the parents as we go through the whole process, not wait until the opening week of school.
LA	What concerns me about the way we transition our fourth graders is there's little to no communication with anybody about these students. There aren't sit-down meetings, in my previous district I was obligated to sit down with the principal

of the junior high and go through student-by-student issues and concerns. I think we send them over and it's a blank slate and then people try to recreate the past of the student after the fact. We don't do enough activities to get all those children together as a group—we just throw them into the mix and we hope they get along and when they do it works out and when they don't we're scratching our heads trying to figure out what to do to help the process. My final concern would be that of tradition and what do you do with traditions that need to change or need to go? How do you deal with people when that happens? I'm sure all of us have fourth grade activities that happen in each building. My concern is that those activities don't get pushed to third grade, because sometimes that's not appropriate, and how does that then translate to the upper elementary with those traditions.

RA That's a good point. Now's the time to make changes to things that have existed for many years in need of change—now's a good time that the district is going through such a large adjustment. Another good point that was brought up is communication. I know with students with IEPs [individualized education programs] we do communicate and there's set up time for communication, maybe we need to look at more communication as a whole.

BA1 I think that's an excellent idea. One of the other things we heard the secretary of education say his goal in Pennsylvania was that every child be known by name. That would force the elementary principals to get to know each of those fourth graders and force the upper elementary school principals to have some knowledge of those kids.

ARP Dealing with the different teachers, the number of teachers they'll have to deal with and the social as we talked about already.

ASP The class size and a new school in general.

KSP I'm worried about changing schools at that young, immature age, the building size, and just the number of students that are going to be there. Pretty overwhelming for a nine-year-old.

PP I think it's what the fourth graders experience, because I think there's a lot of people that think they're too young to move to a big building. Exactly what a year difference in development would be—they're even younger—I think your fifth grade daughter already having those issues—I think it would be those issues that the kids are already experiencing.

MP   The cafeteria—that scares a lot of children—the long lines and everything. Some of them are afraid to go in line and then they're late and they only have a few minutes to eat lunch, so that's a big thing when you have three hundred kids or whatever eating at one time.

ARP   And who they're going to sit with. I don't know how that works at the middle school if they're allowed to sit wherever and that would be, again, the social. You have a child who isn't good at initiating social contact that would be totally overwhelming.

KSP   I don't know how it works there because I don't have a child there, but I would hope that they would keep the cafeteria in smaller numbers with at least the fourth graders just with fourth grade.

MP   Right now each grade eats on their own time. All of fifth grade eats together, all of sixth grade, all of seventh. In the beginning they have to stay on their team and then after a week they can go and sit and like every nine weeks they can switch their seat, but they have to sit in that same seat for nine weeks. That's the way it is the whole three years there.

ARP   Which is nice. There are so many and they have different teachers who supervise an area so it's nice that if you know something's going on at this table you can kind of keep an eye out. I don't know if they have assigned seats, but they have tables for that grading period.

KAP   That seems to not work well with the social issues, but I can see the point that you need to monitor that large group. It's probably not possible to split up lunch even more with whatever schedule they're going to have.

ARP   They almost have assigned seats in the beginning and then once they're familiar with it they're allowed to change.

KAP   My other concern also was timing between classes. Both my kids have gone through the middle school and always complained about not having enough time to get to class, running for the bus, those issues. I would hope with the new building it would be a little less stressful that way. When we first came to the middle school we were told we still treat them like they're in elementary and I thought, "No, you don't." They have to be eased into that eventually cause they'll do that later on, but not the first year that they're there — rushing everywhere. There might be some middle-of-the-road way to go.

KSP   It was my hope that as fourth graders they wouldn't be changing every class. It's important for my daughter to have a relationship with a teacher, and I think if they're changing classes for every subject she's not going to have that bond and as a nine-year-old she still needs that.

MP   This year — my son's in sixth grade — so there are three teachers on a team and the five teams. He has one teacher for three classes, so for the first two periods he has the same teacher. It's better if you only have three teachers so you get to know all three more. He seems to be adjusting well to that, because last year he was on the five-teacher team and they were larger classes. This year on his team there's only 78, when last year there was like 150.

KSP   I think that fourth grade coming from a smaller elementary school the whole team idea is kind of overwhelming. I wouldn't expect a fourth grader to even need a team; they should be with one teacher.

AGP   Do you know what time school will start? That's another thing if a fourth grader now has to be at school at 7:30 or whatever time the current middle school starts.

KSP   I would agree with that. I would hope it wouldn't be too much earlier than what it is right now in elementary.

JP   My son leaves the house at 7:00 to catch his bus to the middle school.

ARP   Concerned!

KSP   We walk and we can leave the house at 8:55 and be there in time, which will be a huge change.

ARP   That is something for them to consider when they're making their schedules also, what the kids are going to be doing when

	they first get there—this is going to be a major change for them.
KSP	We won't be walking then—we'll be catching the bus.
JP	It's a long ride—my son leaves the house at 7:00 and he doesn't get home until 3:35. That's a long day. He's in seventh grade, so he can do it. Another concern I thought for these upcoming fourth graders, they're still so young and they're going to be taking a swimming class. Will they offer swimming to that age group? That's something to think about.
AGP	Keep the swimming for the fifth and sixth graders, but I think that for fourth graders that would be way too much—dry your hair, change clothes, and get to the next class.
KSP	Especially on a six-day schedule where I can't keep track of what's happening on what day.
ARP	If they are going to switch teachers, a smaller team would be good in case there's an issue with a kid they don't have to search out five other teammates, there's only two other people they can confer with—that would be better for the kids also.
KAP	I've had one go through with the three teams of five and now one with the five teams of three, and I'm really much happier with the five teams of three. Another issue I always seem to confront with going to the middle school, I don't feel real welcome at the middle school. The teachers seem kind of distant. If you want to organize team meeting you can, but it does take a lot of work—you don't have your conferences anymore unless something's not good. A little more parent interaction would be nice. I wouldn't let my fourth grader go to the mall by himself, so I would like to know what he's doing all day at school too and know the teachers.
DBT	Sometimes when we move from school to school a lot of information doesn't go with that student. Perhaps they were placed in one program or an intervention was implemented at one level and then they come into the next level and for some reason that information doesn't go with them so the teachers are privy to know what's already been tried. We need to do that at every level, especially with our seventh coming up to the intermediate as well, to make sure that that information follows

them somehow. We have guidance counselors now at the elementary so that should help make a smoother transition than it was in the past. Sometimes you end up spinning wheels that were already spun and we're wasting time. In special ed. we have a meeting at the beginning of the year where we tell our regular ed. teachers about our special ed. students and their goals, so maybe something like that should be implemented with everyone so that the teams at least know what their students are going to look like.

JWT   I know we do a little bit when they come to meet with the administrator and guidance counselor, but I do feel in my building that's a frustration that I wish we could share more and have a chance to share more and we just don't get that opportunity. Having that open communication like the special ed. does go up and meet for a day, it would be nice as a team to go up and be able to discuss specific issues about certain kids. Some of them just need that little bit of extra help that we've already been giving them. I have actually heard about two or three kids this year that are really struggling that if I would've been able to share more information rather than just one or two words on a piece of paper it would've been a little bit better I think.

SDT   I don't know if you're aware of this in elementary we have always met at the end of the school year—the special ed. teachers and the principals and the current guidance counselors—with ____ so we have in our hands before the end of the year every Instructional Support Team [IST] file at least, so those kids we are definitely on top of and we have their names before the end of the fourth grade school year and we have all of their accommodations and our guidance office places those kids accordingly on appropriate teams. For instance I'm an inclusion team this year and kids who have had IST intervention were purposely placed on the teams with the special ed. teachers, maybe not in all of my classrooms but on those teams. So we are doing that and I'm sure that will obviously continue. I think with guidance counselors in the buildings we'll even be getting more information than what we were able to get through IST.

MOT Don't assume that's going to continue, because the ESAP [Elementary Student Assistance Program] is totally different than IST and we do not get to share the information that we would normally share if we had IST. You're not going to get the same information; you're not going to know about the kids who are struggling, because the ESAP process is very long.

SDT Why couldn't we just do something like a summary sheet? We don't have to reinvent the wheel here. They take a few minutes to fill out and they are confidential, so we could look at individual teachers not a Student Assistance Program [SAP] coordinator but we could do that just as teams and we could do that at every grade level. A summary sheet could even be a positive of this child's strengths—if you had the time to do them you could do them for every child in your class still probably within an hour, an hour and a half. Maybe we should just make that part of the process of them moving from grade to grade.

CT I think the point you made is excellent. I think a lot of what has to happen is communication, but I don't think it should be every week. The other thing that might sound strange to some of you but the whole idea of having the third/fourth graders go to the middle school five times or whatever, I think that giving everyone parents and kids the message that they're going somewhere strange and they have to prepare. Really it's just like moving on to school and if all the teachers are willing to treat the kids at the developmental level that's appropriate for them, I know it's a big deal in terms of structure, staff, and rooms and I'm honestly not trying to underestimate that, but I think in psychological terms the kids moving from one school to another unless we turn it into something big, I don't think it has to be.

MKT I agree with that. I think a lot of the transition problems—I get to work with fifth, sixth, and seventh, and the incoming fourth graders—a lot of the anxiety that parents have is sort of created by the teachers. I know it happens when we have go to special ed. IEPs, like in seventh grade, it was easier in fifth and sixth, it was real hands-on—seventh grade is more like an intense note-taking skill, and we're the ones who set the parents up and

68　CHAPTER 10

MOT　say "start getting worried about this," and your kids get anxious about it. It shouldn't be thrown up like a warning alarm.

MOT　In my building, we are very positive about the middle school. The parents already started asking questions, and we try to tell them that your kid's going to be fine; the transition is great, we've already started doing that. We just keep encouraging and saying it'll be fine. But the more the kids see the places they're going to go, the more comfortable they become. Especially if it's a third grader—they'll think "Oh, I've been here, I know how to get to the office." I think the more comfortable you become the less anxiety you have. There are a lot of little kids with anxiety, and I think it's going to give a comfortability to that child.

JWT　Maybe they should come to the building as a guest for a holiday concert or maybe they come and participate in an assembly.

DBT　Maybe make a video too.

Discussion

Anytime there is a transition there is some anxiety on the part of the students and the parents. Some of the issues that we're going to see include: orienting students and parents to the programs and to the physical layout of the building so that they know where they're going to be, they know what their program's going to look like, and they're oriented to the staff. Creating smaller learning communities is crucial to addressing that. The vision is an elementary school where we're going to see two- or three-person teams—people working together with a group of two to three classes of students to make those learning communities even smaller. We need to be prepared. The students need to feel, when they come into a new setting, a sense of belonging and a sense of security in their new group. One issue that fourth graders now have is that they go from smaller elementaries to one large group of students at a grade level. That will be the same issue. We have third graders going into fourth grade now who are coming from five buildings all funneling into one building. There are a lot of new people they will be meeting. It's a new environment and so many things are going to be changing.

One of the huge changes that the kids experience now is, instead of being walked to music or walked to gym, the bell rings and 1,300 kids are in the hall. We can do a lot to ease the transition by keeping things similar between the K–3 buildings and the 4-5-6 building. With the idea of progressive independence, the sixth graders could walk themselves, but in fourth grade and fifth grade the class should go as a whole so that when the bell rings kids aren't just scattering. The closer we can make it to what they're used to at the elementary, the easier the transition will be. In the course of transitioning from third grade to fourth grade there are going to be some students who experience difficulty academically, behaviorally, and socially. We need to have programs in place. We're not going to eradicate all the problems and all of the academic issues in K–3. There will still be students who struggle to achieve. We need to make sure that we provide the resources necessary in grades 4, 5, and 6 for those students to be successful. We need to communicate better with parents and teachers at the transition point to ensure a smooth transition.

The cafeteria was a concern for the fourth graders. They will be scared in such a big environment and they will have to decide who they will sit with. We may want to look at smaller numbers in the cafeteria at a time. Participants thought fourth graders should be with one teacher and not a team. Participants were also concerned about the earlier time the children would have to leave for school. Swimming should be kept for fifth and sixth graders and not available to fourth graders. The major concern of all three groups was the communication across all three interest groups: teachers, parents, and administrators. The more informed all are, the better the transition will be for the students and their parents.

Question #4

What do you see as prevalent issues affecting a parent of a student who transitions from grade 3 to grade 4?

RA   I know one always is transportation. Your child is now leaving the area in which you live. They're used to shipping them a short distance and now in some cases partway across the school district.

70 CHAPTER 10

         Now they're going to be spending more time on the bus. When kids are on the bus longer there tends to be more bus issues.

SA   One of the things you might want to look at is holding some events throughout the year in those communities. Community Outreach has opened a facility in ____ and look at doing some different things throughout the course of the year with the 4-5-6 building within the communities. Maybe up in ____, down in ____, something over in ____, just to get back in those communities.

MA   Most of the parent concerns are going to come from the uncertainty that exists with the change that will be taking place in grade configuration. Parents are probably worried about their children going to a large building, just as the fifth grade parents were worried about students going to such a large building. It is critical that we really have a vision for the 4-5-6 building and that it's clearly communicated to the parents. We look like and sound like we know what we're talking about. If we don't have a clear vision and don't have a clear idea of what that school's going to look like, we're going to have a hard time convincing parents that it's going to be good for students. We need to spend a lot of time over the next year and a half developing that vision and getting the word out there positively.

RA   Another concern they may have is how much access they're going to have. One of our earlier focus groups involved how welcome parents felt in schools. In the elementary they feel pretty welcome because there are so many activities that we need their help with—the kids are a younger age and you just need more hands for assistance. There might be some confusion if they're still welcome in the school, what is my role in the school? what can I help with? what can I do? That may be an area that we want to look at, I know the current middle school has worked very hard to change some parents' perception on their role in the school.

EA   That goes back to logistics again. We're talking about buzzer systems, drivers' licenses, all these security systems which put a barrier between the parents and schools. That impacts what we're about to do with this transition because we're actually going to be sending a physical message to a parent, "Do not come to the school without buzzing in." I know they understand that but the reality when parents are inconvenienced they get upset and I think that this transition is a key time to communicate with them strongly and frequently that they are welcome in the school. I go back to some nervousness I have about safety of children. There are twelve exits in that building and there're some safety issues. You must commit to smaller learning communities and then the teachers are responsible for a group of kids at all times.

MA Another concern or question that parents may have is, "Who's in charge?" I think the district needs to identify as to who the leadership of that building is going to be and it can't be at the end of next school year. It needs to be announced at the end of this school year or at the beginning of next school year—a leadership team needs to be identified. Principals, counselors, those types of people so that this hard-core planning can begin in earnest. None of the good things we've talked about will happen without a leadership team being identified and hitting the ground running with focus groups like these or monthly meetings or planning committees.

EA That's absolutely correct—but I think it should be now. We're planning right now; this is the start of it. Those leaders need to be identified regardless of who's retiring, who's not retiring. How can you lead a building and plan for the building if you don't know you're in charge of the building?

LA To add to that, I even think that identifying which teachers are going to go, which teachers are not going to go. We've talked about how soon can you start that staffing decision as it relates even to the full-day kindergarten, that planning needs to take place and I think it's difficult that we're going to be planning with not knowing who the staff is going to be. I just don't think you can bring someone in that just interviewed and plop them into a new full-day kindergarten program unless they've had extensive experience and expect them to be successful. Same with the fourth grade program at the middle school, my staff has asked questions and I'm sure parents are asking questions of them. Will they remain a triad team? will they be thrown in the mix? and will the principals establish new teams when they get over there? Perhaps if some of that work could be done now and even letting that staff know what is their choice if they don't think that transition is in their best career interests. What are their options, or are there any options that they may be able to exercise.

BA1   I think we still have some work to do in just identifying numbers of staff. I don't know how many speech teachers we're going to need at the new building versus how many will stay. I don't know how many special ed. teachers we'll need. I don't know if we're going to have a teacher who works primarily with autistic children. We may need to start something like that in the new building. If a leadership team or a planning team could be identified at each building that might be a way to start to address some of these questions.

EA   It'll be a big mistake if you have subcommittees, planning committees and you put, for example, a fourth grade teacher on that teacher planning for a 4–6 building and then they're not transitioned to that building. I think you will really deflate people and deflate their ownership of these new programs if you do that to somebody. That's why I want to reiterate it's critical to have leadership set up and staff on board prior to your planning.

RA   I think that gives them time to adjust too. To be in the mind-set that we're not hitting people last minute—that's not where they're expecting to go. Obviously there will have to be last minute changes, slight changes. For example, all the fourth grade teachers will automatically be moving up—they can start preparing for that.

KDP   Having had kids go through you definitely feel like you are much less involved when you get to the middle school. You don't have that one teacher to go to—it would be nice to have just one teacher to call and let you know how your kid is doing versus having to meet up with a group of three even. At times even though you feel they're short on time and you don't feel you really get to talk about your kid on a more personal level

Thus, self-serving interests are contradictory to the effective advancement of reform in educational organizations. Consequently, teachers, parents, and other stakeholders must join with all relevant decision-makers in an educational process that tends to close the gap between administrators and concerned, informed stakeholders. The goal is the educational good health of the community, not personal or professional aggrandizement. This educational good health of the community can be brought about by the infusion of input from stakeholders involving school reform and implementation. Even though that balance of power is not generally practiced in American school organizations, it is a socially just means of including all interested, informed parties in decisions that will impact the future of the school and community.

than you were able to with the teacher at the elementary. You can pop in there anytime and see what's going on; you definitely don't have that at the middle school. For a fourth grader you would definitely want to have one person to call on a more regular basis than every nine weeks.

ARP So the communication—there has to be some form of communication from the teachers to the parents maybe through a newsletter—that there's a way to communicate. And also maybe an opportunity for parent volunteers—they're always saying it's so important that the parents be involved.

KDP When you say that, the cafeteria and the thoughts of how complicated that will be, I think that would be a good way for parents to get involved if they can come in and help in the cafeteria with logistics. That way you're there to see what's going on and maybe have a chance to see teachers.

JP I know that they do offer as volunteers to go and monitor the cafeteria. I think they only have two parents, but it would be a nice idea to have more parents if they'd like to do that even for recess. They also have guidance counselors for each grade, and if they break it down to smaller groups that might be something to think about too.

AGP Also the conferences, do you have a beginning-of-the-year conference at the middle school? At the elementary level, we have that beginning-of-the-year conference no matter what— that should still carry over to the upper elementary.

KSP Does curriculum night still happen at that school?

MP There's two different ones—there's one that you can take your child to so they can know where they're going or the curriculum one that's just for the parents and you have what twelve minutes with the teacher for them to give you a brief summary of what's going to happen for the whole year. No personal one-on-one, it's just a brief layout and you follow their schedule. That's sometimes the only time you see the teachers for the whole year.

KAP I understand that numbers make a huge amount of difference— you're bringing five elementary schools into one school so the numbers are going to make some of the issues difficult. I think it can be done.

PP What are the class sizes when they all merge?

MP Maybe three hundred to four hundred. With seventh grade there are 450 maybe.

ARP But even with three teams of twenty-five each, that's more than the elementary kids are used to now—they're used to nineteen—six more kids makes a big difference in a classroom that's another set of issues. To keep the class sizes as small as they can get them would be ideal with all these social issues, academic issues.

MP My son in sixth grade, in a lot of his rooms they've taken the desks out and they have table this year. They're in groups in tables. I don't know how that would be for the younger kids if they're used to a desk.

ARP Their feet would be dangling!

MP Another thing too, there's only certain times that you're allowed to go to your locker, you're not allowed to go after every period. That becomes an issue because you're trying to lug too much stuff.

ARP What about bathroom breaks? They will now be worried about getting across the building, getting to their locker, getting to class on time. Too much time could be a problem because they could get themselves into trouble.

MP I don't think there's a set bathroom break like in elementary. They have their tracker that they have to take with them—that's their hall pass.

JP Keep it more in groups—my second child is going through and I'm still lost in that building!

PP It seems like such a basic philosophical issue—we're talking about how to adapt a fourth grader to fifth and sixth and as drastic to undo what the fifth and sixth graders are used to—to say now you're in elementary school—they're used to changing classes, etc.

KSP I wonder if there's a way to bring the fourth graders in and limit their class changes and their intermingling for the specials. And then in fifth grade let them intermingle for the specials. And then in sixth grade let them do the class changes and the switching among the teams. Gradually wean them in so you're

	not taking it away from the kids who are already doing it, but you're not throwing these fourth graders into a situation that the sixth graders have already adjusted to.
KDP	You don't want to take the fifth and sixth down to elementary too much because they are going to be going into seventh grade and that would be a drastic change for them and the amount of independence they would have to have if their hands are held the whole way through. They need to each grade gradually step up to a little more independence.
JP	I do think they were thinking about this when they put the schedules up for this year, because they made the smaller teams.
JCT	I have a feeling that it will be a lot of the same issues that we have with the fifth grade parents each year, calming them down—the locks, switching classes, not having your homeroom teacher the whole day. It'll be the same issues that the fifth grade parents have now.
DPT	It has been our experience that the transitions are smooth. Bingo on the locks—but after three or four days if a kid can't do a lock, he'll never do a lock. The transitions aren't that bad. You have to understand the majority of fifth grade teachers treat these kids as elementary kids for the most part and it's really not an issue.
SPT	I think we've made a lot of these comments earlier, but we just have to be proactive and keep the parents informed.
DBT	I don't know if the bus is going to be an issue.
MOT	For the parents in ____, one of their concerns is the long bus ride for such little kids. The parents are in our building a lot, so I think that's going to be the hardest thing for a lot of our parents. Like this week I have seen every parent in my homeroom, every day, we have a lot going on. They're in our building all the time, in fact they have their own room where they meet and do their things. I think that will be a little bit of stress for them, that it's not as open arms, come-anytime-you-want kind of feeling.
CT	That's a really big change for the parents, but if the middle school becomes an elementary school then they're going to have to start doing things like holiday parties, etc.

MOT   If it's going to be an elementary setting, that's what elementary schools have always done—parties for all the holidays.

DPT   But it's an "upper" elementary—that upper carries a lot of weight!

MOT   Are we still going to have the Santa Shop? Where are they going to buy their gifts?

DPT   As activities director, I'll tell you right now—absolutely not!!

Discussion

Transportation is always an issue, but may be of more concern in the transition. The children will be leaving the area in which they live. Most of the parent concerns are going to come from the uncertainty that exists with the change that will be taking place in grade configuration. Parents are worried about their children going to a large building, just as the fifth grade parents were worried about students going to such a large building. It is critical that we have a vision for the 4-5-6 building and that it's clearly communicated to the parents. We must look and sound like we know what we're talking about. If we don't have a clear vision and don't have a clear idea of what the 4–6 school's going to look like, we're going to have a hard time convincing parents that it's going to be good for students.

We need to spend a lot of time over the next year and a half developing a vision and getting the word out there positively. Another concern they may have is how much access the parents are going to have. One of the focus groups' concerns was how welcome parents felt in schools. In the elementary they feel welcome because there are so many activities that require additional help—the kids are at a younger age and teachers need more hands for assistance. There might be some confusion on whether or not the parents are welcome in the school: "What is my role in the school?" "What can I help with?" "What can I do?" That may be an area that we want to look at.

The current middle school has worked very hard to change some parents' perception regarding their role in the school. The district also needs to identify who the leadership will be in the 4–6 building. A leadership team needs to be identified so they can work with the committees and subcommittees. We also need to identify which teachers will move to the 4–6 building. Parents also identified communication as a key factor. There has to be some form of communication from the teachers to the parents, perhaps through a newsletter. There should be an opportunity for parent volunteers to assist in the school. It's important that the parents continue to be involved. Locker and bathroom breaks were also identified as a concern. There will be a lot of the same issues that we have with the fifth grade parents each year: calming the students down about the locks, switching classes, and not having your homeroom teacher the whole day. It'll be the same issues that the fifth grade parents have now.

Question #5

What can the school district do to ensure a student's transition from grade 3 to grade 4 is smooth and successful?

BA1   Make the grade 4 as similar to grade 3 as it can be in terms of the routine.

SA   I think a lot of things we have in place now already with the principals and counselors traveling down to the elementary schools, and I think using the counselors at the elementary school level is an important piece of communication. In the spring, open house with the parents, in late summer doing something again where the kids come out and just do a walk-through of where their classes will be, where the cafeteria is, where the gym is, etc.

RA   I think we also need to develop a vision of all of these grade levels of what we expect it to look like and how it's going to run as quickly as possible. Then we can get that information out to the staff, out to the parents so they know what to expect. For example, all-day kindergarten, the sooner we can get that plan laid out and what the day's going to look like and get that information out to parents that will relieve some of their stresses. Same with the third and fourth grades, if the staff knows what the upper elementary is going to look like and the parents know everyone can be sharing that same vision and preparing the students for that next level.

MA   The other thing that needs to happen is that the staff of this new school need to be goodwill ambassadors for the building, they need to be supportive of what's going to happen and programs and they need to personalize education. That means bringing parents in the summer—making personal contact with parents as frequently as possible. With the 4-5-6 building we need to make sure that the teachers are communicating positively with the parents, giving them opportunities to see what the program looks like and returning phone calls, simple things like that are so important to give the parents a sense of security that the 4-5-6 building is indeed an elementary school.

BA1 Maybe it would be nice to get the new students together for some icebreaking in the summer, but maybe the new staff could have a couple days of that too—some work stuff, some fun stuff (cookout).

SA   It would be really nice to have a staff outing where you go out and take a new staff of people like the fourth grade coming from all the different buildings to do something like that.

BA1 When you talk about the 4-5-6 building, are you seeing it as the fourth grade would be in one place, with a principal and a counselor, and the fifth grade would be in one place in the building and the sixth grade in another place? They would share some things like the art and tech.

SA   I think the fourth grade would have that wing where the fifth grade is now; they would be separated and only walked out to the cafeteria and gym class. There's not going to be a principal's office down there or a counselor's office down there. Maybe there are plans in the architect's plans to create an office down there.

MA   I think it's too early to say that. I think this vision is going to evolve in terms of what's going to happen—that's why we need to identify the leadership team for the building and also a core group of staff who will be going there to begin planning this sort of thing.

BA1 I would be concerned if the fourth grade is going to operate in the elementary wing and the fifth and sixth grade are following a bell schedule and scattering to all different rooms.

MA	That's exactly what I meant when I talked earlier about consistency. That program needs to look like an elementary program—not a middle school program. Fifth and sixth need to look like fourth.
SA	Our fifth and sixth grade are really starting to look like an elementary school right now.
MA	Right—with what you've done with the communication arts period. That was a great segue into what the district needs to accomplish the next couple years.
KAP	Our fourth graders always went through an orientation where they went up to the middle school to look around, I think that was helpful. Orientation night where we go with our children was very helpful. My daughter felt a hundred times better after going through her schedule and knowing where her classes were. Even though she had a sister up there and she's been in this building a number of times, still half of it she was never exposed to. The issue, too, some sort of social opportunities that they could get to know some of these new kids. The opportunities for them to socialize are important.
KDP	Having a daughter in fifth grade, she definitely wishes there were more icebreaker-type situations to get to know the other kids in class, basically she felt they got to school and just went right to work. You're dealing with the school and the lockers and all that the first week. The second week you're into classwork, and she didn't feel like she got to know the kids, other than their names, in her class. She was wanting more of a socialization within the classroom so you'd feel comfortable around the kids you did have class with.
JP	Instead of having one big curriculum night for the whole school maybe have it in sections by grade level. It would probably take more time over more days, but at least it would make the younger ones feel more comfortable and the parents.
KSP	Kind of like an old-fashioned open house.
JP	Exactly.
MP	Then the hallways wouldn't be so crowded, the children can find their way without being overloaded with all these people.

ARP   I also like the idea of an orientation their last elementary year to go with their class to see the new building and then have that opportunity again with the parents so the parents can feel confident.

KS   Kindergarten orientation—that was one orientation that was it—if you couldn't go you missed it. It would be helpful if they had a couple on different weeks so that if you're out of town one week you catch one another week. Maybe also different hours of the day and different days of the week.

ARP   We know how important test scores are right now, but give the kids the time to get to know one another and be comfortable so that they will do better on the tests. They won't have all these other social and other anxieties going on. They can actually enjoy learning and get something from it.

ASP   Maybe have a guidance counselor follow up with all the parents a month or so later just to see how everything's going.

KAP   The first teacher conference is really important too. It helps the parents to kind of know the teacher they're dealing with. You got a kid coming home saying my teacher hates me, and then you meet the teacher and you find out it's really not the teacher, it's the kid. I miss that conference, I really wish we did have that again because that was nice. Another thing I was upset about was that they lost the chance to have art and music. Gym is five days a week, which I understand, we have an obesity problem, but recess might be able to relieve some of that. Losing art and music was not a good thing.

MP   They took away family and consumer sciences [FACS]. My son had last year in fifth grade, but now they took it away from him this year. Also tech, which is wood shop, they don't have that this year, only in seventh grade.

KSP   I would like to see the fourth graders still have those basic classes like art and music. I would hate to see them lose that.

ADP   That surprises me . . . I just assumed that upper elementary would have art and music classes.

MPT   I think that when we do this orientation thing it's going to be hard because you're going to be showing them a school that is not the school they're coming to. You can't walk around and say, "That's Mr. ____ and he teaches Spanish," he might not be there. That'll be an issue. If you can emphasize the structure—the library, the cafeteria—but what happens there is going to change drastically.

NT I think that the district needs to inform the parents about what we know.

JCT A lot of the concerns from the parents will fall on the fourth grade teachers, and if the administration can head some of that off then hopefully not as much will fall on the fourth grade teachers.

JWT I have a question. I'm hearing about all this construction, is it going to be done by the end of next year? It seems like a very short time frame for a very large project. Is it realistic that next year is the transition year!

SDT I have the same concern. Is there any fallback plan that by a certain date if it looks like that nine months ahead of time that this construction is not going to be even 50 percent finished is there any talk of them delaying this to the following year? Is that even a possibility or do we have to make this transition?

MOT I also think that we need to know who the administrators are going to be. How can you introduce parents to someone who's not even going to be there when they get there? Or teachers, they need to do their staffing well before August 30 of that school year, so that everyone can get together whoever's coming there, what teachers are going here; let's not wait until August to make that determination.

JWT If the fourth grade teachers are moving up, it's not going to be such a huge transition for the third graders because they're going to be used to seeing us as fourth grade teachers anyway, so that may be easier on the third going to fourth. I agree that having the staffing done ahead of time is going to be a big challenge, but it's a definite positive because then we could work together and figure things out.

SDT Administratively and not teacher-wise, I feel it's imperative that the building administrator should be a person who's already been in our building for a time. I do believe that bringing in all new administrators would not be the best way to go. There should be some consistency with our administrators;

people who have been in the middle school would be better prepared for this transition than somebody new.

Discussion

Make the grade 4 as similar to grade 3 as it can be in terms of the routine. We also need to develop a vision of all of these grade levels. What do we expect it to look like and how is it going to run as quickly as possible? We must get that information out to the staff and the parents so they know what to expect. Fourth graders always had an orientation where they went up to the middle school to look around. An orientation night where parents could go with their children would be very helpful. Icebreaker activities for the incoming fourth graders would be good to include. Instead of having one big curriculum night for the whole school maybe have it in sections by grade level. It would probably take more time over more days, but at least it would make the younger ones and the parents feel more comfortable. Perhaps a guidance counselor could follow up with all the parents a month or so later just to see how everything's going. Parents would like to see the fourth graders still have the basic classes like art and music, FACS, and tech ed.

Question #6

What do you see as advantages of going to a K–3 elementary model and a 4–6 upper elementary model?

LA   I think the advantages are you can focus on specific curriculum aspects with those grade levels. At times when you have a K–6 model, one particular grade drives how the school looks and it's usually sixth grade. When we become a K–3 we will be a primary center and primary children and how to best educate primary children and best practices for elementary children should be our driving focus. The same thing with intermediate-level kids, best practices for the "tweens" should be what is driving that school. You can focus much more on that age group and give them the best they need. I think it has great advantages to making that division because typically when you're in a K–6 or K–5 or even K–4, you can't be that focused, because normally the oldest grade in the school drives how the school is established. I think it has great curriculum advantages.

SA At the 4–6 level, I think also it's a little more age appropriate to have fourth graders with sixth graders than fifth graders with seventh graders. There seems to be a smaller gap between the fourth and sixth, than the fifth and the seventh. The fifth and seventh are on very opposite spectrums.

MA The K–3 setup lends itself better to the philosophy of learning to read. That transition from reading to learning takes place in fourth or fifth grade. In K–3 we can really focus on having the students learn to read through all the things we're going to be doing and all of the interventions that are currently taking place. What I'd like to see us do is make those interventions even better and stronger and more appropriate for K–3. The whole focus in literacy for K–3 can be learning to read.

EA One advantage to having fourth grade in one building, it lends consistency. It's very difficult with five elementary buildings to have consistency just because of the nature of the beast. When you put them together and centralize it's a lot easier for me to pull all the fourth grade teachers together and say here's the program we want to do. We have all kinds of professional development problems when you have people scattered everywhere. This is so much more advantageous to have them in one place—it's going to add to consistency and centralization of that grade level.

KAP The idea of having the fourth through sixth progress into intermediate seems like a nice idea. From fourth to fifth you have two classes, maybe three you might change for, but the teacher's right next to you so you don't have to walk anywhere. That adjustment is big so if we can bridge that gap but still build to the intermediate that would be really nice and I think it will alleviate a lot of stress for the kids.

KSP I have heard people say that they are more comfortable having the fifth graders not with the seventh graders because it's such a big age difference. The fourth graders are more closer socially with what's happening in sixth grade.

PP I've heard that too—that the middle school—those are awkward ages to be together so moving seventh up is good. But the reason we're here is what is 4-5-6 going to like? Ideally it would be an elementary school; if the elementary schools could be big enough they could just stay.

KSP   When I was asking people for their opinions on this that was what was suggested go back to the local elementary schools with K–6 all in one school.

JP   I agree with that, but I also think that if this is the way it has to be done, then I don't see any way of turning back. I think seventh and eighth grade together—they are in their own world—and I think that is wonderful. Seventh and eighth grade should be together.

KAP   Having sixth graders on the bus with seventh graders—that's like a hormone cutoff—I think it would be nicer to have fourth through sixth on a bus. On a developmental stage—they're all on the same page.

PP   The advantage of a K–3 building would be some breathing room! My son goes to ____ and, oh my gosh, it's crazy. I know they'll appreciate having a little elbow room there. I wonder how they'll treat the third graders. Now fourth graders take their special things and you're moving on up, it seems a little funny to be graduating from third grade.

KAP   Is the idea for all-day kindergarten to be an option?

PP   I had heard from one of the meetings with Dr. ____ was that it was going to be optional. That's how they were starting it anyhow.

KAP   For my child if she had jumped into five full days every day that would have been too stressful.

ARP   I think with a lot of working parents—the kids are in day care. We are pushing them to grow up much more quickly—they're learning to read in kindergarten, that used to be a first grade skill. I think that's where that's coming from.

KAP   I think the option is nice.

KSP   I would like to have that option also—I'm not a believer in full-day kindergarten.

SDT   I'll say one thing about the 4–6. I have never been an advocate of 5, 6, and 7 in a building. I would not have wanted my fifth grade daughter in a building with seventh graders. I would have never allowed my children to attend social events with seventh graders. I am very much in favor of this and I think it's just a better mix developmentally for 4, 5, and 6. There's too much developmentally—the gap between fifth graders and seventh graders is huge and I've just never been comfortable with it.

MOT And the curriculum fits better. Like you said seventh grade science is totally different, we do hands-on science until sixth grade, so it makes sense that we're together—we can share materials. Kindergarten all day is a great plan for our kids who aren't making it to the half-day program because of transportation.

DBT I suppose our kindergarten curriculum will have to be changed.

CT I was just thinking of the advantages—this is probably what everyone has said just in different words. The K–3 buildings will still be elementary, but it was a real challenge for the middle school teachers because what you had was the elementary teachers and the middle school teachers. So I would think that would be much more difficult to be a teacher the way the middle school was then, then the way it will be with the upper elementary.

Discussion

You can focus on specific curriculum aspects with those grade levels. At times when you have a K–6 model, one particular grade drives how the school looks and it's usually sixth grade. When we become K–3 buildings, we will be a primary center with primary children. We must determine how to best educate primary children and best practices for elementary children should be our driving focus. The same thing with intermediate-level kids, best practices for that level should be what is driving that school. You can focus much more on that age group and give them the best they need. The K–3 setup lends itself better to the philosophy of learning to read. That transition to reading to learn takes place in fourth or fifth grade. In K–3 we can really focus on having the students learn to read through all the things we're going to be doing and all of the interventions that are currently taking place.

Removing the fourth graders from the elementary schools will also give us a little breathing room at those schools. Several of them are so close and packed.

Question #7

What do you see as disadvantages of going to a K–3 elementary model and a 4–6 upper elementary model?

EA   The whole middle school concept was set up for no more than five hundred students in a building. I think that would apply to a 4–6 building. Over a thousand kids in a building is ridiculous. You could still do smaller learning communities and schools within schools, but if you look at any of the problems in the eight years I've been around, I can always come back to the building's too large.

MA   I don't know if I see this as a disadvantage, but it's a concern, particularly on the 4-5-6 side, that we're creating an entirely new school and way of thinking and way of teaching in 4-5-6. Right now just the uncertainty of it is something that raises concerns and questions and anxiety among students, parents, staff, and administration. I think the whole uncertainty of all this change is a disadvantage that was created by us doing this, but we need to seize the opportunity to turn that into an advantage by being clear with what the vision is and identifying a group of people to develop and then address that vision.

RA   One area we're overlooking is how the third grade is going to transition into the new building, what we need to look at is the students that are going to be there in grades 5 and 6, the year of the change. Is that going to be a dramatic change for them too? Changing from a middle school to an elementary, are you going to lose privileges, and things that you're used to all of a sudden are different. Maybe what we need to look at in those areas, and the staff at the middle school is already starting to do that, is slowly start to transition it over to where in two years it won't be that big of a change other than one grade moving up, a new grade is moving in, but what you're used to is somewhat similar to you're already used to. If there's too big of a change, not only are we going to throw off those fourth grade students that are coming but we're going to throw off the fifth and sixth graders.

LA One of the greatest disadvantages is the issue of communication. Once again the communication needs to be tight and structured, and it would be great if the principals from 4–6 meet collectively. That's how you eliminate some of those communication issues, because you're having monthly meetings to talk. Presently, other than a cabinet meeting, we don't meet with 5-6-7 on a regular basis to talk about issues and kids and curriculum issues. Perhaps that's because nobody ever thought about it.

PP The main thing we've already said is that the fourth graders still feel like they're in elementary school—it's not pushing them forward too quickly. If they're all of a sudden in middle school a year earlier that would be a big disadvantage.

KSP Going along with this, I hate the thought of pushing my kids to grow up too quickly.

KDP Not to say I want to push my kids to grow up too quickly, but I don't want fifth and sixth to be too dependent upon having their hands held, they have a tougher transition to seventh grade. It definitely has to be a gradual transition. Fourth grade—hold their hands, yes it's an adjustment; fifth grade give them a little more independence; sixth grade even more than that.

KSP I think the mind-set comes with the change in the schools. You move to the bigger school you think you have to grow up. Your kids were all still in elementary school at fourth grade, mine will be in a big school. That's overwhelming to me because I wasn't in a big school like that in fourth or fifth grade. I transitioned into sixth without any prep, without any transition. At that age it was fine, but I don't think a fourth grader is ready for that.

MP Another thing too, they have to be prepared because there's going to be two grades moving at one time. There will be two completely new grades up there.

KSP One of my concerns when I thought my daughter might be in that first grade at the middle school, that that class isn't going to get the chance to be the big kid on the block in that elementary school. They're going to go from being just a third grader to all of a sudden being the youngest in the school. That is pretty important to be the oldest in the school. They're going to lose that. Hopefully the Parent-Teacher Organization [PTO] will, when they have the fourth grade picnic, will have a third grade picnic also. Whatever that school does that's special they need to try to make sure they incorporate that third grade class.

ASP I'm concerned about the same thing because my daughter's in second grade now so she'll be in the same situation. I think it's just going to be up to the parents of that grade to make sure that, and believe me I'm going to be right on it, to make sure that they get the same privileges as the fourth graders.

ARP One of the disadvantages I think of is that our elementary isn't in the greatest of conditions to begin with. We need new windows, new doors, the furniture is very, very old, I don't know that we're solving that problem. This came up with the renovating of the high school, but yet the elementary buildings don't really get touched. Now that it will be K–3, I don't know that they ever will be, that's a concern we have. We'd rather see the mileage go up a little more but cover all the bases, get them all renovated, the heating systems, cooling system because even in our building there's a concern with safety.

KAP I see earlier schedules as a detriment to the middle school. That is a huge adjustment. In our house it was over an hour difference and for fourth graders to have to get up an hour earlier, this is the time when we say you need sleep and it seems kind of silly—why not reverse it—make the younger kids go earlier.

DPT The initial onslaught of the complaining parents. I see that as the biggest issue and that has to be dealt with quickly because we need the support of the parents—especially with these little kids coming into the building.

JWT Time change for a third grader to start at 7:43 in the morning, rather than 8:45—that's a completely different time frame for

	eight-year-olds, if we keep with the current middle school schedule.
MOT	If we keep fourth grade in a six-day rotation.
MPT	I think just by virtue of changing schools, the fourth graders are going to feel like they're much older than they would if they were staying in their regular schools. The sixth graders are going to feel like big dogs now, just like our seventh graders do now.
SPT	That's where we have to have more of an elementary focus—if we have playground we can teach them that you're still kids, you're still in elementary school this isn't a middle school anymore.
DBT	We haven't talked much about our sixth grade staff. There will be issues for them.
MPT	Will we make sixth graders have recess? If fourth graders have it and it's an elementary you would assume it's going to be consistent.
NT	I was at another school which was 4-5-6 and the sixth grade did recess on a rotating basis so that one day out of the five two classes went out together. Fourth grade went out every day, and fifth grade teachers decided what they wanted to do—even like a fifteen-minute break.

Discussion

The whole middle school concept was set up for no more than five hundred students in a building. That would apply to a 4–6 building. Over a thousand students in a building are too many. You could still have smaller learning communities and schools within schools, but if you look at any of the problems in the eight years at the middle school, they occur because the building is too large. One area we're overlooking is how the third grade is going to transition into the new building. What we need to look at are the students who are going to be there in grades 5 and 6, the year of the change. Is that going to be a dramatic change for them too?

Changing from a middle school to an elementary school might mean losing privileges and other things that they're used to; all of a sudden it's different. Maybe what we need to look at in those areas, and the staff at the middle school is already starting to do that, is slowly start to transition it over to where in two years it won't be such a change other than one grade moving up. A new grade is moving in, but what they're used to is somewhat similar to what they expect. If the change is too dramatic, not only are we going to throw off those fourth grade students that are coming but we're going to throw off the fifth and sixth graders as well.

One of the greatest disadvantages is the issue of communication. Once again the communication needs to be tight and structured. It is recommended that the principals from 4–6 meet collectively. This will eliminate some of those communication issues, because they're having monthly meetings of face-to-face interaction. Presently, other than an administrative cabinet meeting, the 5-6-7 principals do not meet on a regular basis to talk about issues, students, and curriculum development. Perhaps that's because nobody ever thought about it. We should put some money in our elementary buildings. Some of them need renovations. Also, the earlier schedule for the fourth graders will be a problem. They will have to get up much earlier and that will be difficult for them.

Question #8

How would you view the six-day rotation and its effectiveness with fourth, fifth, and sixth graders?

RA   We need to take a look at that—obviously I don't think you can have fourth grade on a six-day rotation and then five and six on a five-day rotation—that's going to create a lot of confusion. Maybe what we need to look at is with the elementary losing some students, what would it look like if we go to just a five-day, take a look at what that would mean—does that require additional staff, what could we do with the current staff or do we need to stay with the six-day rotation.

LA   Along that same line, if in fact the full-day kindergarten structure remains as is, we will all be forced to have afternoon preps for kindergarten teachers. Logistically, I don't know how you can do that with the amount of traveling staff we presently have—to put every kindergarten teacher's prep in the afternoon means that we all have the need of having staff members in the building in the afternoon. I don't know how you make that work given the amount of traveling staff we presently have on the six-day rotation.

EA I believe the six-day rotation was brought in to increase the amount of time students would have in those special subject areas. However, in my experience with scheduling with the elementary and with the elementary principals, we do so much work having teachers travel that I have yet to see the advantage in the six-day rotation. If we did a study of the actual minutes that students are in these specials and compare, I would venture to say they are not getting more instructional time in special areas. I do not see the six-day rotation as advantageous, I see it as a scheduling nightmare, and I see it as problematic for parents because they don't know what day they're supposed to wear tennis shoes or what day they're not. It does not give them the advantage we hoped it would. The only thing I did see it do was save us money with staff, which didn't work either because we spend more money paying for travel time and trying to hire half teachers. You'd be better off to have the teachers rotate into the classes within a nine-week rotation.

MA I disagree. The six-day rotation was originally created not to increase special area time, but to equalize the amount of time that the students have in art, music, and physical education. Prior to that when we had three specials we ran on a Monday through Friday scheduling which meant they got one special twice another special twice and another special subject only once. The idea behind it was to equalize the amount of time the students spend in a special. That goal has been accomplished. We have equalized the amount of exposure the students get to the arts. One of the things the six-day rotation has done in the district, it's created a structured schedule and I think parents are used to it, I think the staff is used to it, I don't see the issue of kids forgetting their tennis shoes. They still forget those tennis shoes and instruments; doesn't matter whether it's day 2 and 5 or Friday and Monday. Equalizing the exposure to these specials has happened, and I think scheduling-wise it's easier to schedule on a six-day rotation because it's really a three-day rotation—you schedule for three days and repeat the schedule for the other three. We eliminated or reduced the amount of time in some specials and increased in others. I do agree that we need to look at the amount of travel time that our teachers are spending on the road between schools to cover all these classes.

BA2 I think the six-day rotation schedule in its initial implementation did in fact increase instruction time in the specials. However, over the years the manner in which people are selected to fill a class period here or travel across the district from there has gone against our individual building schedules when we would like to do common preps for our staff, programs that are currently existing, and trying to bring somebody in for a forty-minute class and send them across town really does take away from the meeting. I think the six-day schedule in itself had positiveness, but it's been bastardized and we are to the point that it's not doing what it could do.

EA Music education. You look at music and instrumental—they have to get pulled from certain academic classes or science time to do music. That's not appropriate. It's not appropriate for a kid in elementary school who wants to play an instrument to have to be pulled from an academic. That's why the six-day rotation does not work. It also eliminates common plan time. If you do this six-day rotation, fourth grade will never have a chance to have common team time. That's extremely valuable—that's when you discuss integrated approaches, science lessons—I think the six-day rotation eliminates those kinds of things. So respectfully, I disagree with the six-day rotation.

MA You can have common planning time in a six-day rotation. As a matter of fact you can have it easier in a six-day rotation than in the regular schedule, because it helps if you have three sections or less, if we only have three subjects to schedule for then you can only have three people on common planning time.

RA One thing that was mentioned was that you can plan three days and then repeat that; from my standpoint and probably from all the smaller elementary standpoints that could not exist for us. We have to piecemeal a schedule together because quite often we're sharing a lot of staff with a lot of different people—we don't have someone full time. Over the last couple of years it's gotten worse, we try to schedule so they're only traveling once throughout the day, but they're traveling a good bit and it's not consistent in my building. We're not able on day 1 and day 3 have the same schedule, because of how we're sharing so many staff with so many different buildings. At times it makes it difficult to put together a cohesive schedule.

LA It would be my hope that when we make these transitions that somehow ____ can successfully get out of the mix of sharing staff with the middle school. Unless we run periods the same exact time it does not work. That person spends more time running back and forth across the street then they do actually teaching children. What seems to drive the schedule is the middle school and their needs and we get the leftover pickings to have what we have. I also think at times the six-day rotation doesn't work to help give common planning time so special ed. teachers can get in with those grade levels and really meet with those teachers. Special ed. teachers have to take their preps wherever they can, sometimes not having the freedom to put people where you need them to be doesn't allow staff members to all be free at the same time to sit down and engage in conversation.

Whatever type of scheduling system we go to, we need to look at and be sure there's some kind of system set up so we reduce the amount of shared staff between buildings where we're not on common time.

MA You can get the common time in the six-day rotation—it's easier to do than in the five-day.

LA We have the common planning time at ____, but when you're forced to work across two buildings that operate on different times, it doesn't work. It also doesn't allow for freedom and flexibility to move preparation periods for testing and other things, because inevitably somebody's missing their prep when you have all that shared staff across buildings. If you eliminate

94　CHAPTER 10

	that you can open up more creativity with scheduling than you can with that kind of sharing just to have more dollars.
EA	And to go back . . . that's why I can't have one grade level on a six-day and the other two not. When it comes to testing and those things, it's impossible. Believe me, 102 teachers, doing a schedule it's already cumbersome and they are on the same bell schedule.
KDP	I say to get rid of the six-day rotation.
KSP	I agree.
ARP	I agree.
JP	I don't even deal with it anymore but it just sounds like another thing to add to the confusion. I'd get rid of that.
KSP	I understand the reasoning behind it and I'm not going to protest if my daughter misses a gym class because there was no school that day. I'd rather have the sanity of knowing it's Monday, we need to send your library book; it's Tuesday, you need to wear gym shoes. That's the way the real world works and if a holiday falls on a day that you regularly have your meeting at work and you don't have it then you don't have it. I think the six-day schedule is a lot to ask of families to keep track of.
KAP	I was under the impression that was because we shared teachers. So if we're at one school we wouldn't have the need to share teachers, there wouldn't be any reason to have the six-day schedule.
OT	The six-day rotation is a nightmare, especially when you have physical therapy coming in and they want to pick a Monday at 10:00 and Monday on day 2 your kid's doing something else and on day 3 he's doing something else—it's a nightmare for occupational therapy [OT] and physical therapy [PT] and any other person who comes in to give outside services.
JWT	Nobody else follows it in the district. Even some of our special ed. teachers don't follow the six-day rotation; they follow a Monday through Friday schedule. It is a scheduling nightmare.
MOT	Speech is also an issue. They work Monday through Friday and so does occupational therapy and physical therapy.
MKT	I don't know anything about the six-day rotation—I couldn't even understand it! I wouldn't want it, but it should be at least

	consistent, if they're going to do it, it should be 4-5-6 and not fourth grade on a six-day and fifth and sixth on a five-day. Whatever they end up doing it should be consistent.
MOT	We don't want it, and I know it's a money crunch and that's why we do it in the elementaries because it saves money.
SDT	One of the biggest concerns that the middle school teachers have right now is not moving fourth graders over, it's going to a six-day rotation.
JAT	I know from a special ed. standpoint to schedule meetings it is horrendous because you have to think about who's on a Monday through Friday schedule and who's on a six-day rotation and you're dealing with parents on a business schedule—it's horrible to schedule IEP meetings conferences on a six-day rotation. Somebody always messes up.
JWT	The administrators who are involved with the ESAP process are on a Monday through Friday schedule, but the elementary is running on a 1 through 6 schedule and they schedule meetings on certain days, but that doesn't coincide with any days for the rest of the whole team, because some of the team members are only here on days 2, 4, and 6, and it just makes it very difficult to make scheduling happen. I couldn't even imagine doing it in the middle school.
OT	Also for scheduling outside programs or assemblies, you have to think months and months ahead if you're planning a program in January what day rotation that is, and hope there's not a snow day or a gym day when someone's using the gym. It's a nightmare.
DPT	The consensus of this committee is that we want to eliminate the six-day rotation—next question please!

Discussion

We cannot have fourth grade on a six-day rotation and then fifth and sixth on a five-day rotation. That will create a lot of confusion. Maybe what we need to look at is the fact that the elementary schools are losing enrollment. What would it look like if we go to a five-day rotation in the elementary schools? If in fact the full-day kindergarten structure remains as is, we will all be forced to have afternoon preps for kindergarten teachers. Logistically, it is difficult with the number of traveling staff we presently have. Preps in the afternoon mean that we have need of staff members in the building in the afternoon. It will be difficult to schedule given the traveling staff we presently have on the six-day rotation.

As a conflicting viewpoint the six-day rotation was originally created not to increase special area time, but to equalize the amount of time that the students have in art, music, and physical education. Prior to that, when we had three specials, we ran on a Monday through Friday scheduling. This meant students had one special twice, another special twice, and another special subject only once. The idea behind it was to equalize the amount of time the students spend in a special. That goal has been accomplished. We have equalized the amount of exposure the students have in the arts. One of the things the six-day rotation has done in the district is it has created a structured schedule and parents and staff are used to it. It has equalized the exposure to the specials. Scheduling-wise it's easier to schedule on a six-day rotation because it's really a three-day rotation—you schedule for three days and repeat the schedule for the other three. We eliminated or reduced the amount of time in some specials and increased it in others.

One thing that was mentioned was that you can plan three days and then repeat that. From one standpoint, and probably from the standpoint of all the smaller elementary schools, that could not exist. We have to piecemeal a schedule together because quite often we're sharing a lot of staff with a lot of different schools—we don't have someone full time. Over the last couple of years it's become worse. We try to schedule so the teachers are only traveling once throughout the day. But in actuality they're traveling a good bit and it's not consistent across buildings. We're not able on day 1 and day 3 to have the same schedule, because of how we're sharing so many staff with so many different buildings. At times it makes it difficult to put together a cohesive schedule. The consensus of this committee is that we should eliminate the six-day rotation.

Question #9

What do you think we should do in the _____ School District in developing a plan to transition from a K–4 model to a K–3 model and from a 5–7 model to a 4–6 model?

DATA PRESENTATION AND ACTION-PLAN DEVELOPMENT   97

RA I think just in general we need to get the plan ironed out as quickly as possible and get it out there to the parents, to the staff, to everybody so everyone has a vision of what that model's going to look like and there's no confusion. The sooner that we get it out there and share that with the public, staff, and students the better it can be put into place and people can be prepared for it.

BA1 One idea would be the way we came up with that vision for the future; we all met as a group in here and then split into the subgroups. Have a K–3 subgroup, 4–6 subgroup, and so on. We can all be in the same room and we can hear what the other ones want to do.

ARP To allow for parent conferences at the upper elementary and also smaller class sizes.

AGP We talked about a general orientation time having time for the kids to get to know each other.

AP The whole idea of every year building upon their independence.

MP In elementary, parents are more hands-on, helping more, and in the middle school they don't ask for much help but with the new fourth graders I think the children need to have more parents up there helping.

PP If there are willing parents or if it's the philosophy of the school—just the whole PTO at the middle school issue. It does feel that needs to be looked at again and fired up with younger kids to allow a more active PTO. My other comment as far as transition I wasn't able to go to those early meetings in June, but I appreciated that and there were dates to choose from, and just more of that over the next couple of years as things are happening. It is a work in progress—send letters out, group meetings like before—so as we think of more questions or issues so we won't be surprised.

JP Be a little more creative in social events—skip those dances and put something else in there. I think it was a stretch with fifth to seventh graders and with the ages that are coming in there now, it would be ridiculous.

AGP I agree, there has to be some other social functions beside a dance that would also involve the families coming in. Even if

	you did something just for the fourth grade one time, something for the fifth grade another time each month a different grade you wouldn't have so many people there. The dances would have to go.
JP	And also have an opportunity for the parents to be involved if they chose. Right now parents are not even welcome at this time.
ARP	I think having a guidance counselor for the kids—someone they know they can get to.
AGP	As much communication with the parents and families as possible, either on the website or mailing things home to read.
KAP	I would like to have the gray envelope—I would like to have more information coming home. That envelope makes a big difference—it gets home to you. It was a big shock entering kindergarten and being smothered with all these papers and then going to the middle school and nothing.
KSP	I'm wondering if there's a way of transitioning the new guidance counselors they brought in to the elementary schools. I think if at least in the beginning of the year they could stop in the upper elementary school, it would be a familiar face, somebody that they know for the kids.
JP	Right now in the middle school the guidance counselor you're assigned to stays with you the whole time you're in that building. It's been really nice after that many years they get to know them a little bit.
MP	Will all the fourth grade teachers be moving up?
JP	Will they need that many fourth grade teachers that are in place right now in the elementary buildings. That might be something you want to keep.
SDT	I know that when we transitioned the fifth grade to the middle school, the principal at the time organized a committee of teachers in the current middle school and then the fifth grade teachers from the elementary schools. Every elementary school was represented. We met for two hours twice a month—all these issues were discussed and I think it is imperative to have this time together because that's where we worked out most of the kinks and that's why the program was as successful as it

	was. I think we do need to get those committees together. They were comprised of administrators, teachers, and parents.
SPT	And I think we need to establish that group soon. Once you have that group then they can take care of all these concerns—sitting around like this is great, but we need action now.
SDT	It was not always smooth sailing—there were times we left there and there were definitely splits—so we had a lot of compromise, a lot of give and take, but in the end it proved to be quite successful.
MOT	I don't think the transition for K–3 will be anything—I think the whole thing is 4–6, 7–8, and 9–12. One of the things brought up in our staff meeting what about furniture in your classroom and what about your materials and what about books that the librarians bought for your class, are we going to be allowed to take that stuff with us to the middle school. That's something that needs to be discussed in this transition. How is the district going to help us with that transition?
SDT	When we moved over we brought our stuff.
OT	The librarians are already asking us to earmark stuff that we use in fourth grade so that it can be boxed up for the transition. So they're already looking at that.

Discussion

We need to get the plan ironed out as quickly as possible, and get it out there to the parents and staff so everyone has a vision of what the model's going to look like and there's no confusion. The sooner that we get it out there and share it with the public, staff, and students, the easier it can be to put into place. People will prepare for it. We should allow for parent conferences at the upper elementary, smaller class sizes, and a general orientation time for the students to get to know each other. In addition, parents need to be involved in the school and they need to be kept informed. We need to build a strong PTO at the 4–6 level. We should be more creative in social events—skip those dances and put something else in there. Dances were a stretch with fifth to seventh graders, and with the ages that are coming in there now, it would be ridiculous. We need to be aware of furniture and textbook needs. We need to look at what furniture and books we will be moving and what will have to be purchased.

Question #10

Explain your views on recess for fourth grade versus physical education class if run every day.

LA   I'll speak to that. Having been a principal of a 4-5-6 building, our children did have recess every day, in comparison to only having phys. ed. twice a week so they did get the recess every day. My concern is always when you have that many children and the physicalness at which they will engage, I think logistically it becomes a very serious issue where do you physically put them all to successfully have a safe recess. I don't think having five hundred children running full speed on a field is a successful recess and I don't know how you would do that given the logistics of how it would work. The only solution I can envision is that someone would have to be eating lunch at 10:00 to phase them out in smaller groups. From a safety perspective it would appear to me that phys. ed. every day would be the better option. But I also know if we want to look more elementary, recess should be a part of that.

BA1 I think the phys. ed. would be a better option. From my perspective we always have a problem with the special-needs kids at recess—you need an aide to watch some of them, parents are afraid about them running away. They can have a much better experience if it's structured, there's a game or there's some activity to be done, they have a specified role in that activity. A lot of times these kids are just walking around not doing much of anything at recess.

SA   Most kids don't do well in unstructured time.

EA   I think this goes back to six-day rotation again. We're only talking about fourth grade, fifth and sixth graders do not have recess—leave it alone—they're used to it—there's no problem there. I would envision fourth grade having structured phys. ed. every day. I would also envision maybe they had a period time where they have an activity period where you have structured activities. Whether they go to a room for chess club, they go to a room for game room, whether they have a kick ball intramural program going at that time. Clubs, activities—that way you're serving two purposes—getting the phys. ed. energy level, and by the way we have an obesity problem in this country and recess isn't working, so I think structured phys. ed. is better for that problem as well. I think the activity period will give them enough outlet and social time where you don't have to worry about them going out and killing each other on the kick ball field. Every problem I've ever had in elementary dealt with something at recess. There are more problems going on at recess—because they're not supervised. There could be 380 kids out at recess at one time, even if you go down to thirds that's still a hundred-some kids. How many staff members are going to be out there—you're going to pay all those staff members to be out there. It's a logistical nightmare in a building that size.

MA   I totally agree. To take it a step further, to expect a teacher to do a club for 180 days might be a little much. I think working out a rotation of day 1 is your club period, day 2 or Tuesday may be something dealing with literacy where we could get AmeriCorps involved with the teachers. Maybe the third day would be a guidance type of activity.

RA   I think we have to look at our goal. Is it for physical activity—we're not achieving it by doing that. Close to four hundred kids on the playground is just asking for trouble. If you're going to have a recess, somehow those kids are going to have to be divided up whether it's several recess areas or different recess times—you can't have all of those kids out there at one time. You're asking for mass chaos and injuries on a daily basis.

EA   What do you do on the rainy and snowy days?

LA   It's been mentioned to me a few times that what angers parents most is that there was a commitment made to fifth grade recess that was never followed through on and I don't know what kind of commitment has been made to fourth grade recess, but I know several parents have approached me and said that was a big issue when fifth grade was moved to the middle school. A lot of parents were angry that commitment was not followed through with.

RA   If a decision that recess is not the best option, you present the reasons why and a lot of them are what we said today just the logistics of four hundred kids running around a big field together. Hopefully parents will understand that we're looking out for safety issues and safety concerns. If there's an alternative plan parents would be more willing to accept that. At my previous school we had an activity period. Each teacher chose an activity that they would like to run. Some were physical activities and some expanded on what they were already learning (math club); kids were given an opportunity to sign up for where their interests were. You could do it on a quarterly basis and rotate that.

PP   Recess is do what you want to do and not so structured like a PE class. I think they need that time to do whatever they want. When I've observed their lunch it seems to be very structured, not as free as I envisioned lunch. Really all they have is recess. I don't think they're the same.

ARP   I agree, and I think PE is important, but it is very structured—swimming, track, where recess gives them the opportunity for social. I think a playground is important—some place where they can play kick ball or something other than standing around because we know that can get them into trouble too.

JP   I agree with that.

KSP   I agree—I don't think you can substitute recess for gym or gym for recess. They're two separate ideas.

JWT   If this is an elementary setting we should not have gym every day. So then recess would have to be implemented. If you do gym every day, are they going to have two specials, which means two classes for the elementary teacher, which is not acceptable.

OT   If they're looking at having gym every day, then what is a typical day? Do you have one period of math, one period of English, what's a typical day and how long do you teach that period? I teach a forty-minute period for each one and we don't have a bell that rings at the end of forty minutes, we just close our math books and pick up the science or we switch for social studies. So what is a typical day going to look like? That needs to be predetermined with this committee because if you're having gym every day does that mean they have art when they're not doing gym? How's that going to work with an elementary group?

MOT They're still learning the basics of music and art and PE—they're still learning how to skip in fourth grade.

SDT I don't know that that's happening. I don't know that we are even looking at continuing rotations.

DPT I think that what's going to happen here is that they're going to create things that don't exist now, to fit this building. Geographically and physically if they go through with the renovations and they number these rooms correctly. I've been there how many years and a kid will ask me for a room number and I have to look at a map and I still can't find it on the map—that's how bad it is. Hopefully this will all be ironed out once these things are built and people can see where certain things are going to be and if they plan accordingly and put the fourth grade where they're supposed to be and if they have to go to this special, it's right there and not 250 yards away.

MOT If we don't have PE every day we have to have recess because that's the health initiative. We're not even allowed to have recess denial anymore. I think recess is a great plan after lunch.

OT Recess is also used as social time. In fourth grade they don't get to interact with the entire fourth grade except at lunch time.

MOT It's a very awkward time for fourth grade—they're just starting to approach thinking that the opposite sex is kind of cute and I think they need that social development.

JWT I agree. Having sixth grade be on a completely different thing because they're also getting ready for seventh grade and they're obviously not going to have recess in seventh grade. So I think sixth grade would be OK in having their own schedule.

SDT Our sixth grade is not in the best building. In a perfect world we wouldn't want our sixth graders doing everything and following

	the same schedule as our fourth graders—then shame on us—we're not preparing them for their transition.
MPT	That's going to be a real problem because we have sixth graders who are in elementary and then all of a sudden they're at the intermediate building then they're high schoolers.
SDT	We need to be consistent—we are now an upper elementary school and we're going to be working on the premise of whatever they develop for this building. We need to be united as one but we are separate grades. We may not have to have the consistency that everybody thinks amongst the three grades.
CT	There has to be a basic consistency, but then if you look at kindergarten and you look at third grade—they're certainly not doing the same things—there's lot of differences—probably more than between fourth and fifth.
SDT	It's quite evident that our team time we have found to be probably the most beneficial educational move that we have made. Whether we're a middle school or not, and that was a middle school philosophy, we have found that the team time is the most valuable time that we spend in dealing with individual needs of children, dealing with situations. I believe that even if some of our day is going to change and we might be a little more elementary, there's no grade level—kindergarten through 12—that wouldn't benefit from a daily team time.

Discussion

We're only talking about recess for fourth grade only. Fifth and sixth graders do not have recess—leave it alone—they're used to it—there's no problem there. Envision fourth grade having structured phys. ed. every day. Also envision a period of time where they have an activity period with structured activities. They go to a room for chess club, or to a room for games, or have a kick ball intramural program going at that time. With clubs and activities you're serving two purposes—getting the phys. ed. energy level, and addressing the obesity problem in this country. Recess isn't working, so structured physical education is better for that problem as well. The activity period will give students enough outlet and social time so you don't have to worry about them going out and killing each other on the kick ball field.

Many problems at the elementary level deal with recess. There are more problems going on at recess because they are not supervised. There could be 380 students out at recess at one time. Even if you go down to thirds that's still a hundred-plus students. How many staff members are going to be out there? You're going to pay all those staff members to be out there. It's a logistical nightmare in a building that size. Parents were more convinced that the children should have recess, with possibly phys. ed. a few times per week. Children need some unstructured time, and if this is an elementary school, we should have recess.

Question #11

What will the 4-5-6 building look like in five years?

MA   It will look like an elementary school. There will be smaller learning communities. Teachers are going to know their students well. The curriculum is going to be developmentally appropriate, more elementary based. The programs and activities are going to be centered around the needs of the elementary student as opposed to the needs of the middle school student. If we do the staff development correctly, the staff is going to have more of an elementary orientation to their thinking. There are going to be programs in place to support students who are still struggling after they get out of the K–3 program. We're going to have interventions in place to meet the needs of students who are struggling academically and socially. We can't forget that we need to meet the needs of the students who are excelling.

LA   I would agree that that's the utopia of how it will be. I perceive it will look like whatever the leader of this district deems appropriate. I think with leadership transitions we know change happens. We know someone could come in with a different vision and model for how they see things being. I also think that the federal government drives a lot of what we do and depending on NCLB [No Child Left Behind] and how it gets reauthorized I think will have significant impact on how things look as it does now. Things look radically different than they did ten years ago due to legislation that was beyond the realm of our control. I agree those things are important and we would want to hold that regardless of leadership or legislation, I think part of it is going to heavily depend on what happens with testing and accountability.

BA1 I think one of the things we can predict no matter what changes occur is that we're going to have kids with academic needs. No matter what kind of assessment comes along, there's going to be kids who aren't making it. We're also going to have social, behavioral, emotional needs. They bring baggage in with them. The 4–6 building should be a place where those things can be easily addressed and programs in place to address them. In general, the vision of this upper elementary school could be ____ leading the Halloween parade in costume with ____ bringing up the rear in costume! It's going to be an elementary school—a fun place to be!!

AGP Hopefully it will have a playground, better security.

KAP It would be nice if they could keep each grade in a different hallway. There would have to be some mingling, but to keep one grade in one hallway and one in another—that would be good.

ARP More parents there to help.

AGP Right now at the elementary schools it's a kids' world–everything's small, toilets are small, lockers are small. I'm assuming at the middle school everything's big. For a fourth grader it might seem really, really big. Maybe in that fourth grade hall they still have smaller lockers.

MP My son last year had a hard time getting to the top shelf of his locker. He had to keep everything down because he couldn't reach it.

JP I think definitely more parents up there to help and a playground. It should be like an elementary—just a different building. Same focus—just a different building.

MP Forget it was the middle school.

MPT In five years it'll be working perfectly and hopefully we won't remember any of these problems.

DPT   All due to this meeting!
OT   And the well planning of the administrators!

Discussion

The 4–6 building will look like an elementary school. There will be smaller learning communities. Teachers are going to know their students well. The curriculum is going to be developmentally appropriate, more elementary based. The programs and activities are going to be centered on the needs of the elementary student as opposed to the needs of the middle school student. If we prepare staff development correctly, the staff will have more of an elementary approach to their thinking. There are going to be programs in place to support students who are still struggling after they leave the K–3 program. We're going to have interventions in place to meet the needs of students who are struggling academically and socially. We can't forget that we need to meet the needs of the students who are excelling. One of the things we can predict, no what matter changes occur, we're going to have students with academic needs. No matter what kind of assessment comes along, there're going to be children who aren't making it. We're also going to have social, behavioral, and emotional needs. The 4–6 building should be a place where those things can be easily addressed with programs in place to address them. Hopefully the school will have a playground and better security. In five years it'll be working perfectly, and, hopefully, we won't remember any of these problems.

Question #12

What safety measures should be in place for the 4–6 building?

EA   I think that's so broad of a question. First of all I think a leader needs to be chosen for the building. Secondly there needs to be a safety committee formed and those decisions can be made by them.
SA   One of the safety issues that you could start out with—the teachers could wear the identification badges. That's something small and easy—the students can start recognizing employees of the school.

CHAPTER 10

MA A building that big should be accessible and inviting to people. The setup of that building needs to change from the way the current middle school is. There needs to be a greeter or receptionist or secretary who's available to greet parents and send them on their way to where they need to be. Not just parents, any visitors. The building is large and it's very difficult to manage if there aren't procedures in place for visitors. It's going to turn people off if there's not someone who is a friendly face who greets them in the building. Needs to be someone who's positive, someone who recognizes trouble when it happens—that's going to be critical for that building. If it stays as it is now, you walk in and you look for the office. People need to be greeted.

BA1 For somebody who's looking for trouble, there's nobody to stop them.

EA ____ and I talked about this yesterday. If you come in the middle doors right now, the first door to the right is my office. What they need to do is gut the whole office area, redo it, put in bandit-proof doors so that when they come in there's a mini lobby and my office becomes a reception area. Everything else is locked.

KAP I think they're looking into the idea of a password. If a parent calls in to say I'm getting my kid at 2:00, what's the password?

KSP Except I have five passwords I have to remember for work!

ARP Everyone needs to be told—the teachers, the kids—you don't open a door for anyone, no matter who it is. I teach at an elementary building and if the kids see an adult at the door, they'll let them in.

MP Right now when there's after-school activities, the kids just come out. A lot of times there's no teachers there with them, and if you're not there to pick them up on time they're just standing out there.

KAP That was a big shocker too. The first time my daughter stayed after and I asked her where are you going to be and she said out in the parking lot.

MP I don't know where the office is there, but can they visually see the door?

KAP No.

ARP There was a suggestion at the school board meeting last week that they have video cameras and not just tied in with the secretaries, perhaps a couple other people in the building, perhaps the nurse—someone else who might be at a computer that they can confirm who's there.

JCT I think the bus issue that has already been discussed is very problematic. We need to address the fact that we can't just let these students run free as they do now. Particularly the first year when you have two-thirds of them that are unfamiliar with the school.

DBT Parents need to come in and out of the building and with the way things are going in the world, we're probably going to have a buzz-in system.

JWT I think safety in all buildings is right now being looked at. Right now in the elementary setting there are a lot of us who can't even lock our doors if there's a lock-down situation. I know what we're trying to do at the elementary level is what the middle school is trying to do to make it a safer building.

DBT I think there need to be phones in the classrooms.

OT We have a buzzer that if we get in a crisis we can call the office. At ____, fourth grade is totally away from the offices. If something happens in the front of that building we would never know it, and if something happened in the back of our building the office would not know either.

MPT The building's so big we discussed having the grade level principal in the area where the grade is, but they would have to hire another secretary. We have two now, we'd probably need two more for the main entrance.

JWT Isn't the high school looking at separating the building in half and having two separate administrations in that part of the building? I think that should definitely go hand-in-hand, because if it is an elementary setting and the building as big as it is, having an office in each section would definitely make it a lot easier.

MOT Another concern that we have on our safety committee is when kids have custody issues and no one in the building knows. Keep the teachers very well informed if there's a custody issue.

SDT   Good point. We need to make sure of that in our new building. That's not a concern for us because we have an attendance secretary so that's really not an issue. So it's imperative that our building still has the guidance office—the three guidance counselors and the attendance secretary because that's why we are so successful in sharing custody information. Another big issue is the phone system. I know we're talking about the parents moving over to our building and the high anxiety. One of the issues I still occasionally hear from parents is that they can never make contact with anybody. They'll call for an hour, an hour and a half; the phone will either ring and then go to a voice mail. For anxious parents that can be an hour of sheer dread. It would be really nice if there was one person in each of the buildings—I know other districts that do that—that have a line that doesn't go to a voice mail that is always answered by a person.

Discussion

First of all, a leader needs to be chosen for the building. Second, a safety committee should be formed and decisions can be made by them. One of the safety issues that you could start with is to have the teachers wear the identification badges. That's something small and easy—the students can start recognizing employees of the school. A building that big should be accessible and inviting to people. The setup of that building needs to change from the way the current middle school is arranged. A greeter, receptionist, or secretary could be available to greet parents and visitors, and send them on their way to where they need to be. The building is large and it's very difficult to manage if there aren't procedures in place for visitors. It's going to turn people off if there's not someone who is a friendly face who greets them in the building.

Entering through the middle doors right now, the first door to the right is the principal's office. The whole office area should be redesigned with bandit-proof doors so that when visitors come in there's a mini lobby, and the principal's office becomes a reception area. Everything else is locked. The bus issue that has already been discussed is very problematic. We need to address the fact that we can't just let these students run free as they do now. This is particularly important the first year when you have two-thirds of the students unfamiliar with the school. Having phones in the classrooms was also mentioned.

Question #13

Can you offer any other suggestions on how we can continue to improve our plan to transition students from grade 3 in the elementary schools to grade 4 in an upper elementary school?

EA   Choose leadership—we need to know who the leaders are now. We need to find who the stakeholders are and let them lead.

BA1   I think this was a good start. We need to do more of it.

MA   Not only choose the leadership, develop a vision for the school, talk about some things that are going to be put into place, and get the positive word out to the community and the parents that this is going to be an exciting change. It's going to be a good thing for our children and a great thing for our community to have an upper elementary school on ____ and make it look like it's the best thing in the world. Start with leadership, move to a core group, and then you develop vision and a plan and get the word out and make it positive.

EA   I think we need to be in the communities and churches, every rotary, I don't care where it is you need to go there. Don't expect them to come to you—the same parents are going to come to you that come to you every time. We need to actually go to them—this is going to be a critical transition.

MA   Put parents on the committees too. Give them a voice and give them some small victories; whenever they're on the committees truly listen to what the parents have to say and give them real input into what the program's going to look like. I'm not saying to do everything the parents want for the school, but make them have an active voice and truly listen to and implement good, sound practices and suggestions from parents.

BA2   Could there be an informational taping being that we have that capability. And then have that run on the TV through this process so people could see what's happening.

MA   Use public access television channel 13, channel 98—get it out there early—here's what the programs going to look like and make it positive. Before even the school opens, make sure there are contacts—folks that parents can communicate with and meet with about the program and that should involve the counselors who would be part of that school. We need to the sales team for that.

KAP I have one specific request. My kids are in gifted education and I found that when we went from the elementary to the middle school it was very disappointing. I figured well we've got all these other classes we were going to get more gifted education and we ended up getting less. You get a nine-week period where you get it every day and then nothing for the rest of the year. It just sort of amazed me that it gets sort of squashed and everything else expanded. At the intermediate they have it every day, they can opt out of it if they choose not to do the activities in gifted education, but I think the fact she has it every day is much more productive and for the most part most gifted education kids usually reading their best asset so why not have them not have reading, let them have gifted education.

ARP The communication. More parent meetings, mailers, just to keep the parents aware of what the plan is and what's going on.

AGP It might sound silly about the gray envelope, that's another thing I never even thought of. I just assumed we would keep doing that—it's elementary school and you should still have that weekly information.

KDP As I said back in the beginning, for the fourth graders going in, the whole school should have a little more socializing at the beginning of the year to get to know the other kids in the class. That way they are comfortable in the class before you even jump into a lot of the academics.

KAP Getting more liberal arts elements in there. Keeping that from the elementary school rather than having it be an elective.

AGP The fourth graders should have art one day a week, music another day a week, library another day, etc. Rather than do languages for ninc weeks and computers for nine weeks, I think it

	should be the same all year because they have enough adjustments to make.
KSP	I would agree with that plan. I think expecting a fourth grader to adjust to a schedule change every nine weeks is a lot to ask.
KDP	Maybe you could do art twice a week, maybe computer once a week, library once a week and whatever else you could fill in for that other class so they get some of those experiences.
PP	I'm just wondering if like we talked about phasing them in, if the fourth grade at the new building could look like fourth grade and then at least they're already there. They now have the three hundred kids the same age, then those transition issues of what sixth grade looks like now they just deal with that one issue at a time. Just pick up fourth grade and put them in that building and fourth grade be fourth grade. Keep the sixth like it is.
KSP	I think the hardest transition is going to be the first few years where everybody has the mind-set that this is really like a middle school. I think it's important that it's not treated like a true middle school. These are elementary-age kids.
AGP	They have to make sure that every time they address it, it's upper elementary. It's not the middle school anymore, it's upper elementary and that will reinforce that these kids are elementary kids.
ARP	Back to the recess thing then, are we thinking just fourth grade has recess? I don't know that they'll do a playground for one grade level.
JP	I think they should keep it for all three—maybe more structured if they see the need for more structured recess. Today we're playing kick ball, something like that. They could have different stations—kick ball here, hopscotch over here, just different things that they could choose what to do.
MP	Another thing too you have to fit that into the schedule, so is the day going to be longer—or cut out another period. One whole grade out there at one time, that's three hundred kids, how many teachers are out there. In the cafeteria, you're contained.

AGP	At least keep the fourth and fifth.
KSP	In an elementary mind-set they don't have periods—they have before lunch and after lunch.
MP	You don't know how they're going to change it. You still have the bell and the three minutes to get to class.
KSP	I guess we need more information. We need to know what their structure is going to be and what they're going to do with the periods, and the time between classes.
MP	And then you can't go backward for the sixth graders, so are they going to be different.
KSP	Maybe they could be different until the kids who are already there leave that building, and the kids who are new in the building would just continue with the way they started.
MP	Or have a school within a school. Let fourth grade be on their own schedule.
KSP	We need more information. We don't have answers here.
MP	We're just giving the ideas—they have to figure it out. They'll have to design it to the curriculum of that grade.
JWT	Developing that committee to make the transition smoother. I think once you get a core committee together a lot of things could be sorted out and a lot of anxieties could be smoothed drastically.
DPT	Hopefully led by the administrators who currently lead that building. That would be pretty paramount.
SDT	Last year we had a lot of changes in our middle school and will be changing again in a couple years. That's been sort of difficult but the reason our transition has been as easy and smooth as it has been because we developed within our own building a task force committee where we were given time in school but many hours were spent on our own time and that really was what made our transition I believe much easier.

Discussion

Identify leadership now. We need to find who the stakeholders are and let them lead. Not only choose the leadership but develop a vision for the school, talk about some things that are going to be put into place, and get the positive word out to the community and the parents that this is going to be an exciting change. It's going to be a good thing for our children and a great thing for our community to have an upper elementary school. Make it look like it's the best thing in the world. Start with leadership, move to a core group, and then develop a vision and a plan. Get the word out and make it positive.

We need to be in the communities, churches, and every rotary. Don't expect them to come to you—the same parents are going to come to you that come to you every time. We need to actually go to them—this is going to be a critical transition. Put parents on the committees too. Give them a voice and give them some small victories; when they're on the committees, truly listen to what the parents have to say and give them real input into what the program's going to look like. Give parents an active voice and truly listen to and implement good, sound practices and suggestions from parents. There could be an informational video. Have it run on the TV so people could see what's happening. Make sure gifted education is not affected, and avoid relinquishing some of the resources we currently have.

VIEWPOINTS AND AREAS TO EXAMINE

This investigation encompassed the viewpoints of administrators, parents, and teachers regarding the future transition of students in grade 3 at their respective elementary school building to grade 4 at the future upper elementary school where the present middle school is located.

The responses, in this researcher's opinion, were candid and contained valuable information that will, hopefully, assist committees and subcommittees in the process of developing a plan and creating our "vision for the future." The participants in this study identified forty-three assertions related to the future transition of students in grade 3, at their respective elementary school building to grade 4 at the future upper elementary school. These assertions will become the basis for future planning to create a smooth transition:

1. Each school needs to incorporate time in its schedule for interventions. This should be approximately one period in length.

2. We need to continue to look at incorporating early interventions (which we currently have such as the RAC program, Sonday, and using Intervention Coaches). More interventions should be seriously considered.
3. We should investigate the possibility of including a Head Start program within our existing framework at the K–3 schools.
4. As we move to a K–3 model, primary education is an area to be explored.
5. All groups envisioned the K–3 model much as it is currently with emphasis on preparing appropriately for the full-day kindergarten programs.
6. The new 4–6 school should be an elementary school. Everything about it needs to be like an elementary school.
7. Schedules for grades 4, 5, and 6 need to be similar in terms of the way instruction is delivered, and the way teachers and students are grouped. The whole building should be on the same schedule.
8. The new 7–8 building should be our middle school.
9. Programs K–4 that are operating and working well presently need to be transitioned appropriately into the 4–6 building.
10. We should keep recess for grade 4 and even consider extending it to grades 5 and 6.
11. Anxieties that our current fifth graders experience when coming over to the 5–7 building are the same as the fourth graders will experience in the future.
12. We must decide who the administrators will be at each building as well as which teachers will be moving. We must do this now.
13. Anytime there is a transition or change, there is some anxiety on the part of the students and parents.
14. We must do a good job of planning and communicating to parents and students what the programs and procedures will be. We need to provide orientation programs for parents and students.
15. Creating smaller learning communities is essential to the academic success of the transition.
16. The closer we can emulate what the fourth graders experienced in the elementary school; the smoother will be their transition.

17. We need to have programs in place to help the students academically, but also for those students who are challenged socially and emotionally.
18. There are concerns about the large environment in the cafeteria, and efforts should be made to make that environment smaller for the fourth graders.
19. Parents expressed a desire for the fourth graders to be with one teacher and not a team.
20. Swimming should be a part of the fifth and sixth grade program, not the fourth grade program.
21. The communication among teachers, parents, and administrators at the transition points is critical for a smooth transition.
22. Transportation procedures will need to be examined. Student arrival from the bus and dismissal to the bus should be revamped.
23. We really need to communicate the vision for the 4–6 building to the parents.
24. Parent access to the school and their children must be examined. Currently, parents are very involved at the K–4 level. Will that level of involvement be provided at the 4–6 building?
25. Parents should be involved on the committees that make recommendations for the vision of the future planning process.
26. Parents expressed a concern over restroom and locker breaks for the fourth graders.
27. Grade 4 at the new building should be similar to grade 3 in terms of the routine.
28. Instead of having one big curriculum night for all the schools, we should plan it by grade level.
29. Parents would like to see the fourth graders have classes such as art, music, FACS, and tech. ed.
30. Guidance counselors may want to follow up with parents of fourth graders about one month after the start of school to see if everything is going smoothly.
31. The K–3 buildings will be primary centers, and best practices for elementary children should be the focus.
32. In K–3, we can really focus on learning to read. Since the transition to reading to learn takes place around fourth grade, the configuration is conducive to this model.

33. Going to K–3 buildings will give us some breathing room; some of the elementary buildings were packed.
34. The size of the new 4–6 school is a problem. There needs to be a "school within a school" concept applied to break it down into smaller learning communities.
35. We need to examine the changes that students in grades 3, 5, and 6 will experience as well as those experienced for the grade 4 students.
36. All three groups agreed that the K–3 buildings should operate on a five-day rotation.
37. We need to restructure social events for the 4–6 building to more elementary-type offerings.
38. We must be aware of such things as furniture needs and what furniture and equipment will be brought over from the elementary buildings.
39. Grade 4 should continue to have recess, with some time for a structured activity period. Grades 5 and 6 should have structured physical education.
40. Staff development should be within the parameters of an elementary-based program.
41. A playground should be built.
42. Security needs to be increased and each classroom should have phones.
43. The office area needs to be renovated to create a more inviting atmosphere.

THE FOCUS-GROUP PROCESS: AN IDEAL METHOD FOR BREAKING THE SILENCE

The focus-group process was an ideal method to use in efforts to break the silence of these populations. Arranging the participants into similar groups appeared to create an atmosphere conducive to the discussion of information that normally would not be shared in other settings. I believe the participants were comfortable enough with one another that they were able to respond candidly to each question. The participants were also most appreciative of having the opportunity to express their feelings about this issue.

Action Plan Development

You can develop your action plan similar to how I did in this study. Each school building developed its own action plan based upon the assertions that emerged. Then, at our monthly principals meeting, each principal presented their plan. By doing this, ideas were exchanged and each building plan was refined and ready for implementation.

Once all your data are analyzed and broken down into your list of assertions, you can reasonably manage it into a workable action plan. In the case of this focus-group study, our action plan involved the development of a number of committees to address the many aspects of the district grade configuration change. One of these committees was the transition committee which used the data from this study to make recommendations to our education committee and board of education regarding the smooth transition of students from grade 3 to grade 4. As you can see from the number of assertions, there were many aspects that needed consideration to develop a successful transition.

An action plan can be developed in many ways. You should develop your action plan in a format that you are most comfortable with. The important aspect of any plan is that it is *user-friendly* and produces measurable outcomes. If a plan is so complex that it looks good on paper but those responsible for carrying it out cannot fully understand it, then there will be confusion, lack of communication, and frustration. This will lead to a plan that ends up in the circular file with no measurable outcome, or outcomes of little significance will be the result. The key question you must ask yourself is: "Is this action plan reasonable and manageable for the people who will implement it?" If the answer is "no" or "not sure" then scrap it and make changes to it that will produce a "yes" answer to that question.

Your plan should minimally contain the following:

Goal or goals (must be measurable)
Objectives
Person/persons responsible for implementation
Time/resources needed
Timeline for review and completion
Measurable outcome/outcomes

FOCUS-GROUP CASE STUDY #2

Communication and Parent Involvement in a School District

Abstract

This investigation was conducted by Dr. Joseph D. Latess, Assistant Superintendent, at a suburban school district in Pennsylvania. This research encompassed parents' viewpoints regarding parent involvement and communication in a school district. Focus groups were used to gain viewpoints of parents. Four focus groups of six to nine participants were formed with members from each of these sample populations:

Focus group 1:	Parents of elementary school students.
Focus group 2:	Parents of middle school students.
Focus group 3:	Parents of intermediate school students.
Focus group 4:	Parents of high school students.

Parents were sent a letter describing the research to be conducted and were asked to return a form indicating whether or not they desired to participate. Focus-group interviews occurred during the month of June 2004. Interviews were conducted in a conference room in the school district, utilizing an independent facilitator.

Participant's responses were audio- and videotaped. To protect their identity, all participants were identified by their initials. In the event of identical initials, participants were given an identification number as well. In addition, only the researcher viewed the transcripts. Once the audiotapes were transcribed and the videotapes viewed, they were locked in a storage cabinet. Forty common assertions were discovered that relate to parent involvement and communication in the schools. From these assertions, schools are able to develop and implement strategies for increasing parent involvement and communication.

The Purpose of This Study

The purpose of this research was to assist administrators in the school district in making better decisions about increasing parent involvement and communication in their schools. One of the district's goals for increasing academic achievement is to "involve parents in their child's education."

Parents exercise great influence over student success in achieving educational standards and in increasing student performance on assessments. As a result, it is necessary to examine the viewpoints of parents regarding their involvement and to explore ways to improve communication in the schools.

This study was limited to the following:

1. The research for this study took place in one suburban school district in Pennsylvania.
2. This study was limited to a purposive sample of six to nine parents from the following levels:
   - Elementary school parents.
   - Middle school parents.
   - Intermediate school parents.
   - High school parents.
3. This study was limited to the responses of purposively selected samples of six to nine parents elicited from focus-group interviews conducted by one facilitator.
4. This study was limited to the viewpoints of purposively selected samples of six to nine parents regarding parent participation and communication in the schools.

This study was limited by the following:

1. This study was limited by a fixed population in one suburban school district, which prevents the results, but not the process, from being generalized to other suburban school districts.
2. This study was limited by a purposive sample in one suburban school district, which prevents the results, but not the process, from being generalized to other groups or samples.
3. This study was limited by the effectiveness of the researcher's ability to gather data through focus-group interviews.
4. This study was limited by the capabilities and consistency of the facilitator in asking questions and in prompting group members in order to elicit responses.

5. This study was limited by the purpose of exploring parent viewpoints regarding their participation and communication in the schools. It is not the intention of this researcher to provide normative data or master narratives for the purposes of prediction and control.
6. This study was limited by the conditions under which the focus-group interviews were conducted as to facilities, setting, and the setup for audiotaping.

Focus-Group Interviews and Discussion

Data from each of the four focus groups were compiled into similar categories. Only participants' first initial is indicated along with the grade level of their group as a coding procedure (e.g., E-elementary, M-middle school, I-intermediate school, and H-high school). Material included in this summary was information that was directly related to each specific question. Information that was extraneous or, in this researcher's opinion, not related to answering the specific question was not included. This summary encompasses group participants' similar responses to each question, with a discussion specific to each question following each set of responses.

Question #1

Elementary school parents (grades K–4) are generally involved at the school during those years. What do you believe prompts parents of children at that age level to be more involved in their child's school?

PE   I think probably because they're so young and so enthusiastic about everything you want to watch your child experience that. As they get older, they get a little bit jaded, you get a little bit jaded, it's not quite as exciting and new. And sometimes I think the kids have something to do with it, they don't want their parents around—you know, don't talk to me when I'm with my friends kind of thing.

LE   I think it's more the kids who prompt us to do it. Because it's new for them and they have a fear maybe they feel better be-

	cause we're there. Maybe they want us to be a part of their lives at that point. More so than when they get older.
VE	I also think there's more time when they're in elementary school. They're not as involved in other activities and so there's more time to focus on their activities.
AE	I also think that there's a lot more opportunities at the elementary school level than there is as they get older.
JE	I see higher expectations—younger parents have very high expectations for their children in the beginning. Everybody starts as "Einstein" and then as things may not go as planned you see things drop off. It's a harsh reality but I see that quite a bit.
KE	Every parent thinks their kid is above average and is like "Einstein" and you want to find out how they're doing as soon as you send them to school. All As, right! Everything's going good so you want to be involved and make sure when they're starting out, they're starting out on the right foot.
JE	I think that the teachers are a big key with that because they request parents to come in. I know from my point I was able to go to my kid's kindergarten class and read for an afternoon. I think that as that goes beyond elementary school you don't get requested to come other than a parent-teacher conference or something along that line. They're requesting that parent involvement, I think that's what makes that so successful.
VE	I know with the middle school when they have field trips there's only a certain number of parents that are allowed to go. So you don't have a choice in that matter, they only take the first couple parents that respond and that's all they let.
RM	I think because parents have more time. They're at home more and a lot of them aren't working. They're more excited when they're younger. As they get older they have a lot more teachers at the middle school.
CM	I think there's more opportunity in the elementary schools to be involved. I don't think the opportunity is there. Not so much even in the middle school as when you get up to the intermediate school. I don't know about the high school—I'm not there yet. At the intermediate school I know they don't involve parents at all. It's not that there wasn't parents who wanted to be

involved; there was nothing to be involved with. There never was an opportunity to be involved. We pretty much didn't do anything. It's kind of sad but we really did nothing as far as parent involvement. We were allowed to decorate for homecoming and that was it. We got no phone calls, we got no information at all as far as what was going on in that school.

LM   I agree with what ____ is saying to a certain point. I think once as a parent being involved at the middle school or the intermediate school that's the highest level my children are at, maybe too because the kids don't want parents visibly in the school, but to me behind the scenes there's a lot of things that we can do if the school is accepting to us being involved. I know there are fewer parents because a lot of parents do work when their children get older, but there are still parents like myself, a stay-at-home mom, and I like to continue to be involved. I have two at the middle school coming up this year and one at the intermediate; I'm still planning on being home and still would like to be involved always. Again, I did not feel they really gave us the opportunity at this level. Middle school a little bit, but elementary—doors are open pretty much.

SM   I have elementary, middle, and intermediate. I feel the same way. In elementary you are welcome. I've actually been told by middle school teachers themselves that you got to let your child grow up a little and you need to back off and you really shouldn't be so involved. I want to be involved, and I've actually had such a difficult time understanding why that would be a good thing to discourage parents. Whether it be in academics or in activities. We are still the ultimate educators, we are still responsible—that is our role, and that's a definite problem that I've faced. Elementary, they're like, "Please anything you want to do."

LM   I agree with that. They shut the door at the middle school. The doors are open in the elementary school and they shut the door on you in the middle school. They don't want you there and they outright tell you that. I agree to the point that I've heard that many times, more so at the intermediate rather than middle school level that they're old enough to start doing things without parents being involved. They have to be responsible. They're fourteen, fifteen years old, how much responsibility are they really capable of right now with their mind-set going through their changes? I just think they expect too much, I honestly do. The middle school, somewhat but I've given my personal opinion to the principal at the middle school as to how I feel. They still need to have parents involved—looking at what the kids' homework is every day—instead of just letting them be responsible. I think they're giving them a little too much responsibility for a young age.

SM I also feel the same way. Information like in report cards, we don't see much more than that, at least I didn't with my one child. He's not one to give me a lot of information. Even in dropping a grade from an A to a B, after it happens it's too late. I just think the teachers have so many students unless there's a red flag seen that a lot of the good children get unnoticed.

RM I just think that there's not enough or any communication. Good students, bad students, any students—you're a number. I really don't like to be a number.

SM I was told, and this was a direct quote from the team leader, the well is dry. We have no other suggestions for you and I find that appalling. I work in the health field and if I told someone who had just fallen and broken their hip that wasn't progressing real quickly, sorry, the well is dry, that would be a serious breach of my ethics. I was also told about the numbers—your son is one of many and we have 450 kids here and there's not another kid here that has problems with turning in homework. You're made to feel that it truly is your problem; your child is choosing to deliberately defy. I am disappointed that there's not a program in place to help the child who needs the help the most.

CM Those bubble tests—I mean you get no information from them. If he fails the test wouldn't it be nice to know what was on the test. I mean you get a piece of paper with one through five and little bubble answers and then the test grade.

JI I think the reason why most people are involved when their children are younger is because for a lot of them that's their first child going through the school district—they want to see how it works. A lot of times, perhaps, they want to be involved because they're afraid, they don't know what's coming up, this is their only way to see what's going on, it's their way of getting into the school, it's their way of interacting—getting to know other people in the school, getting to know how the school works.

PI   I agree with you that it's new to them—that they're excited and this is something new for their child to experience and they want to be there when their child goes through. They want to be there for the parties, they want to be there for the field trips. Safety's an issue too—if my child's going on a field trip I want to make sure I'm there so I know that my child is well taken care of. It's a part of your child's life that you want to enjoy and be there to share with.

CI   I think at the beginning more moms or dads have an opportunity to be home. They can be involved. As the child grows older that's when a lot of parents will go back into the field of work or work part time. The opportunity to be involved, physically, is there. The elementary teachers need the help of the parents at that time. One teacher to a class of twenty to thirty-four kids—so they invite parents to come and be involved a little more than they do later on.

PI   Unfortunately, I've been out of that area for a long time, but I suspect also that the parent is wanting to get the child to have a good foundation and that's why they tend to be a little more involved at that age.

SH   One would be that you have more time when they're younger—maybe you're home more with them. You have the time to do it; you don't as they get older. Then it's fun—the kids are having fun and you're having fun, it all changes after that.

MH   Plus they want you then, as they get older it seems they would rather you not get as involved. But when they're younger they do want you there.

CH1   Also the grade school provides opportunities for the parents to come in—you're able to come in and volunteer for parties and to help with the book donations, and so on. As they go on through school suddenly you're not really welcome at school. Plus, as ____ said, you're supposed to be invisible once the child is older.

SH   I feel it is a learning process not only for the child but also for the parent on school procedures, learning names of teachers and administrators in the district, things like that.

DH   I think it's part of the separation process—they're so young you just don't want them to be on their own at that point and it's easier to stay involved—you're there, you can see what's going on.

SH   I agree with you that you do feel as they get older you do feel very unwelcome. There aren't as many opportunities to get involved but also it doesn't seem like the school reaches out to get parents to volunteer for things in the classroom, chaperone field trips. As your kids get older they need you more. My youngest is six, my oldest is seventeen, so I go all through from first grade to senior high school. As they get older they need you more, but the school doesn't want you. My younger kids are in Catholic school where I'm there almost every day doing something—the teachers know me, I know them, there are tons of things to do and when my kids came here suddenly parents are the enemies. When you walk in, it's like, "What are you doing here, why are you here?" It makes you feel very bad, and I'm trusting my child to these people who don't even want me here. It's very strange. Even the communication thing is very regimented—you must talk to this secretary and leave a message and maybe this person will get back to you and it's all very formal. You don't feel like you can ask a question or have a problem addressed or work something out because it's very formal and this is the way we do things because this is the policy. It's not like "How can I help you—I know your child's here and you think it's very important that this be addressed." It's mostly this is policy and this is what we do. There's no sort of working things out.

CH2 I do agree, but I think what happens is the numbers change as the children get older. The elementary schools have a lower number, and I think more parents are home when their children are younger so they have the time to get involved. When you get to the middle school, PTO meetings are during the day, which working parents can't get involved at that level so it makes it harder. Occasionally a teacher would contact me to help out. The other thing is when they're younger they don't mind you being there but as they get older they don't want you around as much. I agree that they do need you, but I think the social thing of their parents being around a lot of times embarrasses them. I remember when I was that age, so you don't want your parents around.

SH1 With the communication, I think the teachers feel that it's the children's responsibility like when they get in to eighth, ninth, tenth, eleventh grade it's their responsibility to have these papers. It no longer becomes the kids need help with this or that or they call you because they're having trouble; it's more like, well, the children have to take care of that themselves. They make them more responsible, but some of them aren't quite ready for that level, at least mine aren't!

CH3 What I found was when I ran against these walls that you're talking about, I stayed active in the PTA, and what I did was I would suggest that we have after-school activities at the middle school. To some extent it is true—people don't want to change. Change is hard. So when you tell them that as parents we want to come in, we want to be with our children even though they are older in such a way that we're not obvious. You're still there, your presence is there, but you're not obvious. So we formed a PTA at the high school. And then they had the awards for the students, I was never president of the PTA at the high school or the middle school, but I was president of the District Parent Council. Some of the things we talked about are how do we stay viable and active with our children. That was one way we did it. But the point is your children do need you more at the upper levels than they need you at any other time. They need you actually to be home more to chaperone their activities and what they're doing and to give them guidance. Elementary is fun—it just is—I mean you go to the parties, and everyone's so thankful and happy and the teachers are so very nice and receptive. And as you go up further, and I'm not putting any blame on the teachers, but at the middle school there seems to be an attitude there sometimes that students are guilty till proven innocent. I've said this for years. And I think that's kind of the thread that goes through. It's a shame because I think at the higher level parents need to know more than ever, because students are going to transition to college, to work, to a military career—whatever they're going to do. Once you lose that touch, it's harder and harder to regain it.

MH About being involved—there are other ways to be involved. There's the band thing and the booster club. There are ways to be involved; however, you're not necessarily in a classroom but you are with students, you are with teachers, again, you get to be with the other students. So I feel that if you choose to there are ways to be involved it's just not like when they're in the elementary school. Every day you could be up there if you chose to be.

SH2 It's not necessarily that I think we should be involved in the classrooms all the time or anything, but I would like a more receptive attitude to a parenting group—keep the parents more informed about what's going on in the high school. Often when I call the office to get information—something my son has totally missed like senior photos—they'll tell me, "Well, he got that, it's impossible that he didn't get that." They just don't take your word for it that he has no information about something like senior photos. About half the teachers have been receptive if I contacted them and they've gotten back and been very helpful. Often the administration doesn't give you enough information—sometimes I think parents are overly involved in some of the things like band and musical and so on. The children should be doing more of that themselves. We need to support our children and to do that we need to know what's going on, when do they have to sign up for the tests for college, just the basic information doesn't often make it to the parents.

Discussion

The reason that parent involvement at the elementary level is so prominent is that the children are much younger and enthusiastic about school. Parents are also usually younger and in many cases experiencing their own children in school for the first time. Younger parents seem to have higher expectations for their children. There is more time for parents at this age to be more involved because there are not as many activities for the children. The parents are not being pulled in as many directions as they are with older children. Everybody (referring to children) starts as "Einstein" and then, as things may not go as planned, you see parents dropping off in involvement as children get older. Teachers at this level are more tuned in to parent involvement, plan activities for parents to be involved in, and give more encouragement for parent involvement. Children at this age really want their parents to be involved. As they grow older, children become more independent, and do not want their parents around as much.

Parents may also have more time at this point in their lives. Parents seem to feel more welcomed at the elementary schools, while they often feel involvement is discouraged at the other schools. There is less communication at the upper levels. Keep in mind, students at the upper levels are expected to bring information home to parents and often that information does not get home. At the elementary level, parents are more likely to check their child's book bag each night and read all the information that is sent home. Often, at the upper levels, the school populations are much higher and that may affect the level of communication and encouragement. Often, parents in the elementary levels have more opportunity to be at home, whereas, as their children grow older, many parents go back to work and do not have the time to get involved. Also, the activities they have at the elementary schools are hands-on, and require many adults to assist and supervise.

It should be noted that some participants felt that as children grow older, they need their parents even more. Involvement must continue through the secondary levels. Again, often after elementary school, the teachers don't make the parents feel as welcome. The attitude at the upper levels is that the children need to take on more responsibility for communicating, so the parents don't have to as much. At the secondary levels, there are other ways to be involved. It is not the same as elementary, but if a parent wants to be involved, there are ways to be actively involved. Communication needs to be improved between home and school at the secondary levels, which can provide parents with ways to get involved in their child's schooling. This researcher found that parents are often accustomed to having a lot of communication and contact at the elementary level. As their children grow older and advance to secondary levels, the communication and contact is not the same because of some of the variables mentioned above. Often, the communication is different or disseminated by a different medium, causing a feeling of what I will refer to as *communication variation*; sometimes it seems like nothing is happening. The communication medium has changed, causing a feeling of communication deprivation.

Question #2

As students become older and move to middle school (grades 5–7), intermediate school (grades 8–9), and high school (grades 10–12), there seems to be less parent involvement. To what would you attribute this occurrence?

PE   The teachers in elementary school like you there more. They make you feel so welcome and they're excited to have you, the kids are excited to have you. As you move up, maybe the teachers aren't quite as receptive to your participation, that's how I feel. They almost want to run the show and they want you to a certain extent but they also want you to let them be in charge more or less.

LE   I agree with that, but I don't think they do it because they don't necessarily want us to be involved. I think it has to do with they're trying to establish the kids' independence. They're telling you, "Back off a little, don't help with the homework as much," or "Let them make their decisions," and I think that's what they're trying to do. It's not necessarily that they don't want you to be there for field trips or they don't want you to volunteer for parent-teacher, they don't want you to be there for that, I think it's more that they're trying to get the kids to be more independent. I have a daughter now going into fifth grade and that was the big thing. Whenever we went to orientation, they were stressing they have to be together, they have to know where they're going, you're to give them a little bit of leeway. Being the tight parent that I am, that's going to be a little bit hard, but I see their point, they need to be a little more independent. And I think that we take it too far, we say, "OK, fine," then they don't want us there, or they don't want us to be as involved and maybe that's just our perception. I agree they don't ask and I think it goes back to a lot of the teachers too. If we feel welcome then we go, if we don't then we stay back.

KE The way the structure is set up, I think it tends to go that way. We have all these elementary schools and pretty much your son or daughter has the same teacher for the whole day. My background is sales and the key to sales is building a relationship. When you're in these small, little schools and you have the same teacher you build a relationship and there's a comfort factor and you feel comfortable going to talk to that teacher. When you get into the middle school, and it starts earlier and earlier now—fifth grade—they've got a bunch of teachers, they're changing classes, you as a parent I don't think you feel as comfortable, because you don't get to know the teachers the way you knew your little elementary teacher there and there's not that comfort factor there. I think the district sets up that way based on their structure. It makes it so that it's harder for parents to be involved at that level.

JE Elementary school teachers, they may be responsible for maybe sixty kids—a kindergarten teacher thirty in the morning, thirty in the afternoon. When you get to middle school and you're changing classes daily you may be responsible for 120–130 kids depending on the class size numbers. With parent involvement with 120–130 kids, building that relationship with that individual parent and teacher becomes almost an impossibility. We see that quite a bit and it is a frustrating thing for teachers as well because we feel that we would love to have more parental involvement but we're limited on our time to make that phone call. With a kindergarten or elementary school teacher you have more time to make those phone calls if you're not dealing with this many kids. Sometimes there are kids that just as we know fall through the cracks because there's no time to make that call and make that contact all the time, as much as parents would like. Then there's the confrontation factor. No one likes it—parents don't like it, teachers don't like it. I think things get let go because we don't want the confrontation factor. It kind of gets let off and no one does anything and then the kid gets in real trouble—academically.

LE I think that's where the parent comes in. You must get on the phone and you must take the initiative. The teachers have too many kids and they have not enough time to pursue each child. That's where the parent comes in. And there's been many times that I've gotten on the phone and I've said, "Hey, this happened or that happened." The only place you're going to get the straight story sometimes is from the teacher, you're not going to get it from your kids because they're all jaded. They come home with the story the way they saw it, or how they felt and many times I've gotten on the phone just to straighten something stupid out but it works.

KE Just to kind of summarize, I think what we're hearing is that it's not the parent's fault, it's not the teacher's fault, it's the structure. What scares me is it used to be kids didn't go off to high school until ninth grade where you had all this big bureaucracy and this big structure where they're changing classes and it keeps getting lower. I wouldn't be surprised if in a few years we'll have them go the middle school in fourth grade, then third grade, then there won't be any elementary schools and we'll have these big factories where we send these kids where the parents don't know what's going on and the teachers don't know what's going on.

LE We, as parents, really agree with that. But why do all these parents who are eighth and ninth grade homecoming go out and buy the $300 outfit and suck into this. She's not an adult but it's homecoming. It's parents too.

VE I agree—everyday dressing. But also with me trying to fight this situation the parents don't want to be involved as far as the

	academics are involved. I've called many parents and said look, I will go to the school board, I will be the spokesperson, I just need people to back me up. Well, you know what, I don't have time—and it doesn't really matter if my child doesn't have recess, it's not that important. It's not an issue to them.
LE	Doesn't it make you more angry at parents than the educators? Having the amount of children at my house—that's what I'm up against. I'm up against parents. It's all in what you want for your child.
VE	The teachers and the administrators, unless the parents come to them and say, "Look, this is what's happening," they're not going to know that.
LE	I find that I'm fighting parents more so than teachers.
LM	The school district shuts the door on you. The principal in my school has already warned me because I'm a very hands-on parent at elementary school. Don't expect this treatment in the middle school, you're not going to get it. Other parents have told it to me. I went to orientation, they outright said it. Send your kid to school here, we're going to move them around nine times to ten different classes, call the homework hotline if you want to know what the homework is and we'll see you on conference night. That's it.
CM	Don't look for conference night. There is no conference night. Unless your child is failing miserably, I guess, I've never actually had a conference. I had one go completely through the middle school, I have one going into seventh grade, I have never had a conference.
LM	I agree with that. I requested a conference when my oldest went into fifth grade. None of my children in the middle school has had a situation that warranted, as far as the teachers were concerned in their teams, I still feel as a parent that to touch base with us throughout your child's school year that year, is not asking too much. But we're not really even offered that, as a parent I think that should occur at least one time throughout the year. Rotate it, I know it's 150 kids per team but somehow it seems like other than curriculum night you really don't have an opportunity to talk to the teacher. I'm looking at it from a dif-

ferent angle. My kids have all been very good students and it seems they've been able to take on the additional responsibilities and I've been able to pull back. Every teacher sends home a paper at the beginning of the year telling their phone extensions. I know I could look up their phone extensions if I need to speak to someone. I don't really feel myself that the teachers or the guidance office has been inaccessible. Whenever I've had a question I've been able to contact the teacher and get that question answered.

SM I have not had that success. My son was struggling with math, not with the actual content but he had handwriting issues, things like that, that affects grades. So I've tried to discuss that we have a 504, some of these accommodations are on here, I don't see feedback returning. Certainly there have been some teachers that have gone above and beyond the call of duty, but that was mostly in computer and art oddly enough. I have found it to be very difficult, even when I had a problem with my son coming home with welts on his arms from being bullied. I am still waiting for two months. I have yet to hear from the principal after sending a note and leaving him a message.

LM I've had that same experience where I have made a phone call to a teacher or whoever and have had to do it at least two or three times before they address my concern and actually have had to get a little bit nasty about it. I would appreciate if you would return my phone call, and I don't appreciate when someone doesn't return my phone call. I just feel that that's uncalled for. If you're a parent and you have a concern no matter how little it may seem to someone else, obviously if you're calling you're pretty concerned. I've had that experience as well.

RM I've had no problems with them calling us back but, catching something before it's too late — we just had an experience, my son who's in seventh grade — As and Fs. Nobody called us; we had to make the call and then you start hearing all these things. If you had the opportunity to meet with the teacher, at least once or twice a year, it's amazing what you can find out. Your child may not be a problem but he could end up a problem 'cause you're not involved, you're not hearing, you're not knowing what to look out for. You're not sure what you should be talking to him about because you don't know what's going on. I think all children—there are no perfect children—and I think from a parent's point of view you would like to hear it from the teachers where they could use some help. I just think every parent would like to hear about their own child. Especially the younger—fifth grade is really a big adjustment. They're very young children and I don't know any of them that are perfect, I'm sure they could all use some swaying in one direction or another. I don't think they have the time to pay attention to every single child. But if you went in for a meeting at some point during that year, I think fifth grade is a terrible adjustment for the child and for the parent you kind of lose control there. You're not finding out enough information.

EI I think that parents have a tendency to think that their kids are older and don't need their involvement as much. I personally don't agree. I feel that my freshman going to be a sophomore—that I need to be more involved with her in probably the last five years. That's my opinion, but I don't know that that's the opinion shared by a lot of the other people in her age group.

SI I think it's harder to get information on what's going on in the schools the older up they get. It's harder to get information because you have your parents that are always there to help and they are more active and maybe not as like parents, like myself, if I go into the middle school and OK, I might catch a little flack—Mom might be there too much or whatever. And I gave him a little bit of flack thinking I was still going to get all the information that I had in the elementary schools home, and OK, I'll be able to figure out what's going on at school, and that's not true. If that child does not want to give you that paperwork, you have no idea what's going on at school. My son, at the end of the year, I was amazed what I found in his book bag. I said, "Hello, I would've went to that." Their awards ceremony, he had it in his backpack and I had not a clue that there was an awards ceremony. So I think you have to call the school district more and listen to the activities, see what's going on, be able to find out what's going on in school because I didn't

	know half the stuff. That's my fault for not calling and asking. These kids don't want to have to bring that paperwork home 'cause it was in all in the book bag.
EI	That was my experience too, with the awards ceremony. I have only one child and have never been to the district and we didn't know. He came home with awards and oh, ____'s mom was there, and all these other people were there. "I would've like to see you get an award." "Oh, I didn't want you to be there."
CI	It's really important to be proactive as parents as they get older. Having one that graduated, it's a very fast year, fast pace. You have to be very involved or you miss a lot. It's important to keep them on a schedule if they're going on to college or a trade school to keep on top of the records and the way things need to be. It's hard if they're not one to communicate with you or if they want to be real independent, they're trying, but they just don't know it all so you have to go behind their backs or behind them and just go ahead and go up there. Go to the office, ask questions, call, and inquire. The communication with the teachers gets less and less so you have to be the advocate and it does make a difference.
JI	____ does have a website that does list some stuff, but some of the schools, such as the high school, I've noticed, does not list everything that's going on—it's not updated enough. I have found updated information a lot more so in the elementary and middle schools. I even found some of it on the intermediate schools, but I don't see much change on the high school level for the website being complete. With a daughter going into high school, I'm going to be looking at that. It's not going to be able to tell me anything. I think they really need to keep that updated too to help inform us parents.
MI	I think there's a little less opportunity to get involved in the middle and intermediate schools, there aren't any class parties, there's a lot less field trips, I found, and I know with my son who's in high school sometimes I'll ask him a question about what's going on or this or that or I need to ask a teacher about this and he said a lot of the teachers in the high school prefer to talk to the student about a problem or questions because they're

treating them more like adults now, and they don't get as involved with the parents as they did in the younger years. I find that if I want to know something, I'll call anyway.

CI   It depends on your child's activity level. But if they are involved, it really benefits you to go to the parent association whether it's with band or chorus, musical, just to hear what's going on. You don't really have to participate but it does a lot of times you can see in any organization, the small core group that does all of the work. Sometimes you're a good facilitator to go out and grab more people to help—even if it's just baking something.

SI   In reference to your core group, sometimes what I've found if you don't get it on that core group level, you're done. Because my daughter tried out for the musical and they asked for parents to come in and help. I went in and helped, well, there's a core group of parents and they expect you to already know what everything was and I had not a clue. Well, they had one meeting that I went to and then apparently they had other meetings that they felt I didn't need to go to. It was like, "Well, you signed up to volunteer but too bad"—sometimes that core group of people is bad. It's good that they're willing to help and do a lot of stuff but they assume that everybody knows what they do and that can be a bad thing too. That's been my experience.

EI   Touching on what you just said—I know when ____ first came to the school, I went to the first parent-teacher meeting. The first one is in the evening and all the rest are in the morning. I work full time 8:00 to 4:00 and so does my husband. There's no way that I can make it, when I asked about it was told that, "Well, we tried having it in the evening and it didn't work out any better so we're just sticking to the schedule." That was kind of a negative experience and I probably wouldn't have made every one, but I really would've attempted to go on the days I could had they been in the evening. But just the attitude that we're not even going to consider this, they don't really want anybody's input other than the core group that are here who can make it in the morning. I think that was probably the worst experience that I had being here in the district in this school.

JI I used to be involved in going to PTA meetings on a regular basis in elementary school. When my daughter went to the middle school I went to those meetings as well. I didn't go to any PTA meetings for the past two years. This year I went to one PTA meeting at the middle school and it was the last meeting I'd go to. Because what was argued upon was the most ridiculous thing, and I wasted an hour and a half. Unfortunately a lot of these organizations do fall into cliques like every organization has. And the cliques are what deter people away from things. It was a very ridiculous meeting—I think they were arguing over how you get to be elected homeroom parent. It is amazing how many people have to be homeroom parent or they don't feel special enough—I don't know what it is. Me, personally, I am a very busy person, I would love to come and help out and help my child out in school, if the teachers need me, I'm here. I am a stay-at-home mom and I do have a flexible schedule, but at the same time I cannot be bothered with because I'm not homeroom parent. They fought over how you elected this homeroom parent and it was suggested to put all the names into a bag, someone picks a name, and that's how they got it. They didn't want repeat people, they didn't want them having two in one year. It was a dead end. I got up and I left and I said this was unbelievable. Not to pick on a certain grade or anything, but it was 90 percent of the fifth grade moms because they did not understand. It's a huge change—going from fourth grade to fifth grade at the middle school. I've seen it happen year after year—it's always the fifth grade. It's a huge change coming from elementary and throwing your child who's an elementary student into a middle school scenario, where they don't have the parties they should probably still be having. It's a huge change for the parents to accept as well as the child. I don't want to get off the questioning but that's a good reason why a lot of parents don't get involved is because of the cliques. The same people have to be running it or they're not going to cooperate with the school at all. Then they start

SI	spreading bad things about the school. That does make a big difference.
SI	We just moved here for my son to start seventh grade. He came from a very small Catholic private school over in ____ where there were about ten to twelve kids in a class. This was an immense change for him. I realized that it was going to be a much bigger school district. They do have an awful lot more opportunities than he had at the private school—a lot more computers, the athletic program here is immense compared to what he was used to. I do miss the personalization, you can get to know the teachers better. A lot of the teachers don't want to be bothered. I have tried to get involved—trying to talk to different teachers and things like that because my son has struggled. Partly his fault and partly the school's fault—it's just so huge it was a major adjustment. Yes, I was also very put off by the PTA—meetings that were only in the morning that I can't attend either. He's going to be going into ninth grade now and I'm hoping that things might change because I would like to go to the PTA meetings and be more involved and, hopefully, the teachers will be a little more willing to talk when I call. They give me yes/no answers and that's it—very short, if they return my call at all.
MH	Didn't we address that? We kind of like went the broad range there didn't we with the previous question?
CH2	We probably discussed everything....
CH1	Come on, give us a hint (laughter).

Discussion

Again, the teachers at the elementary school make parents feel more welcome. As the child progresses to the upper levels, parents are not as welcomed. Often, teachers at the secondary levels want their students to be more independent, and as a result, do not communicate with the parents as much; they expect the children to do that. It may not be that upper-level teachers don't want parents involved, but if the parents perceive that they are not welcome, they will not come in. Elementary teachers are usually responsible for about twenty-two children. At the upper levels, teachers may have 120–130 students, which makes communication more difficult. It is easier to deal with twenty-two sets of parents as opposed to 130 sets of parents. Because of the number of students, it is more difficult to find the time to communicate with all the parents. Also, at the secondary levels, there is the "confrontation" factor. Teachers and parents seem more likely to have conflicts and, because of that, each shies away from communication to avoid any confrontation. It may not be the parents' fault, or the teachers' fault; it may be the structure. Schools are too big, which interferes with effective communication.

In other schools (assuming smaller districts), students go into high school from ninth grade, and the schools feeding into the high school are usually smaller, whereas here, the middle school and the intermediate school are rather large buildings. Another perspective that was presented was that parents who do not get involved have a profound effect on those parents who do get involved. Parents need other parents to support them in their efforts for reform and often, not enough parents want to or care to get involved. As indicated, it is not a school problem as much as it is a lack of involvement by many parents. The following telling statements were made: "Doesn't it make you angrier at parents than at the educators?" "I am up against parents." "I find that I am fighting parents more so than teachers."

Some elementary principals tell parents not to expect the same level of involvement at the middle school, intermediate school, and high school. Other parents say the same thing. At the middle school, parents really don't have an opportunity to talk with the teacher. The teams often tell parents that a conference is not warranted. Parents should have some structure to touch base with the teachers even if their child is doing well. Many teachers go above and beyond the call of duty in contacting parents, and yet others give no communication at all. There is a website that lists some things, but not enough to be reliably informative. Much involvement depends upon a child's activity level. The more involved a child is, the more opportunity a parent has to get involved. Often, meetings are held during school hours. If parents work, they cannot attend. There are no provisions for people who work normal jobs (8:00 a.m. to 4:00 p.m.). PTA meetings at the middle school were not productive at all in the past. Frustrated that they talked about the most ridiculous things, one parent said, "I stopped going."

Question #3

How do you feel about parent involvement in the schools? Do you see parent involvement as a significant factor in increasing student performance? Please explain.

JE I think the schools, especially the elementary schools, the performance level of students when they start looking at things like standardized tests, the more parental involvement you have in the schools the higher your scores are going to become. The more parental involvement you have with students the achievement's going to be, because sometimes even the parent is learning along with the child. It's when you start seeing that lack of involvement you start seeing the drop in the scores.

LE1 I also think that for every one parent there's two kids in that classroom that need parental involvement. And I think that if, as parents, we could pitch in and pick up the slack because it doesn't matter if I or you go in there with parental involvement, if there's five other kids with no parental involvement, you're not getting anywhere. It's like they don't work together as a community, it's all about me, my child, instead of, well, these three children really need this. I just feel there's a lack of caring. Intense feeling of it's not a community effort.

LE2 I think the school has to find some happy medium to deal with everybody from the worst and slowest to the more mature and fastest and brainiest. They stuck it somewhere in the middle and it's our responsibility, only ours, because we know our child.

LE1 But what I'm saying is you can't individualize just to a child. These are the children your children are going to grow up with in this community all the way through twelfth grade. If we do

	not work as a whole to make everybody a better parent or a better student or a better teacher.
LE2	A lot of parents will take offense to your trying to bring their child along with yours.
VE	It shouldn't be up to us to bring the other children along. We're trying to get the parents involved to bring their own children and work together with all the other children.
LE1	Like you said, it's hard to get people to open their eyes to what you say. They're so busy with their job, with this, with that, it's not about you, lady.
LE2	At a very early age, everybody needs to care just a little bit more. It's one, I don't know where it went, but if everyone could care. _____ has five children, why aren't we watching out for _____ and her five kids. They are going to be growing up in this society in this community with all your children. It's so selfish.
VE	I can see just for the fact that my second child is the type of child that really needs pushed and so I called the teacher from the get-go and I had a team meeting and I said, "Look, you really need to come down on this kid. He really needs pushed." So the teachers knew from the get-go and I said, "You have my permission and anything you need to do to get him to do his work," and so from the get-go they were on him. Now with my daughter in fifth grade I didn't say anything; I didn't contact the teachers I just let it go and she's the type of kid who really doesn't need much. But I saw that she was starting to fall through the cracks and none of the teachers were doing anything about it until I got involved and then all of a sudden it turned around. I called the teachers and said, "Look, she's having a really difficult time with this responsibility and she's crying every day," and then the teachers only took notice. She was this way through most of the year and nobody really noticed and when I talked to the teachers about it they said we didn't know. I don't expect them to, it's not their fault. Unless the parents point out to the teachers what the child needs, they're not going to know. So if there is no parental involvement....

JE Kids in classrooms do very well in masking and hiding any kind of problems that they're having from their peers, unless they're very close friends or especially from an adult. They very rarely want to confide that they're having these difficulties. But they will do that in front of a parent, it'll manifest itself in all kinds of different ways. Again, when the parent involvement comes in and contact made with the teachers then they are aware of those kinds of things and automatically that sets that in motion. When we don't have that parental contact with not knowing about these kids it is easy for a kid to slip. Because it's the old "no news is good news" kind of thing. I'm not having any problems—unless it's manifesting itself in a disruptive behavior in school or something along those lines, that's the one who's going to draw the attention and that's the one that the teacher is going to be active in calling that parent, getting an administrator involved whatever you have to do.

LE1 That's the parent that says, "Well, I don't need to be involved, the teacher's on top of it." It's just like the situation here—why were you chosen, why were you chosen, why was I chosen. Are we getting some of the parents that aren't involved? How do we know?

LE1 This is the breakdown I'm talking about. You can't sit here and say those parents don't care. You have no right to say that. They care, they don't know how. And to me it's a disgust factor with the educators—oh my God, there's twenty who don't care and five who do, who's gonna ride this wave with me. I do not know what going to happen.

JE What it's coming down to and what I'm hearing is a lot of people maybe a little nostalgic with the way it was—the good old days—but you have to remember in those days we're talking about a different social country, communities are different. We had smaller schools—think before the merger of this district.

LE1 That's what killed it.

JE Now you had smaller schools—you had a high school down in ____, you had a high school down in ____, you had a high school in ____. You had small communities, they knew each

	other. Those communities knew each other, they grew up together. Now things have changed socially, economically, all of those things have gone to super districts. Everything's got to be super-sized and it has been.
KE	The assumption is bigger is better.
JE	And now we're seeing a change in community. I see it even in kids; they have a loyalty and a pride in their area. It doesn't matter whether it's a low socioeconomic area or it's more affluent, they have a pride in their area and that's pretty much it. For the whole thing, they don't have a pride. We see that in the school district. Certain areas, the kids are not involved in school pride.
LE2	I think that's because people in one community make that hard for people who do not live in that community. You're almost a minority.
JE	Well, what it's gone down to is communities. You can go as far as looking at racial problems and things like that. You see that it's a taught thing. It's not nothing you're born with—you're taught these things. You learn these things, and who are you learning them from?
LE2	I disagree, I don't think it's all the parents. I think it's on the whole. If their community thinks they're better than anybody. . . .
VE	It's the parents who are putting that down to their children—"Well, you're from ____, that child's from ____."
LM	Absolutely. To me it's just so obvious that parental involvement is important. I guess it just depends on how you define parental involvement because in a lot of ways I feel I'm not "involved" in the schools, I don't go to the parent meetings and so forth, but in our house it's just an expectation that you're going to work hard, you're going to do well in school, you're going to be responsible. I don't do more at this age than say, "If you have any homework, you better get started on it now before the game tonight." As far as projects and so forth, they schedule their time—if something's due a month ahead, they're responsible for getting it done. So I would say definitely parent involvement is important.

SM I agree—parental involvement is essential and I know that ____ had mentioned this earlier—you don't always know though where to be involved. And it very difficult—I mean in the elementary school you kind of bebop in after class and pick them up and talk to the teacher directly if you find that you're having problems. Here you'd like to be more hands-on and all, but at the end of the year you don't even know what skills is lacking if you're not getting any feedback through the year. I have a child that can go through without any problems, but the other three need varying levels of adjustment over the summer—a tune-up over the summer—and I really don't have any idea, you get a little bit of an idea from the state tests, but I don't think it's even our job as parents to guess 'cause that's how they were on that one day. When I did request information to what would help, any suggestions—the third grade teacher was wonderful, but fifth grader all they said was tell him to read. Read what? Is it reading comprehension, big words, vocabulary, and with my seventh grader they just never even returned a call and I had homeschooled him in sixth grade and was amazed that the areas he got As and Bs in that he understood basic fundamental things I had to back and work on. I don't mind doing that 'cause that's my role as a mother, I'm more than willing to do that, but if I had known that earlier, I could've avoided so much. I was not aware of how bad his handwriting was, for instance, or how much he really was reading—one word, next word, next word—well, no wonder he couldn't remember what he read in the sentence before.

CM Like we said about the bubble sheets—I can't help my son if I have no idea what my son's having problems with. It used to be they would send home a test; I could look at the test, see where his problem was and help him with it. I can't do that with a bubble sheet. If he fails the test, all I know is he answered this many questions wrong. His math teacher in the intermediate school kept all his tests. They kept all the papers—what did you get on your test?

RM They do it because they reuse them so that the kids aren't passing them to the kids in the previous years. There has to be a better way, because they're passing them to the students but then the parents can't help them.

CM   They just basically tell them what the grade is; they don't tell them what they had wrong with them. And if I don't know where he's having problems, I surely can't help him. Yes, I think it's very important that we reinforce their education.

LM   At elementary I was much more involved, hands-on, working with my child. Number one because the papers did come home and you could work with them, and number two, I understood very easily what they were doing. As they're getting older, they are not bringing papers home and even if they did, I may not be able to help them with that homework assignment or that test where they maybe did not do a good job, but at least if I saw it I would know that this needs to be addressed somehow. I would like to know that the teacher did that and I wouldn't even have to ask for them to do that. I would hope that they see that my son or daughter didn't do well on a test, there's a problem, and we need to address this—not me having to initiate that. I'm certainly always concerned that they were having problems.

LM   To answer the question—absolutely. When you as a parent are involved that shows your child you care and that you're watching and you're helping; they care, they work harder, they know that you're right there and you know what's going on. They can't get as much stuff past you. Sadly enough the further along they get in their education, the school does not allow you to become as involved.

RM   I think there would be a lot of children that would be better suited if their parents knew more of what they were doing. The more we could help them, it would increase their test scores, which the school is worried about, we can't help them if we don't know where to help them. I think it would be significant for the school along with the parents, everybody needs to work together. I think it would be a much better solution to the problem if you knew what was going on. My son's pretty self-motivated and you get used to a child like that, then you have another one that is totally the opposite and it's a real struggle as a parent. Bright, very bright, but just not as mature and not as responsible. It can be a real problem when you don't have the information.

CI I think it does. I think it benefits your child and I think it's carried my children through at a higher standard because they know I'm interested, they know I want them to achieve and do better. We set higher standards for them, it's important to us and I want them to be involved and try their best. I think it does come from the home. You're going to have situations where you have conflicts with teachers here and there, but I think it's important that those you do have a rapport with and show respect, that child's going to do the same. It's very important to be aware whether it's in sports or music or the arts—just get in there and be a part of it.

SI I agree. I think parental involvement is 100 percent you have to do it. If your child knows that you care enough to know and sit there and do homework with them even just to review it, or ask how their day went, they're going to know that this is important to Mom and Dad, I want to make Mom and Dad happy, I want to be happy—they're going to do a lot better. My children, whenever they don't do well on a test, say, "Mom, I tried I couldn't understand this," then we'll sit there and go through it. They care for their grades, they're into this grade point average now, they think this is the greatest thing. They are in competition with each other, which is good in a way, but sometimes not a good thing. They care about their grades because they know that that's their job, they have to care and they have to be responsible for it. Mom and Dad go to work, and this is your job—this is what you're supposed to do. You need to do a good job. The more information I know that's going on at school or the more information I know that's coming up, even if I don't know what it's about I can talk to my kids about different things and they're amazed that I know what's going on. It keeps them on their toes. Even just a little information is a good thing.

EI Definitely it makes a difference. I think you have to set the atmosphere—you create an environment where they're going to want to do well and they're going to want to follow through, then I think it will be easier for them to be successful because you are there and you're involved. My personal experience is that when I have not bugged her and not been on her and not been really involved, she just hasn't done as well. An example of that was her finals—she has a high grade point average and did well all year, struggled in some classes, but brought those up. I didn't really bug her about the finals—didn't really make sure she had her nose to the grindstone, she didn't do as well as she could have. And I really think a lot of it was my fault, because I didn't force her to do it. I didn't really push it. I think that I saw from all the years of babbling at her about it is that she was kind of disappointed at some of her grades—she was disappointed that she hadn't done better here or hadn't done better there. The fact that she cared about it more than we did—I can't tell you how pleased I was. What I say to her is, "As long as you're doing the very best that you can and you bring home Cs and Ds—I'm not going to care as long as I know that you're doing your best." You know when your kids are slacking off and that they're just getting by and that they could be doing better. To try to get her to feel like that, I thought was great.

JI I think if you care they'll care, that's the bottom line. Even if you can't be involved in this stuff during the day, as long as you're still involved in some aspect of their education, still showing an interest in them, if they don't feel you're interested, they're not going to be interested. I just think that's human nature. I think it's very important—taking an interest.

SH1 My number was on speed dial from the high school with the guidance counselor, speed dial at ____ Technical School and I know with my son you have to be right on top of them. I say, "Do you have homework?" "Nope." "Test?" "Nope." "How are you doing in English?" "Fine." You don't get a response early enough from the teacher saying you know that his English isn't fine and he skipped going to the technical school three days in a row. He decided he didn't like gym so he just wasn't going to go. I think it's real important, I spent more time at the high school and technical school than I ever did when I was going to school. I appreciate it and I had very good results with and even his HVAC teacher at ____. I think it's real important—they don't like it, but for me, I work three twelves a week, I'm a nurse and I'm not home. He wasn't telling me nothing. OK, you can go through the book bag but all you find are notes from this girlfriend and miscellaneous papers, and I'd say you got to get yourself organized here. Sometimes at seventeen they're just not ready to be organized.

DH I agree with you on a lot of that. You do find out too late that your child's possibly failing something. But I think that what the school does is that they look at the students that are mature and are straight As and can do well and do bring all the papers home to their parents, and they don't look at the ones who don't do it. It is important to be involved, but it is hard to get involved because you don't know. I've talked to several counselors this year myself—you just don't know how to get your foot in there and find the right people to talk to.

CH1 Like you're afraid sometimes I think that you'll overstep your bounds. I think that first of all being involved at home is number one, being involved at school is also very important, but I think it starts at home. You can't put everything off on the school and the teachers—they can only do their jobs too. You're afraid a lot of times to question or the teacher will take it out on the child, which tends to happen. Then your children don't want you to do that because they're the ones who will suffer from it.

SH2 On that I think that when they're at school they're at school the majority of their day. There's people whose job it is to teach them to help them. When they come home, some of the stuff I don't know how to do it, or I'll show them how I think they should do it, and it's like, "Well, that's not how we do it at school." Sometimes I think the teachers want too much of it to be sent home and done at home as far as projects and different things. We've done so many projects and they're not getting my kids' work, they're getting my work. You really have to do a lot more at the school I think.

DATA PRESENTATION AND ACTION-PLAN DEVELOPMENT   151

SH3   I completely agree with ____, where a lot of these projects that are supposed to be done at home are actually being done by the parents and it becomes a competition amongst the parents on who has the best projects. If they were actually done at school at least that would be the child's true work at school.

MH   I agree with you; in elementary school, I had an issue and chose to go to the principal and it went down from there. I had a meeting with the teacher, my child, and the principal. Very soon after that in the classroom the teacher said, "Contrary to what ____'s mother said . . ." She said that in a full classroom. After that I never volunteered to do anything, my son forbid me to do anything, because I thought, "I'm not going to have my child crucified in a classroom." It's a catch-22.

CH1   I feel the need to comment on that. Confidentiality is an issue always. I'm not going to turn this around and be answering questions, but as a parent, I have felt this. Me of all people, a little high profile there sometimes. My child doesn't ever want me to come and say anything—he wants his autonomy. It's interesting because I have two sons and my oldest is twenty-five and he came through the system. My youngest is seventeen and he'll be graduating next year. It's really interesting because I have found this in our system—if your child wants a good education and they want to perform, it's here. We do have good teachers and I'm not here to be a poster child for our district. So what I'm going to say to you is this—if your child wants to perform and you're a parent who's on them and you're with them, they're going to excel. But you as a parent even if you want your child to perform and they don't want to, then they will circumvent you. My oldest son just wasn't motivated in school, he was the classic underachiever. Great social butterfly, great human being, he has a work ethic, but school wasn't his thing at that time. And so what happens to those students at that point is they kind of fall between the cracks. As a parent you want to be able to feel that that door is always open and you can get in here and you can get them any help they need, that's what you want. Because you figure that's what they're here for, to help you. Sometimes what you find is the brick wall, and it's just very upsetting because you think, "Well, the guidance counselor should be here to answer all my questions. Why aren't they returning my phone call?" It isn't just you, it's everybody, and everyone's treated the same in that respect. If you're not your child's advocate, then your child suffers. In order for your child to have good performance in school either way, no matter what, if your child's an underachiever/overachiever, you still have to keep tabs and the school still needs to be very open with you and receptive and if they're not, then that's where the problem lies.

KH I have a comment on that. I find the majority of the teachers are very receptive. The frustrating part is when you have a teacher who isn't and you have the principal who backs them up, and gives the excuse, "Well, he's older and set in his ways." This year I had a real problem and I have been on the phone and I have been in touch with everybody—guidance counselors, social workers, principals, superintendent—and still not getting anywhere. And now I'm told, "Well, gee, it's the end of the year there's not much we can do." Excuse me, I want accountability. I want accountability from that teacher, and I want it from the principal, and I don't want to be blown off and I don't want my son swept under the rug. And that's where I'm at now. I really believe that the majority of the teachers are very, very accessible.

SH2 I totally agree with you. Parents have to be accountable for their children, but the teachers have to be accountable and responsible not only to the parents, but to the children. I had a problem at the intermediate school this year, where the math teacher, of all things, didn't come to school the day before a test. He didn't come to school the day of the test so if these kids had questions, they were out of luck because they had a substitute who didn't know how to answer their questions. The man never sent home progress reports. My son said that he just doesn't fill these out. We came to every curriculum night there was, tried to talk to the teacher and he was trying to impress everyone, telling everyone that he has been a teacher longer than I have been alive. I think maybe it's time to retire, or move on, or get an assistant who is competent, because my son went from a B the first quarter to an F the fourth quarter. I had no clue. He can do the work—he just chooses not to. He's got friends, he's got a job, he's got more important things to do than his homework. It's not a learning disability type thing, although I do have a younger son that has that problem and I'm seriously considering homeschooling my sixth grader, because I don't want him to be swept under the rug. I'm the first one who will come up here yelling and screaming and demanding what he needs, but when you run into teacher after principal after counselor after administrator who backs these bad teachers up and says, "Well, that's just the way it is, that's the way he's been teaching for 150 years," you get nowhere because you can't change it if they're all backing each other up. I'm considering not sending him to school at all because we've made so much progress with him, I don't want to lose it all.

CH3 I agree with you on how they back them up. I think that legality-wise because of the union they have to. I'm sure that once you leave I would think that they would have a private meeting, hopefully, with the teacher, but I don't think they can say to you, "Oh, we're going to fire him."

SH2 I know they can't, legally they can't. The principal has to back them up. But backing them up to a point of telling you basically that you are wrong and your child is lying to you. Not, "We will talk to the teacher and we will find out what's going on." No, it's like you are wrong and your child is a liar.

SH3 I agree with that accountability thing. The minute your kid gets in trouble you're responsible and you better be up here letting them know why this happened or what did or didn't happen. When the child comes home and says to you, "Well, this teacher did this or that," and you go up there, they look at you like that couldn't happen here because we have perfect teachers and they all love children and that's a lie. I mean it takes a certain type of person to be a teacher—you got to like kids and teenagers are obnoxious and you got to like to doing that or you're not going to be very good at it.

CH2 There's a book called *Adolescence Isn't Terminal*, I'd like to buy a gross really. I want to get the book and read it, and I should've gotten it long ago, I am going to get it this summer and read it, because you're right, teenagers are trying to be their own individual. The problem I see, what happens at the upper level is this they expect them to be responsible. But then on the flip side, if they do something and try to be responsible and it doesn't turn out right then they come down on them like a ton of bricks. There's no latitude to experiment and try it, and if it fails you're not a terrible person for it. We all learn from our mistakes and rather than embrace the mistake, sit down and say, "Hey, what was the consequence because you did this? Wouldn't it have turned out better if you had done this?" No, you did it, you're labeled, and you're going to be this from now on. It shouldn't be. I try to say this all the time, but as a parent even when you're having problems in your own house, right away it's the blame game. Sometimes it's really important to train yourself to step back and look at it and say, "Hey, wait, that wasn't so bad. Could've been a lot worse." That's what we tend to do and what it does is just kills their spirit. I hate for the students to have their spirit killed. That's something I see. The elementaries are so nurturing here, they take care of them. They come out of that elementary and they go to the middle school and it's like I told you, you're guilty till proven innocent and it kind of just kills it along the way. Then by high school you look at their identity and we need to question ourselves have we beaten the fun out of them, the creativity, the spontaneity, that's wrong.

Discussion

Parent involvement has an effect on student performance. The more involved the parents, the more likely the students will improve their achievement. Also, the parents learn as well as the students, which helps them become better prepared to help their children. For every parent who gets involved, however, there are two students without parent involvement. We must work together as a community and get more parents involved. In many cases there is a lack of caring. Because the schools address the smartest and the slowest, there really isn't anything for those in the middle. Parents should not shelter their child. Children should grow up with a wide cross section of peers. We must be willing to help all children at various achievement levels. We need to bring other parents along. We all need to care just a little bit more. It's obvious that parent involvement is important. It depends on how one defines parent involvement, because in a lot of ways parents are not "involved" in the schools and don't go to the parent meetings. But in the home it's just an expectation that the children are going to work hard, do well in school, and be responsible.

Definitely parent involvement is important because it is essential, but parents don't always know where to be involved. As one parent lamented, "When requesting information to what would help children perform better on the state test, any suggestions—the third grade teacher was wonderful, but fifth grader all they said was tell him to read. Read what? Is it reading comprehension, big words, vocabulary?" The school needs to be clearer on how parents can help. Parents need to be accountable for their children, but the teachers have to be accountable and responsible not only to the parents, but to the children. Parents need communication on how they can help, both at home and at the school.

Question #4

What do you believe are the advantages and disadvantages of parent involvement in the schools?

PE   If you feel comfortable walking into the classroom, introducing yourself to the teacher, that opens the door for every other problem she may have with your kid, you may have with her, your child may have with the other kids. The main thing you should do is get to know that teacher, and if you don't that's your fault. If you don't take that opportunity to get involved, you can't be blaming the other kids, can't be blaming the other parents. It's up to you to take responsibility for how your kid interacts there. You can't leave it up to everybody else.

AE And I think the key word was you need to feel welcome. The problem is now that 9/11 happened and they have all the new rules, and you have to sign in and you have to wear badges. That's all fine and I think it's a great idea, but it's starting to be carried to such an extreme that you can't ever go into the schools for anything anymore. It seems like we pick our kids up outside, drop them off outside, don't walk them to their class. It's just now starting to be a problem for us, we're not allowed in the building.

AE The thing is with the standing in the lobby, it seems like such a minor thing, except it's such an opportunity to see the teachers and talk to them, see the principal and talk to her, see the secretary and talk to her, see other parents.

VE As far as the advantages of the involvement, my kids know I'm always there so they're less apt to try anything or to get over because they know I'm always lurking in the background. Just like my son got an F on his report card, well, I tried, I really did this, well, he knew the second I got the report card I was on the phone. So the teacher said to me, "No, he didn't hand this in, this in, that in." So my kids are less apt to try anything because they know. If the parents are involved, they know they are not going to get over. I am very forceful about that, I call parent-teacher meetings, whether they're doing well or not, I want the teachers to know I'm always available—I'm a stay-at-home mom and I want to be told everything. Even to the point where if they're doing well, fine, they might be doing well academically, but socially they might not be. I want to know that. My kids come home, I ask them questions and my husband will say, "I can't believe you asked them that." How else am I going to know, unless I am involved. My son says, "Mom, you're like everybody's mother." I have kids coming to my house telling me things and their parents say to me, "My kid will never talk to me. He never tells me." Do you ask them? Not only do I ask my kids, I ask parents of their friends, I ask their teachers, I am very involved. I am involved with the sports, I'm the snack mom because I know what goes on. And it's not that I'm overprotective or overbearing, they have their independence, but I want to know what's going on in their lives.

JE One of the advantages that I see with parental involvement is dialogue. When you have that, you have a dialogue with the teacher and the parent. I'm sitting here trying to think of disadvantages of parental involvement because you asked for advantages and disadvantages. I can't think of very many disadvantages of parental involvement other than if it interfered with the workings of a classroom or something along those lines, but I don't see that happening and I don't hear that happening. Even in the elementary level where my son goes to school we're very welcome. The teachers have been open with my wife and myself about being very welcome in the classroom. I've never heard of anything where a parent has actually disrupted a classroom. I really can't think of any disadvantages.

KE We all agree that the advantages are wonderful. The only disadvantage I could think of, is there a way that a parent could be so involved that they actually interfered? Sometimes I've run into parents where they feel their kids can do nothing wrong, and if their kid does something wrong it's never their fault, it's always that person they're hanging out with and they want to put the blame somewhere else. That's the only disadvantage I could think of and I think that's very rare.

RM I can't see a disadvantage.

LM I agree I would never say that why would there be a disadvantage. I guess some parents may overstep their bounds a little bit in certain areas, I guess that could be a disadvantage, but to me as a parent, physically at school, I would never see a disadvantage to that.

CM I agree. I know that there are parents who go in. Are you talking with the school or are you talking with your child? Because there are people that go in and pretty much hover over their child, and that's a bad thing. To be in the school and know what's going on, I can't see where that would ever have a downside.

LM I agree with that. There's only advantages to parents being involved. They help their kids, they give them encouragement.

They show that they care, kids need that. The only disadvantage could be if you were so overprotective and hovering that you can't let the child have any responsibility and not let go so that they can't form their own opinions and be responsible and remember their books on their own, remember their homework. They need to be accountable at some point. The disadvantage is not letting go enough or not knowing when to let go—when to transition them into this is your job to remember your homework.

CM I'm very involved, everybody knows that, everybody knows who I am, that I spend a lot of time at the school. If I see my son it's like an event. I go into the schools and I do the book fairs and I do the parents' association events, and I do the extracurricular events, but as for seeing him while I'm there, sometimes. I might run into him. He might come in and buy a book while I'm there, ask me for money, but I'm not in his classroom, I'm trying to improve the situation in his school for all the kids, not just him. And I can't see that being bad for anyone.

PI The cliques can affect the way the parents operate within the school. That's the disadvantage. The advantages, if you're involved, are that your child will recognize that—that you're interested in their well-being and what they do in the class and so forth. I think eventually you hope that that's going to translate into them trying to do their best or better than they were doing prior to that.

VH I think the advantage of being involved is if you know the teachers, the teachers won't have a problem coming to you. I've seen that at the elementary, halfway through my son was diagnosed with ADHD, got put in learning support, and has been unbelievable. His teacher has not been afraid to say Mrs. ____, you need to go back to the doctor and get ____ medicine adjusted or he's doing this today. I think they're more apt to send a note home, and I think at the middle school you need notes sent home from time to time. Those kids are still kids—they're babies. My eleventh grader totally disliked the middle school—did not like it, it was too hard for him. My daughter loved it. I don't know how my fifth grader's going to do next year. I'm very concerned—he's only in learning support until he is technically caught up and then he's phased out, so they say. I'm very afraid that he's going to get lost in the shuffle and ____ just loves to follow the gang, he likes to be a part of the crowd. My only good thing is that he likes to please, so hopefully he likes to please the teachers, not other students. I think that middle school is too rough on them and I don't think there's enough parent involvement.

CH3 Hopefully the middle school administration is going to change or you might be in trouble. They need at least three principals or get someone who knows how to communicate with the children and the parents. Number one issue down there.

VH Any time I've had problems with my daughter I've been lucky to get them addressed. I've had a couple problems with her with teachers where my husband has called the teacher and the one teacher called him back and he told her that she was coming across really rough and here she didn't even realize it and she didn't realize that half the classes were afraid of her. She pulled my daughter aside and talked to her and my daughter said she's totally changed. But we've had problems because my daughter has a problem with her shoulder—she's been out of gym for three months and she has difficulty trying to find somebody to help her to class, and if you don't have a note because she wasn't wearing a brace. Any time we had a problem, I have to say, the principal has been a help.

CH3 You're the first one to say that.

VH I know because I asked him a question when he was at the intermediate and I didn't like his answer, but I have to admit at the middle school when we needed help we got it from him. Now my daughter's involved up there, maybe he knows her, I don't know and I think that's part of the thing. If your kid's not involved they don't care. My son in eleventh grade isn't involved in anything and he doesn't want to be involved. He's involved outside the school with the fire department. How do I get involved if my kid's not involved? I'm lucky enough and I'm young enough that I still know half the teachers up there;

my daughter had my sixth grade teacher. My son had Mr. ____, who is a wonderful teacher. He sent home notes every semester my son made an A. But how do you get involved if your kids aren't in band, aren't in football? My son tried out for baseball—didn't make it—so OK, now what. You can't tell me the majority of the kids are involved in something. Not every kid's a cheerleader or a football player. How do you get involved? Granted they don't want you around, but you can't tell me there's not things behind the things you can't do just to get to know these teachers.

SH3 One of the disadvantages, I think, and this might be off course because I guess we're supposed to be talking about parents of our children. I have a real pet peeve, and I'm sorry if this is your job because I don't know what everyone does here, but the moms who come in and work as aides in the classroom. I have two sons who are both in special ed. and I feel like you have a mother in there who has no educational background, and she's just gone and got a job so she can work when her kids are in school, and she's helping as an aide in the classroom, and my kids are already behind. I think they need the best teacher they can get, not just a fill-in to work with them. I know this is kind of off course—but those are parents who are involved in the school—they're up there every day as an aide, but I don't often feel that they're the most qualified. I think that's a disadvantage. And then I go to baseball and I have a mom say, "Oh, I was in with your son in math and he didn't have his papers and he didn't have this but he's a good kid." Another mom told me she saw all the senior report cards this year—I don't think that should be allowed.

KH I have to really agree with her. There's one mother in particular that's up here in the intermediate school and who goes around talking about the children who are in those classes. When you live in a small township or a small neighborhood and that stuff goes around, and then once again it comes across as your word against theirs.

SH3 I had one teacher who told a friend of mine a story that happened to my son, so it went from this aide to my friend to me.

I went up to the school and I said, "What happened?" and the aide said, "Oh no, that's not what I said." Meanwhile my friend thinks my son is a big goofball, because she heard this story from one of these moms who come in there as an aide.

CH2 They are to keep confidentiality. They don't have a form per se but they are told and they are in-serviced with that, I believe. We talk about this a lot and it is an issue and everyone's well aware of it. The point is that controlling that individual, you understand what I'm saying. Then if you are the recipient of that, what you need to do then is call and let them know that this is happening and you have to. I know you feel you've hit the wall. See, this is what has to change—you can't feel that way, because if you don't do something about it, if you're not your child's advocate, then nobody else will be either. You have to stick up and you have to tell them what's wrong, if it takes a hundred times, you just keep telling them and that's it.

SH3 Wouldn't an aide be held to the same law regarding confidentiality as the teachers? Because I know by law teachers are not allowed to blab about students and things that go on in the classrooms to people not directly related to that child. But if they are it's a breach of that confidentiality and they should be fired. No questions asked, no second chances, because a teacher that went around blabbing in the community about different kids would be fired for cause. They need to know—look, you blab, you're fired.

CH3 Not really they won't be fired. They are in a very strong union.

CH1 There needs to be safeguards.

SH3 I agree that it starts in the middle school and that's where my problems started. The transition from fourth to fifth grade at that middle school—he just hated it. And then that just carried right over into high school and he hates that. He'll wire up a furnace for you at the technical school, but you want him to do vocabulary—he hates it.

VH The funny thing is that my son was in the first fifth grade up there and I was very open about it. I was in the first sixth grade class taken out, but they did it so different—they had you in your teams and you stayed with your class, your teachers, and that's what those fifth graders need. I'm not saying maybe sixth, maybe seventh, but I think that in fifth grade, ten classes, ten teachers the lockers, lunchroom. I just think that's where you start losing these kids. They just start thinking the heck with it, nobody cares, I'm just trying to keep up, I'm running constantly. I think that's where you lose the involvement.

SH2 I have a comment about middle school also. I think some of the basics aren't handled in the middle school—the place is chaotic. I know that age group is a real challenge, but people are running in the halls. I used to go pick up my son occasionally and I was practically killed in the halls after school. They run toward you—the kids are getting big—someone in between classes has to stand out in the halls, the teachers should step outside their rooms and see what's going on and correct kids if they're beating up kids at their lockers. Kids get slammed with the lockers, punched, and so on in the halls and the teachers are blissfully in their classrooms because no one wants to say to a child, "You can't do that here." There needs to be basic discipline, basic good behavior in the halls—walk fairly quietly, I know it doesn't have to be like in the old days with absolute silence, but just some basic good behavior and then the kids would feel like they were safer there. The other thing is to be treated with respect in the lunchroom and so on; you were automatically assumed to be a bad kid and assigned to some sort of lunch detention at the drop of the hat. When teachers and administrators assume that a child is misbehaving and is doing bad things, the big kids will think, "Why should I even bother."

Discussion

It is extremely important for the parent to get to know the teachers. If a parent does not, that is their fault. The key is that parents must feel welcome. Since 9/11, the schools have become so secure that sometimes even parents cannot gain access because of the restrictions. This has had an effect on parent involvement and the fact that parents may not always feel welcome. When the children know their parents are there and involved, their behavior changes and they will do better in school. The only negative factor may be parents who hover over their children and actually interfere. Involvement is good, but too much involvement and overprotection may not be. Students need to be accountable for some things.

Parents who feel their children can do no wrong do a disservice to the children, too. It is important to be involved so the teachers know the parent and would not have a problem coming to the parent if their child were struggling. We must be careful of parents who work as aides in the buildings. There have been instances of some of the aides talking in the community about certain children. Confidentiality is important. In essence, the advantages of parent involvement far outweigh the disadvantages.

Question #5

What kinds of activities do you feel that parents should be involved in at school?

JE   I think at the early age and I know that they do this in my son's class, he's in kindergarten. They have parents involved in the parties. They have snack days, they have parent readers come in modeling things like reading. They do an occupation thing where somebody comes in to speak about what they do. Whenever that happens my son comes home so excited—I met a fireman today or I met a police officer. I think those are great. I think also that field trips—they went to Romp & Roll and they invited as many parents as possible and I think that was a great opportunity. In some districts they allow the parents to come in and assist on cafeteria duties. They stop that after the middle school, they don't do it in the intermediate school. I think those would be great things. They do encourage parents to come in and have lunch with their kids.

VE   Realistically, in the intermediate school, if I went in to have lunch with my son he would be tortured beyond belief.

JE   One of the things here in the intermediate school occasionally what's also nice a couple of the police officers will stop by and come in and have lunch. And they get to know some of the kids in this building. I think those kinds of things should be encouraged more often. Community people should be encouraged more. I hate to quote somebody like Hillary Clinton but it does take a village to whatever. . . . In reality that's what it does.

KE Another way is to have parents involved in curriculum. I was involved on a technology committee and we developed the curriculum for technology. What's nice about that is a lot of the parents have connections out in industry and we know what they're looking for what kind of education our kids should have so they can get a job. Bottom line is they're going to have to go to college and get a job, and we have a lot of input into what goes on out there and it was nice to be involved.

VE That's an excellent idea—that the parents should be more involved in the curriculum. I'm sure, ____, with all your children you understand this, I have five children, three hours of homework a night. I've watched with especially the middle school, the core classes keep getting smaller and smaller because we're adding Japanese and creative expression. The only creative expression my fifth grader needs is recess. As far as that goes and I'm going, "Wait, wait, wait, and this is going to help you how?" I truly believe that parents should have more of a role in the curriculum. I totally agree with that.

LE1 That's good, but there again there's those kids who have no mom or dad that are at school.

VE But if you and I or this group goes and forms a curriculum, it's going to trickle down. Even with the children whose parents aren't involved, they're going to see a change in the curriculum. If we all get together . . . I'm spending three hours a night with homework. If these children don't have that parental involvement, they're going to fall through the cracks.

LE1 I'm spending more time on elementary homework than I am on the other levels.

VE My first grader's doing fractions. This is ridiculous. That needs to change.

LE1 Lower standards?

VE No, no. You don't see that much in elementary that's still the core classes, but as far as the middle school goes we have

Japanese, cooking, sewing, creative expression. She needs longer core classes so the amount of homework that comes home is cut down a little bit because they have more time in the core classes.
LE1 Tutorial.
VE Exactly.
LE2 I agree with all that 100 percent. My thing is get them when they're coming in the building in kindergarten and start forming and shaping them. If we instill all that at a really young age....
VE I don't think we should overload them either. The responsibility is trickling down where we have to keep giving them more and more at a younger age so they can keep up by the time they hit middle school. They need to be kids first and foremost. Their creative expression—they're losing creative expression because everything is so structured. It's to the point, and I agree with parental involvement, but you go to an elementary holiday party, OK, we have ten minutes to hurry up and make the craft, ten minutes to eat, ten minutes to play games. All the parents should get there, bring food, and say to the kids, "Go play. Do what you want to do." It is so structured.
LE2 There are parties that I've been to where us mothers have said, "They're having a good time, leave them alone." Hey, I have a second grader doing multiplication tables and not only is it a multiplication table, it is a timed multiplication test. Timed ... you talk about pressure. The kid had hives for a week. I'm not kidding.
VE And even at the middle school my son says to me, and I hate to keep going back to the recess issue again, but this year the first hundred kids that went through the line at lunch got to go stand in the courtyard. And I literally mean stand, they could not do anything but stand. As far as that goes, the state tests, the principals are letting these kids out for that hour, so apparently they know that that helps them learn. So why are we only doing it the week of the state tests? Why aren't we doing it all the time.
JE You're talking about the middle school, right. In this building there are no tutorials, there's no study halls. They go eight out

of nine classes a day. I'll probably get in trouble for saying this but it's a bone of contention with the staff in this building—has been from day one. They don't expect us teachers to go eight out of nine classes. We get a plan period, but they expect the kids to do that. As far as the cafeteria, the reality—there are three lunches with a thousand kids—about 350–400 kids per lunch, five teachers man the lunch. If you have the entire lunch go out you would have four-hundred-some kids standing outside that library doing who knows what at that age. If they don't have phys. ed., they have health class so that's just another class. They don't like phys. ed. at this age because most of them don't like to change at this age, so a lot of them don't even dress for phys. ed., so they don't do the activities, so they don't get any of this energy out.

JE There are ways to change this but every time it's the old we fear change, there's resistance to any kind of change. What is being seen is if it's not broke and they don't see it broke, we're not going to fix it.

VE OK. Now from what I've heard and I'm sure you can attest to this, from all of the teachers I've talked to about this situation, they all want to be anonymous and they said their hands are tied. The school board is only going to listen to parents, which is where the parental involvement needs to come in and say look we're seeing a change in our children, we're seeing what they need.

VE And the teachers I've talked to made that very clear. Please don't use my name. The teachers' hands are tied as far as the administration and the school board and everything. Once again it's up to the parents to get involved. Until we say it needs changed it will not be changed.

CM What I just said. Basically, the book fairs and anything that you can go in and interact with the people in the school but not hover over top of your child while you're doing it. If the teacher needs assistance you go in and assist in whatever they need you to do. The musicals, the talent shows, things like that—you're in the school, your child knows you're there and you're available if there's a problem. I sat next to my son's math teacher at a picnic and he never mentioned the fact that he failed a test. I was sitting right next to him. He got an F on the test and the teacher never bothered, never mentioned the fact that he was failing a test. You would've thought that he would've at least said, "Oh by the way, ____ had a problem with his test. I'll send it home with him"—something, anything, but nothing.

LM I was going to comment on that. Although we're primarily focusing on middle school—in middle school I am involved in some of the committees they have. The involvement sometimes isn't always what we would like to see, the outcome of a committee is not always what our input was, in other words it's overruled. So you kind of feel you're putting your time in on this committee but there's been no advantage to it because they just did something else. At the intermediate school I have to say honestly as a parent that's on the parent group there really were no opportunities for us to be involved. Book fairs, things like that, but I think as the kids get older our concerns are with the bullying and the attitude and the atmosphere, the drugs. I have tried to stay involved a little bit in that area as they get older. Unfortunately, it's a denial thing—this doesn't happen in the school. I don't believe that. From my children, thank goodness, have never had a situation that they've been bullied, but I have heard many other parents and children—by this age they're old enough to tell you what's happening at school. They're not making these things up. That's a real concern with me. My child's not involved in that, but he's being exposed to things that maybe I don't appreciate him being exposed to—he doesn't want to be exposed to—those are some concerns. The schools need to let the parents and the kids be more involved. I think some of the obvious ways to be involved are supporting the kids whether they're in the band or the chorus or sports (attending games), attending things your kids are involved in. I have been involved in gifted education and there've been more opportunities there like to chaperone, to drive to field trips. Sports booster clubs, it's expected that you're going to help and participate. I think there are so many opportunities.

RM   At the middle school, I still think they should have parents being involved with the school dances. I think that's an activity that I would like to go to. They're still young at fifth grade; I guess that's something that they don't want the parents at. Most of the other activities you're allowed to be involved in. The only other problem I would see with the activities, I don't think sometimes you're aware of the things your child could be involved in if they don't tell you. I really was trying to find out information on the track team—how many nights a week. Sometimes kids don't even know what they want to be involved in, you have to give them a little push and some of the activities I really wasn't aware of. It would be nice if they had something at the beginning of the year where you would have a list of phone numbers, names, on how to get your child involved because at that age they kind of take control of all the situations and leave you out of a lot of the decision-making that maybe you would like to be involved in still.

SM   I would like to see more, not even just strictly parents, but family-oriented kind of things. I know they have an Expo night in April. April is such a bad month for everybody. I'd also like to see, for instance these incentives with these Disney movies for seventh graders, I think are insane. Not that my kid ever actually made it to an incentive, but if he were to have made it to an incentive I don't see the value in that. I think we have such amazing people in the community and different parents who would be willing to come in and maybe come in and just talk to somebody it certainly would have to be better than watching the *Road to El Dorado*, some animated Disney film. There's a guy who goes around and does Civil War reenactments, for instance, he'll do it for free. They're learning about Pennsylvania history and Gettysburg, wouldn't that make more sense? I think that might be a way to bring in some people to be more involved. Gets people through the door under a pleasant pretext. I'm not real big on "it takes a village" type of stuff, I feel it's my job, but I think a lot of other schools have a lot of those kinds of interactions with the community. I can't wait till next year for my daughter to be involved in band, because it's another group of people to get to know. My son's on the soccer team and the more activities you're involved in, the more people you get to know. People don't want to come to meetings after being in meetings all day. I appreciate that you guys do that—thank goodness you do it. I'm a single mom, I've got to find someone to watch the kids and it's hard enough to find them when you're working, so that's an issue.

RM A parent brought to my attention that her son was on the track team and he didn't even realize that seventh and eighth graders were affiliated with the intermediate school which could be a real problem for children in seventh grade; her son was taking algebra and missed it every day. He got a D on his report card, and she was totally unaware of it. It's kind of a lack of communication that we need to work on a little bit better if your child is in a sport. Whether you have a sheet that's given to all parents saying about picking them up, dropping them off. She's waiting at the middle school for forty-five minutes and he was up at the intermediate building waiting for her. When it's your oldest kid I guess you're a little more worried and concerned. But with his grade, she was very disappointed and totally unaware that he was missing his algebra class—we're out of sync with them.

CM I think we need parent involvement just because if there are parents in this building and these kids know that there's a possibility that they might walk through, they're going to rethink what they're doing. I have a son at the intermediate school, I've heard some really interesting stories from him—there was a girl drunk—which is kind of scary. She came to school with water bottle filled with liquor, they found out 'cause she fell down. She was knock-down drunk in school. If she even thought there was a possibility that her parents were going to come in to this building at some time and do anything, don't you think she might rethink this? Or someone who knows her parents. The possibility of just coming in hanging artwork. I know that they have all the artwork hung up that the kids do and they have some amazing stuff. I feel bad for the kids' parents who never saw the artwork they did, but nobody knows it's there. The intermediate school office is filled with absolutely beautiful art that these kids did that no one ever gets to see. I saw it because I'm the president of the parents' association, really the only reason I saw it because I make my presence known. If you're not a parent who's willing to do that or able to do that it's kind of sad.

LM I wanted to bring this point up because I have actually asked for next school year. Parents do want better communication, that's very well known amongst all the schools, at least middle school and up. Can't parents be involved in communicating to other parents through the Internet? We even offered to do a district calendar since the district can't do that anymore. I think parents like us who are involved that want to take the time to let other parents know the things that are going on—I don't know how acceptable that is to the school. We've offered, whether it's going to be considered I don't know, but I think that's another way that parents would like to be involved. We want to know what's going on and we want to be able to let other parents know what's going on.

CM They put the administrators' meeting on the website, we begged in the intermediate school to get our minutes on the website. I resigned as parent association president only because of the lack of communication. I felt like I was completely wasting my time, that it serves absolutely no purpose, that's exactly what I put in the letter and I sent one to Mr. ____, basically saying that there's really no point in having a parents' association if no one's going to communicate with them. We serve no purpose. My opinion of a parents' association is to gather information of what's going on in the school. We got no information; if we were lucky the principal would come. I think it's really important to have that communication even on a monthly basis. I have to say the middle school is way better than the intermediate school.

RM Just that school calendar—that alone gave so much information because even if you're at the middle school and your child is involved in the arts and wants to see the play at the high school you don't even know when it is. I think the school is losing

	money because they're not getting people to come to the plays. You are so involved with your children at whatever school they're at; you really don't know what else is available. That was a really necessary tool to give you all the dates and times.
LM	We've offered to do it as parents but again whether they want us to be involved in that area has yet to be decided.
CM	I understand that what they did was really, really involved. We just said can we get something basic that tells us what's going on in the schools. You don't need all the extra stuff—it don't need to be shiny and fancy and have the Titan head on it if you don't want to. Just give us some basic information.
SI	I think that it's appropriate for elementary parents to be there for parties and whatever the teacher needs help with. The older the child gets sometimes they don't want you there. Helping with fund-raisers or even office-wise or whatever. Field trips—I think it's still a good idea for parents to go on a field trip if their child is going on a field trip to a certain spot. As long as it's not the same parents going all the time, a variety of parents from the classroom is going, I think that's a good idea. If a parent could come in during class time and help a teacher out. When my children were in Catholic school, we were able to come in any time and help out because the teacher just needed the time to get things organized. If there were parents there to help, it was a good thing. I don't even know if that would be possible in this school. Just to see your parents there helps the child a lot. I don't think there's really a bad way a parent could help. If there's a way to benefit your child, then that's a good thing. It shouldn't be restricted by, "Oh well, your child's in tenth grade, there's no reason for you to be here anymore." Your child still needs you—it's the most critical time—they've got their driver's license, they're going, they're gone, in two years they're out the door, they're in college. The more involved you are, knowing where your child is and where they need help I think the better off everybody is.
JI	I think it depends on the type of activity, the size of the activity, how many people are involved, for instance, the band, if your child's in the band, the band relies on that parent group to

get through everything. They run that organization and it's been a very successful organization. They work together—they're one of the very few that I can honestly say is a very successful organization. Different sports teams—I don't have a child in sports, but I would assume it wouldn't be a bad idea to have parents on hand to help out with hydrating the kids, sometimes they need someone just to comfort them. I think it just depends on the age, the level, the activity is. The school musical is another thing, there again they need parents to get in there and help to do the job. But as ____ stated, it goes back to that clique thing too where this child's had the lead for so many years and that parent's always done this job, they know how to handle it and sometimes I agree it's easier to handle it all because you can get it done faster, than to sit down and explain to this person or this person or this person. But you have to allow room to let that new person in to help out and to give them a chance at it. Pass it down. I do think it all just depends on the activity, the size, the age, it has a lot of factors involved to determine where it's going to be most beneficial at.

EI My daughter's been in a couple of different sporting groups and I went to as many of her games as I could. It was amazing when we would play ____ at home, the stadium was packed with ____ parents and only a couple of our parents. It was really awful. I felt so bad for the kids—here we are, it's a home game and there were more of the opposing team's parents here than there were of ours. I'm not sure how it all fits into the picture, but something just seems wrong, something seems like it was missing. I've had good experiences with the sports team parents' organizations and I've had the bad. We talked about whether we're going to have chicken or we're going to have sausage—there's been the wasted meetings where who cares, this is not why people come to these meetings. My experience is that there are usually not enough parents, or they'll go once and then if it doesn't sound like it fits what they want to do, then they never go back. From what I've seen and I've been in the district, my daughter came in sixth grade, she also came from a very little school of about two hundred kids. When she came into the district, we were all very nervous about it. It was a good experience for us. She did really well, and the teachers seemed to help her. Now maybe she just got lucky and it all clicked and it all worked out. I think the district was OK and the school was OK and everything was fine, it just seemed that we could be a little stronger with our parental support.

MI I just want to say that I've been very involved particularly at the elementary level and middle school level. But I have carted around a lot of kids whose parents couldn't be there. They were at work, they were taking care of a parent, they had other kids, so I think there's parents that do want to be involved, but they can't be there and I don't know what to say about that. There's a lot more people working these days, and they work odd hours.

JI A lot of times things aren't scheduled at very opportune times. That's not the school's fault either. They have to go by what the activities buses and things like that—you do the best you can.

MI I've also found sometimes I've gotten incorrect information— I live by the calendar and I write things down month by month, and then all of a sudden I'll get this letter home, "Oh, the meeting's not this day, it's this day." I scramble at the last minute— I have to work that day trying to find somebody to switch with me. Sometimes getting the correct information from the very beginning is very helpful instead of getting it the week before and having to scramble.

CI I also teach at a preschool level. It is wonderful to have parent involvement. You can get negative parent involvement—that would probably go with the disadvantages. The moaners and complainers which are detrimental and it spirals down. There is where the administration needs to be stepping in to help support and communicate and be the advocates as well as good listeners. Maybe there's too much of that I don't know. I think it's a difficult balance sometimes.

CH1 Confidentiality is a big problem I guess.

SH3 I believe so. There's has to be confidentiality.

CH1 Do the aides have to sign a confidentiality agreement? I don't know.

Discussion

At the elementary level, parents help with parties and snack days, volunteer as readers, help on field trips, and so forth. It is good at the intermediate school when a police officer comes in and has lunch with the kids. Community people should be encouraged more to come in. Parents should also have an opportunity to get involved in the curriculum. It is good to have parents involved on committees. The curriculum seems to be getting so complex, even at the elementary level. Students are asked to do more at an earlier age. Parents can get involved with school dances, graduation projects, sports, and many other activities. There really is a wealth of activities for parents to become involved in if they are motivated.

Question #6

To what extent are you aware of the principals and teachers in the school district attempting to involve parents in their schools?

JE   I think they do that in the elementary schools relatively well, especially the teachers. Again, and I think it goes back to numbers, they don't have as many students as they're responsible for, so therefore, it makes it easier to get that parent contact.

LE1 When I get my kids out of elementary and put them into middle school, I hook up with their guidance counselor. I call a meeting just so they know who I am and get a rapport going with them. Things can be set up to work for you.

JE   You're doing that OK as a parent. I think in the elementary they do a better job. I think it goes down to the amount of students that that teacher is responsible for.

VE   You're not going to call 130 parents and say, "Can you get involved?" That's ludicrous. So the higher up your children go the less the teachers are able to connect with the parent and that's when it should be up to the parents to take the initiative.

LE2 I disagree. I think the teacher can make some sort of an attempt. They stuff all kinds of papers in my kids' backpacks every single day. Now whether your kid brings it home or not, that's another story, because sometimes they do and sometimes they don't. But between the two of them I get everything. They

	could send notes up saying I need help here or how about you guys get together and do this for them.
VE	But if your child is not a disciplinary problem or a special ed. and they fall in that middle mode, what reason does a teacher have to contact you? According to most of the teachers they don't see a problem unless you point it out.
LE1	Not just for a problem, how about an update? Here's what we're doing, we're studying butterflies or we're doing dinosaurs or we're being happy today.
LE2	What about some teacher incentive program? They might leave here with a hefty paycheck and that's their reward, well, I don't buy that. Their reimbursement for further education—I don't think so. There's no reward system for the teachers to better themselves as educators.
LE1	Our PTO is parent-teacher. It's just a bunch of parents sitting around and no teachers.
LE2	It's like gossip city. I have ____ kids and I can give you an awful lot to talk about. I am telling you that is the last place I want to go in my school.
VE	The PTO at ____, they're more involved in the fund-raising end of it than they are the academic end of it.
JE	You were asking about trying to get teachers to those meetings and I think that if you had professional staff come in to those meetings it might change the dynamics of those kinds of meetings. Again, this would be something that you could work with. I think it would have to go through the school board, and maybe even the teachers' union. There are so many hours the teachers are responsible for putting in. We have to go for technology training, things like that. They're always looking for different things for us to do because there are only so many times they can train us on our web page. I would think it would be a great thing to offer the option to say if you don't want to go do your web page training, how about you do an hour going to the PTO meeting and that would take your hour.
JE	I don't think it's more about what's being said at the meeting, it comes down to a logistics thing, do I really want to spend that

extra hour there after school? I think it would be a good proposition to go to the powers that be. . . .

SM   I didn't even know there was a principal by this guy's name. I don't know when he even came in and I have a child in the intermediate school. I don't even know who the principals are. I don't even know where to go to find that kind of information out. I know from my other child because I've had another special ed. meeting and I met him there.

LM   At least at ____, our principal and teachers always ask for parental involvement. We had a science expo and I had to go up and set up and help put out snacks that they wanted to serve. Assemblies—we're up there for those. Book fairs, Santa Shop, field trips, individual class parties, first grade did an assembly about a big whale in the gym, parents had to come up and help set it up. They had to read a story to the kids, they did these origami things with them. In elementary school at ____, in particular, the principal and the teachers don't hesitate to ask for parental involvement. The doors are wide open and you're welcome there any time. At the intermediate and the high school I think the efforts by the teachers the first day of class sending home the syllabus for the class, what is expected, how things are going to be graded. Phone extensions are included—I always complain that the first day of school I have more homework than the kids! If I need to know what's going on in class I know how to get that information. Those papers always have to be signed so I have to see them—that basically is a good idea.

RM   I agree. I know the principals and most of the women here—you make sure you know the principal. As far as the teachers I like that idea too. Because I feel, too, that's my child's responsibility, but at least it's there and it's available so you do know what's going on in their class. I would never want that to stop.

CM   I think DPC [District Parent Council] is a good way, too. We have every principal, well, almost every principal, here every year, once a month so that you can meet all the different principals. As for the teachers, I think in the middle school it depends on the team how well you know the teachers. There are certain teams that are very parent-friendly. I have to say the team that we were in this year, I was way more involved this year with what was going on in the classroom and information just in general than I was last year. It depends on the team and it depends on the teachers. A lot of the teachers are very parent-friendly, a lot of them don't even want to talk to you.

LM I wanted to say that I think as parents we have tried to make the principal at the middle school aware that we would like to see more consistency among the teams. So when you have a team of teachers that maybe that, like ____ said, very open and then the next year maybe not. That consistency is something that all parents would like to see throughout the middle school. The only concern I have is that we say a lot of things that we would like to see, but never see a result. That's kind of discouraging because, again, I do take the time to go to meetings and give my input, but when I don't see results it's frustrating.

CM And I think that has a lot to do with why people aren't involved in the older class. They're just tired.

JI I'm not aware at all. I've gone and physically involved myself and walked up and asked. This past year at the middle school was the first year. Actually it was the end of the previous school year where the principal had come up and suggested, "Hey, I want to get a parent group together," a small one, like a focus group like us, and we would meet once a month to discuss different things happening in the middle school. That was the first year that I'm aware of that it was done and a lot of piloted programs came through us and were introduced to us and went on to the school. It was very good, it was very nice. I enjoyed sitting on that and being able to have my voice heard in speaking the way that other parents like I would feel. But for the most part, such as the intermediate school here, my son at the middle school got papers on the awards, so I knew they were having awards, but I kept thinking, "What's going on with the intermediate school." They work hard, too, why aren't there awards? We never got an explanation, we never got anything like that. So I went myself because I know if you don't ask questions chances are you're not going to get the answer. Stuff like that they're not going to send home. I went directly to the principal at the intermediate school and was told the teachers want paid to come out to do these awards ceremonies and they're not willing to come out to do them. They tried to do it during the day, kids would heckle, so they did it at night a couple years and I had attended those nighttime awards, and it was beautiful and it was well maintained and controlled. Then this year when I asked about it, because my daughter would stay up till two or three o'clock in the morning working so that she could keep the straight-A average and she wanted to make that top 10 percent. A lot of these kids work very hard—you don't have to be straight-A to work hard, you could be a B/C student and you're giving it your all. It just depends on the child. But they deserve to have that recognition and even if it's not an awards ceremony per se, because they're a little bit older I think it's even more important as they get older to be recognized for it because it's easier to slack off as you get older. But why couldn't the teachers hand them out in their individual classes? Instead they were mailed home in this brown envelope with their report card like yeah, you did good, big deal, here's your award. To hear the fact that the teachers just won't come out because they want overtime, they want paid to come out, I don't believe that—I think I was handed a line. I don't know what the real reason was. Did they forget to schedule this, was it an oversight? Naturally I'm not going to stand and argue, I was quite stunned. And when I went back to one of the middle school teachers and because I had mentioned this to them, she was like, "That's ridiculous." There's other ways around it, I really believe they don't communicate as well when you do get older. I really believe that no teacher or no principal outside of this one situation, I was very surprised that it happened to me—that I was approached to sit on this little committee to help out and it was great. But that's the first time in all these years with the exception of elementary that I was approached. In elementary school those teachers are great they'll call you, "Hey, Mrs. So and So, can you come up and help cut out this or can you come up and do this," and they do need the help, 'cause these kids are little and it's very hard to keep the

DATA PRESENTATION AND ACTION-PLAN DEVELOPMENT 179

little kids' attention. Just because the kids are older doesn't mean they don't need the help still.

CI I think sometimes we forget that as you get older. They're pushing you as the parent—I want to have some distance, I want some independence, and you want to give it a little bit 'cause you can't go with them to college. So it does become a tug-of-war. At the intermediate level we had a good experience. Miss ____ was one who does reach out and does attend sporting events and does communicate with the children and she doesn't even have to have them in her class, she does know them. She gets on other committees, but then again, she's single still. Being a parent and a wife and a working teacher you get pulled in other directions and as that develops in her life, she won't have the energy or the time frame to do what she's doing. I'm thankful that she does now, and it has made a big difference in a lot of these young people's lives that she has helped them and showed the interest—just not my mom and dad coming, or my grandma and grandpa. She's out there and there's some others, too, that have done that as well that have come to this when asked and would love to get out there and see the kids that are young teachers in this area. At the high school there are some that still get involved, but fewer and fewer at that level.

CH3 None whatsoever.

SH1 I don't know.

MH None at the high school level.

SH4 Absolutely none at the high school, but my son was here in ninth grade and to his credit Mr. ____ did send really nice sounding letters saying, "Oh, my door is always open please call me or call the teachers." It's very nice that the teachers have their little voice mail, but having to wait four months for a phone call back is a little impractical. You call and you call and you don't want to appear that you're a stalker calling these people all the time, but after four months and they still don't call you back, it is very frustrating.

DH I actually got a call me back from the school—I'm so glad we're done with this school, finally—just to put me down, and

	say this is what he's doing in class, is what he's not doing in class. He's the class clown—he has all his friends in his class and I find out it's the first week of school and he knows nobody in that class, so how does he have all these friends in his class? It's very frustrating.
VH	I got that too, and he came from ____. He came here where he knew exactly two people out of 550, he knew two people, and the second week of school I talked to one of the teachers and he told me that he's fooling around with all his buddies—I'm like, buddies? He doesn't know anybody. It's amazing.
SH2	It is my understanding from what my child has told me that there doesn't seem to be a whole lot of respect at the intermediate school between teachers and children. If you want your child to be respectful to adults and people in authority the same has to hold true with the teachers and the child. Children are not going to be respectful with the teachers if the teachers don't respect how they're talking to the kids and treating the kids either.
DH	There was an incident in the classroom; the boy stood up who actually caused the problem and she told the boy to sit down because it was my son that did it. So what do you do with a teacher like that, when I'm told, she's new—she'll get there.
SH1	It sometimes hard to hold your own cool when you get up there with these teachers. OK, I'm not your student, you shouldn't be talking to me that way. And then the minute, the minute you change your tone of voice or the minute you change your attitude—well, I can see where your kid gets it. I've had a teacher say, "Well, I can see why ____ reacts the way he does."
CH1	I have to share something with you. When my oldest was in the middle school he had an incident with the teacher and the teacher accused him of trying to skip class, whatever. My son told me he wasn't. I wrote the teacher a note explaining my son's actions. Well, she wrote me back so we started a letter-writing campaign. What was fascinating was it was probably years later that I found out that that teacher shared it with everyone.

DATA PRESENTATION AND ACTION-PLAN DEVELOPMENT 181

CH3 Your letters?
CH1 Yes, my letters. I found that completely appalling. You see you're right if you defend yourself, or you go in and try to be on your child's side, be that child's advocate, then you are accused of being blind to them. Who knows the child better than the parents? I think that should be the rule of thumb and you're right you do need to be respected. You need to be respected because of the fact that you are living here, you're a citizen here, you're sending your child here and if we want our children to grow up to be good citizens, too, we have to have that respect. As the years went on and I thought back to that I actually felt bad for the teacher that did it and for the group that thought it was amusing, because if anything they are supposed to be here for us. We're employing them to make it better. I'm sharing this with you not to put anybody down or anything, but everyone's a victim sooner or later when it comes to systems. And that's what it is, it's an educational system. I feel bad that the public school system has so many things that everybody considers wrong with it. They talk about being an advocate for public systems and I'm sure things like that happen in private too. I don't know what the answer is either, it's the bigness sometimes. The thing about ____ Area School is what they do is they send you that packet home at the beginning of the year telling you that you can join the PTA [Parent-Teacher Association], so I think that's their idea of reaching out to you. How could the principal make you feel more welcome? I think about it too. I've talked about the high school that they should be zoned into the different floors so that the students see them more, that they are more available. I call it the island in the sun when you go up there. Everybody's huddled in that office, nobody's out there. They need to be out there. Counselors need to be zoned out there, too, so that students can get with them and talk to them.
SH2 Also the counselors have to make it clear that it's possible to talk to them. The comments that I've had from my son was that the counselor doesn't want to be bothered. I've had contacts with him and had to call him about scheduling problems and I

was treated very disrespectfully until I stood my ground and said this is what has to be done. I don't think they should treat anyone that way. All through the system my son has complained the students are treated disrespectfully by the teachers and embarrassed in class and so on.

SH3 I think that it seems like from what we're all saying it's becoming us against them—the parents against the administrators and teachers. If we're all there for the common goal of the children, it really shouldn't be that way. Hopefully something like this will come from that. My sons play hockey and ____ did come to their senior night at the hockey rink, but I can also say that most of the parents didn't even know that that's who that was. Most of them didn't even know that that was the principal of the high school.

MH   If he was to walk in this room right now, I would not know him.

SH3 He did put himself out there to come to the hockey night.

CH3 I don't know what the new assistant principal looks like.

Discussion

The elementary schools involve parents relatively well, especially the teachers (a lot has to do with the number of students they have compared to the secondary levels). The higher up the children go, the less teachers connect with parents. It should be up to the parents to take the initiative. It seems that unless one's child is a disciplinary problem or in special education, teachers do not contact the parent. The PTO is supposed to be parent-teacher. In actuality, it is a group of parents sitting around with no teachers. Teachers have certain hours they are required to put in, and attending outside meetings becomes difficult unless they volunteer their time. It was indicated that one of the parents did not even know who the principal was at one of the schools even though their child attended that school. Particularly the elementary schools ask for a lot of parent involvement. At the middle schools some teams are parent-friendly and some are not. Some teachers are parent-friendly and some do not even want to talk to parents.

At the secondary level, some parents expressed frustration at not seeing anything they talked about at the parent meetings come to fruition.

They were tired of making the effort and did not get involved anymore. It seems that from elementary to secondary, there is less teacher involvement in activities and other functions. At the intermediate school there needs to be more respect between the teachers and students. Principals need to be more visible at all levels. Students need to see them and know them. This way, communication can be better disseminated. It sometimes seems like it's the parents against the administrators and teachers. It should be that we are all there for the good of the children. Parents don't often even know who the principals are.

Question #7

How well are school personnel doing with school-home communication in our schools?

VE   I really haven't had a problem. When I contact a teacher or principal and leave a message, I normally don't have a problem with them getting back to me. Everybody's been pretty accommodating, I've had a few higher-ups that are more condescending. My husband gets more results when he deals with a male administrator than I do. I think the teachers, a big issue, is how receptive the parents are. I've said to the teachers, "Do what you have to do." I've talked to a lot of teachers who have said, "We have a problem with the child and when we talk to the parent the parent says, 'Not my son and don't you dare yell at him.'" That's a big issue.

LE1   Because I present myself I even get notes in the middle of a grading period that say this isn't looking too good. But when I talk to other parents they say, "How did you get that note? Why did they tell you that? How come somebody didn't warn me?" I say to them, "Put yourself out there." They don't know every different parent personality—they don't know which one's going to jump down their throat, they don't know which one's going to be protecting their child all the time. You have to go and tell them.

VE   The only problem I have and which I would like to see more of. When my child does have a problem, like there were missing homework assignments, I didn't find out about it until there were numerous missing assignments. All I require from the teacher is that as soon as they see a pattern, more than two, I want a phone call.

JE   I think one of the things that isn't being utilized well enough in the district is technology. Some buildings in the district have a phone in every classroom so that teachers can pick up their phone right then and there and dial Johnny's mom. In this building we have a phone in every classroom; it is invaluable. I know in the middle school when I'm trying to get in touch with a teacher they have to go to a phone center or I have to call the office. I give the parents my phone number so they can call directly into my classroom. I only do that for certain parents, I don't do that for everyone.

LE1 Even if I've left messages on mailboxes, I get an immediate response before the end of the day.

VE   The biggest breakdown so far that I've had with all the schools is the middle school. That is where I've had the biggest problem. Intermediate school is no problem, elementary school is no problem. There is not a single thing I like about the middle school. I detest that school. I've had more problems there. Since my son left the middle school, I've not had a single problem. That's where the communication breakdown is, too, at the middle school. That's where I wait the longest for a phone call, the teachers aren't contacting me when there's a problem. Every other school—no problem; middle school—big problem.

LM   That's our biggest failure in this district. Our communication past elementary school is horrible. Elementary school communication is outstanding but it's that same thing—an open door. You can go in and physically be in their face so they have to communicate with you. We shut the doors at the other schools and then they're bad at sending letters, they don't send the reminders they should or on the progress reports they don't indicate things properly. They'll tell you your kid's doing fine and you get a report card with a C, D, or F on it, to me that's not fine. It comes out of nowhere and then you make phone calls and you do not get phone calls back.

CM   I actually had a letter that was supposed to come home to me that no one ever followed up on. It was my son's homework—he didn't complete so many homeworks—and was to have detention. Nobody told me. I never got the information. He had a paper that he was supposed to have come in and signed and gone back. It never went back because he never brought it home. No one ever called. I had no clue. I asked the principal at the school, "Don't you follow up—if you give them a paper to have signed, if he doesn't get it signed, don't you, like, ask him about it?" He said, "Oh, I have too many of them."

LM   That happened to my sister-in-law. My nephew did not bring the paper home so therefore she didn't sign it, so they assigned him an after-school detention. She works full time, so he couldn't take the bus home 'cause he had to stay after school, but then they wanted her to pick him up at 4:00 when she doesn't get done with work until 6:00. She never knew until that morning when they called. They didn't call her that morning—I think it's when she didn't show up at 4:00 to get him they were calling to ask her where she was. Horrific. I can tell you this much, if that ever happened to me, oh, these poor people, this wouldn't be this same happy face you see here today. It wouldn't happen to me, let's put it that way, I cannot understand how we can be such poor communicators.

CM   He missed his incentive is what he missed. I went to the incentive and he wasn't there. And I said, "Excuse me, where's my son?" And they said, "Oh, he didn't get to participate because he didn't do his homework." And I said, "Don't you send letters home?" "Well, yeah, we sent one home." "Was I supposed to sign it?" "Yeah." "Well, I didn't. Did you notice I didn't sign it?" "Well, we gave it to the principal." So I went to the principal—"Did you notice I didn't sign it?" "Well, that's the teacher's responsibility." "Do you people talk?"

SM   There is a lot of passing the buck because I think since you only have that in the one class, that's the difference too between elementary and middle, you only have two or three teachers on a team there in the elementary, so it is easier to keep track of people. I've had similar problems, I've had Fs on three tests in a row, and the kid had no clue what fractions were so at some point that's going to catch you again. He was just too afraid to show me 'cause he didn't want to get kicked out of soccer. I never got the information. The Wednesday mailbags are helpful in the elementary. I don't see why we can't have something weekly on the Internet. A parent hotline, call in and listen to what's going on.

CM They need to follow up. When there's a problem and the paper doesn't get signed, somebody needs to follow up.

RM I wish they would send their tests home. Every test. Why couldn't we sign their tests? That way they would know if you got to see it, what kids are pulling a fast one. Mine won't show me if she gets anything below an A. I see no papers unless they're an A.

SM We as parents have different ideas on what is important. I have been told by many different teachers there's nothing wrong with a C. When you've got a kid that's getting ninety-eighth, ninety-ninth percentile on state tests, gets a ninety-six on his test, and can't take algebra because his handwriting is so bad that he can't write, then there's a definite failure in communication, so a C is not appropriate for him at all. I think we all certainly have benefited by learning to be moms and we know that different things are important now, but there are things we realize by experience that are more important. We can't expect always to understand without having children. Maybe there's a way we can make it known that these are parental expectations. My child has gotten detentions over and over from losing pencils—he had lunch detention for two months because the teacher got tired of him not having a pencil. I brought in a pack of sixty-four pencils, they would not accept that. The kid's got bigger problems than that—he's got clinical depression, we don't need to worry about the pencil right now. Couldn't we make this compromise here? That's part of the problem—communication. I think there are teachers who genuinely think they are communicating. Just like in a marriage, which I can certainly vouch for being negative on bad communication on that too unfortunately.

DATA PRESENTATION AND ACTION-PLAN DEVELOPMENT   187

LM I specifically have had conversations with the principal at the middle school about communication between teachers and parents and have been told actually sometimes the teachers hesitate to call the parents, they want the principal to do it. Me, as a parent, I would expect a call from a teacher regardless of the situation rather than getting a call from the principal. You get a call from the principal, right away you panic. But for a teacher to refuse to do that is I don't think acceptable.

CM They're not required to do it. I think they're wrong. I really do. I was told that by one of my son's teachers—he was not required to call me. Yeah, he was, district policy required that and I explained that to him. Where does *required* come in to play? I think it should be if the child's having a problem—it's a five-minute phone call.

LM It's a matter of humanity, it's a matter of common sense and courtesy.

CM It's a matter of respect. I mean there's no respect for the parents with a lot of these teachers and I'm not going to say all of them 'cause some of the teachers in this district I can honestly say are absolutely wonderful, they go above and beyond. But a lot of them don't want to communicate and I've left messages for teachers who never called me back. I've left messages for teachers and asked a specific thing and never got a response. That's just flat-out disrespect as far as I'm concerned.

LM I think our district has a true problem—it's not a two-way street. Their expectations of us are so great they are so quick to say, "You didn't do this, you didn't see to it that your son had the right accordion folder." When things go wrong they're quick to blame you or tell you what you didn't do right. They don't want to hear what they don't do right. Or they don't want to hear that they didn't call you back. They'll have 101 excuses as to why, if they even try to excuse it. That's what I find. They want us to be accountable, but they don't want to be accountable. We're supposed to be accountable for our children—the way they dress, their behavior, the fact that they have their homework, and everything they're supposed to do—but they don't want to be accountable for their shortcomings. They can give them a test with a misspelled word on it, but that's OK, but because we forgot to sign a paper if our child gave it to us or our child forgot to bring it home—we're terrible. There's no amount of logic to that to me at all.

SM   I did have a communication from fifth grade along that line. I was supposed to sign a paper after correcting it and I had corrected it—you could see all my little corrections, but right when I got a pen to sign it one other kid came in and threw up all over the floor. I kind of forgot—I'm a single parent with four kids, I'm working, I'm doing the best I can, trying to keep a roof over our heads—and I actually got a note from the teacher and a copy was sent to the principal—the mother will not cooperate with our request for signatures and things like that. That was the only time I fired off two big letters telling them about my day. It turns us defensive too. I'm sure teachers feel the same way. I am so unhappy with the school that I am pulling my son next year and going to homeschool him. The bullying just put me over the edge. I'm here mostly that maybe it would be better for someone else, because it was horrible and yet I will stick up for teachers and you hear some of these people who just are negative all the time. There is one particular teacher that deserves everything he gets without question, I mean, he's telling my son, "Stop making those twitches." He's got Tourette's, what do you want him to do? And so my son has had a horrible year.

LM   I just wanted to say one thing that ___ touched on. There's a protocol for a parent—if you have a problem with your child you are to talk to the teacher, then the principal, then the administrators, then the board.

CM   If you don't they will tell you about it.

LM   Yes, and that should follow suit. If a teacher has a problem or if there's a situation they need to address the parent first, not expect the principal or somebody higher up to do that. They need to communicate with parents more effectively.

EI   I have not had a lot of back and forth with the teachers. I have not had a lot of communication with teachers. When I've called, when I've had questions or I've had issues with what's been brought home, for the most part the teachers have been pretty responsive. ____ was really wonderful—my daughter had her for geometry. I asked if she would be able to meet with her after school and she was more than happy to do whatever she could. All it took was a little bit of extra work, she was just missing some concepts in class, and she came back and I could see it on the papers she brought home. I could see "good job" and "great," just like you would see on an elementary student's paper, but let me tell you it made a big difference, it made a big difference. We were afraid we were going to lose this kid—she didn't like geometry and that teacher's involvement really did help.

SI My son is in an inclusion classroom for special ed. so the teacher involvement has really been wonderful. Granted he has a teacher there that has a smaller group, but she does help the rest of the class also. She has just been wonderful, every year has been very informative, I know ____ grades before ____ does and I know where his weaknesses are. It's worked really, really well. I have nothing but good to say for the inclusion program. They know what his strengths are and they've given me recommendations where I'm like, "Oh no, no I can't do that." And they tell me he's going to be fine and it turns out that he is fine. That part does work well. We had an incident this year that made me very upset with the nurse. My son has a heart defect and he needs to have medication before any kind of dental procedures. I found out that in the intermediate school you have to bring the medication to school and you have to have a note. ____ was not allowed to do this. I said, "Fine, I'll do it." Took off work, came here, and gave them the medication and told them what time to give it to him. I'm picking up my son and leaving to go to the doctor's appointment and he said, "Mom, wasn't I supposed to have my medicine?" I just about died. "What are you talking about?" Went back into the nurse's office, there was an assistant there, and she said, "I tried calling him and he wasn't answering." I said, "Do you realize that he needs this medicine an hour before the procedure?" "Yes, but I don't know where he was." Excuse me—I was clearly bothering her. "When did you start calling for him?" "At quarter to." "Well, he was supposed to have it at 10:30. Why would you start calling him at 10:45?" "I don't know." I said, "Do you realize that if I would've gone to the orthodontist and he would've gotten an infection, he would be in the hospital for a month?" "Yeah, whatever." At that point I just walked out because I could have literally killed her. I had to call the cardiologist and we had to wait an extra half hour because ____ didn't have his medicine on time. So ____ went back to class and I asked to speak with the nurse. She wasn't any more supportive than her assistant. She blamed ____ for not being where he was supposed to be. I was very disillusioned with the whole scenario. I told her, "You will never give my son medicine again." For her total lack of sensitivity to the situation and the importance of it, I thought was very uncalled for.

JI   I find in those cases, in all the schools, if I contact the teacher to ask about what's going on the response is very positive for the most part. Several times if they needed extra help they'd be more than willing to send home a math book for the entire summer or extra packets of extra work to do to catch them up with it. Miss ____ and Miss ____ are willing to stay after school and let you get things done. Miss ____, who runs the career up here, if the kids are on vacation she doesn't think twice about staying after school to let them get on the computer and finish their resumes and things like that. She's one-on-one helping. I find that as long as you take the interest and explain, describe what's going on and if your child's willing to do it, they're willing to work with you as well.

CI   This year was a unique situation where I tried communicating with a specific teacher and was not getting called back. A lot of times you do play phone tag. It's tough to get immediate information. I find it is my place to call the guidance office and then go to the principal because there may be a reason I don't know what's happening here that is facilitating the response I need and if I need it ASAP. Usually I did get through to the guidance office and that helped a lot. I want to know if the teacher is not getting my messages or has he been out ill, which was one of the situations. I think it is up to the parent to go on beyond sometimes, not as a tattletale but as "help me out here." If you have that rapport with the guidance office and a principal then it's going to help you in the long run with the teachers. Because you're going to find with teachers—a lot of different personalities—your child is not always going to be in agreement and that's when you need to teach them that hey, you have to make do.

PI This is the first year that I've gotten involved for many years. I did get calls about midterm where there were weaknesses and where help was needed so forth, did have an appointment with one teacher who explained to me what was going on. I think that if the child needs some help, there is some communication at least in his particular instance.

VH After the elementary school I don't think there is a whole lot. At the middle school we get newsletters, half the stuff in there already happened.

CH3 Everything's coming late.

VH The only thing I've gotten from the high school is on financial aid or starting to go to some of those seminars. In terms of things going on outside of curriculum night—which is sometimes a joke—there's hardly any parents. I was in a class where there was me and one other parent, maybe they all came the other night I don't know, but once you're at the middle school there's not a whole lot of communication. I was involved at ____ Elementary and there was a lot of different ways I was involved. I'm a working mother, my husband stays at home and I work retail—people shop till 9:00 at night so I can't get to PTO meetings if they're scheduled on a day I'm working. I don't understand why they don't utilize the website a little better. I go on the website a lot to see things and why don't they ask a parent who does work, that could maybe do something at home, why they can't put it online.

SH1 If you don't call them, they aren't going to call you. If there's a problem, then that's when you get a phone call. And then if you don't get it the problem progresses till it's like OK, now he's suspended for three days. I didn't even know there was a problem to begin with. If you don't call them, they don't call you.

CH2 I agree with the website. Funny how a lot of the teachers utilize it and then there's others who don't even know how to type. Apparently some teachers don't know how to type because they still handwrite thirty-page handouts. Why not ask the parents to type whatever, get them involved that way. Could you help me do my website, or could you help me type up some handouts.

VH Or even senior projects. I'm sure there's a way to tie that in. I just feel they don't utilize that enough—there's always a click on there to go to the PTA, but there's hardly ever anything in there, might be dance pictures or whatever, but nothing that says this is coming up, this is coming up, or we need parents for this. I just don't think there's enough communication once you hit the middle school.

SH1 I think the school should send home more specific information about activities—not all of us attended schools, not all of us know the band trip is extremely expensive. Any of the details—when money has to be sent in for things—I'd like to have that information. I know some of the kids are very organized and bring things home, but some of us have kids who forget these things and you might get it a month later, too late.

SH2 Why can't they put them in the mail. If you want me to see it, put it in the mail. I'm sure when I get the mail and it says "To the parents of" I open it and read it.

CH3 Unless your child thinks it's a bad report or whatever....

SH3 I think even the middle school, when they go from fourth grade into fifth grade at the middle school it is just such a total shock to those kids. They're treated with tender loving care in the elementary, at the middle school they're expected to grow up so much. In the beginning of the year they learn too quickly because of the responsibility that's placed on those poor kids. As far as communication, at the middle school the parents go from getting things in writing at the elementary and always being at the elementary school but not being at the middle school. Even

DATA PRESENTATION AND ACTION-PLAN DEVELOPMENT 193

	the kids cannot hear the announcement on the intercom. The kids don't even know what's happening, even if they want to get involved in something or if something is important.
SH2	They can't hear the announcements at the high school either.
VH	I think also at the middle school they need to address how they communicate to these kids. Not all kids are like my daughter, who is a big worrier and panics when she's told that the state tests determine how much money they get. My daughter has no concept of how much money a school even takes. But she worries that if she doesn't do well enough there's not enough money for that school. I don't think that aspect of it should be communicated to these kids. These principals or whoever talks to them are college educated to work with kids—maybe seventh graders understand it.

Discussion

Elementary parents didn't seem to have many problems with teachers communicating with them. It is interesting to note, that as the students moved from middle school, to intermediate school, to high school, the communication seemed to be less. Parents at the secondary levels complained about lack of communication while the elementary parents seemed to be happy with the level of school-home communication they received. Communication seems to be situational. Certain secondary teachers were identified as reaching out and being good communicators with parents whereas many others did not even make an attempt.

Question #8

What, if any, connection do you see with the implementation of active parent groups at each school and students' performance on the state test, and with their academic achievement in general?

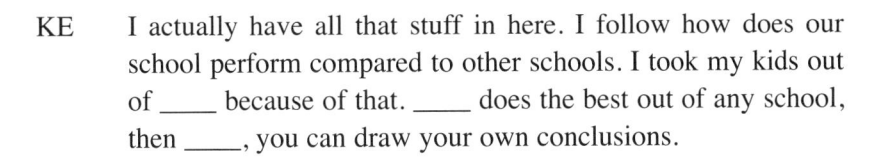

KE	I actually have all that stuff in here. I follow how does our school perform compared to other schools. I took my kids out of ____ because of that. ____ does the best out of any school, then ____, you can draw your own conclusions.

LE   We call ____ the country club of elementaries.

KE   They always do the highest scoring.

LE   We're getting kids from ____, ____; it's not a stable, little community.

VE   Apparently the scores are showing that there is improvement with parental involvement.

KE   I know we really have to focus on those state tests.

LE1   It's all what you read, where you read it, and how you interpret it. I'm a ____. I can read thousands of studies on something and I'm going to get a totally different view of what that person said on that study than the next person. There is no general lump to put everybody in. We can't sit here and say, "Oh yeah, parent involvement is the answer to everything," or "I get treated different because of this or that," there's so many factors and there's so much psychology in the whole thing—there's no way you can cure everything.

LE2   But if test scores account for our funding. . . .

LM   I made that comment earlier. I think when parents are involved children do better—even if it's not their parents. When a child thinks that someone's looking over their shoulder, they perform better, they behave better. When they think you care and when you take the time that you don't always have, that you're finding to put the effort in, then they put the effort in. It goes hand in hand, I think. Would you guys not agree that the children who do better, that are the better academic achievers, are the kids of the parents who are involved?

RM   I agree. Mine always will try to do their best on a test and they do make such a big deal about this state test. What I'm very disappointed for is that they also had the CAT [California Achievement Test] and they did not take as much time or effort in trying to make that test as well. I talked to a teacher about this—they have choral concert, band concert, my seventh grader, I don't know how many tests she had the day of the CAT. Those CAT tests for the child, everything is based on the CAT test so it's in reversal, it's messed up. The school cares about the state tests and they expect the children to care about it because they need their funding. In turn they make a big deal about eating right. It's nice to know when it is, but as a parent we really do know to feed them — we're going to feed them every day, hopefully, not just the day they're taking the state tests. The CAT test — they do all the placement with those tests. They're getting other math tests, spelling test, English. I think she had five tests and then they had their choral concert and that's ridiculous. If they didn't do well maybe the school ought to take a good look at that also.

SM The seventh and fifth grade band concerts were during the state tests and my eighth grader's band concert was right before their test as well. They got out of there at 9:30 — this is crazy. That's not very much time to get a good night's sleep. I try to limit everything a little bit more for any test — not just state tests. Then I've got my son who's getting high scores on the state test, basically the teachers who have half of him all year get a good boost on their potential salary increase and yet he gets Cs, Ds, and Fs. I don't know if you can even give a correlation between the state test and other tests when you really get down to it because in this day of political correctness, it doesn't matter that my son gets As on all his tests, the fact that he can't get his homework in the proper slot in the book counts just as much, so I don't know if you can give a correlation between any of those.

RM I don't think it's particular to that. Parent involvement is life-long learning — not just the state tests.

LM I know in this building, specifically this year, and I brought this up at our parent group meeting. The state test, they decided to change the way they give those tests in the intermediate school building. It's a two-day test that they decided to give it over a week, which is a great idea. The only problem is the way they decided to inform parents was by giving the kids that letter to bring home. I got the letter that my son brought home because he did. I asked every other eighth grade parent at that meeting. None of them knew that that state test was starting Monday. They all based it on, I guess, what they saw initially in their package that was mailed home earlier in the year or whatever. I did ask at that and at the DPC meeting, "Can we make parents aware through a mailing?" They could have stuck it in with the progress reports; that way the parents would've known. The fact that the eighth grade results decide if they're going to be put in a remedial class next year for ninth grade is a graduation requirement I thought was very important for parents to know. There was never a letter sent home saying that. It was sent home just now with their report cards at the end of the year. Inappropriate time—it should've been sent home before. And I have addressed this to the proper people. Whether anything changes, again. . . .

RM I also called the school. Of course the state test results are not back to parents, really, I hate to say it, no wonder the kids don't take it seriously, it doesn't mean anything to them. The numbers mean nothing to the students—they're still using the CATs in the younger grades.

CM Back to the question—do I think parent involvement has anything to do with the state test scores? I think if you talk to your kids and explain to them what's going on with the state tests, and I think you need to be involved to even know what the state tests are. To tell you the truth, I think there's way too much emphasis put on the state tests and that's a whole other story. Do I think it has to do with their education? Sure. Does it make my son do his homework? No. Do I make my son do his homework? No. He's fifteen, nobody makes him do anything anymore. He acts better, he acts more respectful, he's a better person because his mother is a little bit more involved and shows that she's going to be there and pay attention. Sure. And I think any kid who has a parent who cares and shows that they care in some way is going to do better than a kid who doesn't. I've seen friends of his whose parents you never see at anything. Not the parents who don't come to the parents' association because they work, not the parents who don't get involved, but you never ever see them; that's the kids that I think have problems.

LM In regard to that question, I think it depends on how you're going to define parent involvement. Parent involvement just in the schools in relationship to doing well on the state test, I don't think that correlates as well—like I've sat and talked to my child about the state tests. It's not important for your day-to-day grades, like it's not going to take your science grade and take it from an A to a C because you do poor on it, but it is important to the school and it's important that it shows what you know. I let him know it was important and to sit down and do the best he could and to apply himself and to care about it. But also not to panic that it would take one of his grades, 'cause I do have a straight-A student, and that was one of his frets was that "Oh, if I do bad now this A I have is going to go to a C or D or something even worse." So I didn't want to keep that panic because they even tell you—test anxiety. But it's important to the school, it's important for funding, take your time, do the best you can. And he scored above average. Does that help? Is that the answer you're looking for?

JI The parent involvement ultimately boils down to like we discussed earlier—if you care, they're going to care. I don't know as far as state tests if it has any effect—we can't have a state test study guide at home. I think a lot of times the emphasis on state tests in school, yes, they're important, we all realize how important they are, but the pressure is dumped on the kids like you have to do good on these. The pressure on these kids and how it's shoved down their throats makes them more nervous, and I think we need to approach it in another way so that our kids can do better on those tests. My personal opinion is, I think, before state tests, I noticed a ton of homework coming home to these kids, to try to cram this stuff into them to get them to do better on state tests. It boils down to where if they're taught this stuff from kindergarten on up and it's taught in steps instead of jumping from this chapter to this chapter back to this chapter and back to this chapter, they'll get a better grasp on it and perhaps we'll see better scores. I think a lot of it is the pressure that's put on these kids—get home, get a good night's sleep, you need a good night's sleep every day. You need to have a good breakfast every day, not just for state tests. It's not just because it's that time frame—this should be something that should be focused on every single day of the school year in order to make that better. But I do think that there's too much pressure and emphasis pushed on that particular time frame. I'll be honest with you, I think the kids are exhausted and they don't want to do this anymore. I don't know how much the kids particularly care at that point. That's what I've found—I don't know how anybody else feels.

EI We understand why we have it and why it's necessary to have some kind of a measure here, but it almost seems like a separate piece from the total student academic achievement. My opinion is that student achievement should be important regardless of what's on the state test. If what's on the state test is what we should be teaching the children, then we shouldn't have to cram for it. The children should have it, I mean, if this is where we're going and this is what we're doing, I realize that these things change with the wind, the administration, whoever happens to be the Department of Education at the time, but the kids don't see the state test as something they're doing for themselves. I've never talked with my child about state tests, but she saw this as separate, not as her academic achievement. Is this a big waste of time—spending all this time on these tests. I don't have the answer, but I think it should be part of the whole academic achievement for these kids.

SI The question was how would a parent group help the child with the state tests and the total academic achievement, and I don't feel that it could hurt in any way. A parent group would show that the attitude of the parents is strong; they want the children to be strong academically—whether it's the state test or just their grades throughout the year in school. So I think it would help a good bit.

SH3 I think it's very important that they do well and it's just so stressed that at those test-taking times that the kids should go to bed early and get a good breakfast and everything when really it should be done all throughout the year. Not just because if they do well it makes money for the district.

SH1 I think some kids are just lousy test takers, tests stress them out. I know my son is better in a lot of things—he just said it was hard or he forgot, he couldn't think of how to do it. Taking the test is one thing—cramming into three days is a little bit much for the kids to handle.

CH3　Unfortunately they do have to take the tests and they take other tests too, and the state's accounting us for everything. There are kids that can take tests and that can't take tests based on their intelligence level. Then you have the different levels of children, too. I don't really think the school district should place so much stress on the parents and kids about taking these tests. Unfortunately, it's probably the state's fault, that they're making the districts do this. Unfortunately, some schools do not do well on these which make the public question the school system—oh boy, they do really bad on their state test. My kids are doing fine at _____ . But because it's public knowledge and it's published everyone thinks that's really doing a bad job teaching their kids.

CH1　Number one, the problem is that the state test, there's too much weight held on it for the No Child Left Behind Act. We're being held hostage by a test. This is my personal opinion and I'll go on record—I hate the state test. I have fought against this from the get-go and this is the product of outcomes based education [OBE]—remember Chapter 4 regs? And then they went to Chapter 5. The premise behind it is good—they want to be sure the children are performing, that they know their information, but by placing schools on watch lists, threatening them with being taken over, then the confusing reports that go out to parents, that's all bad. You have the disaggregated numbers, the aggregated numbers, you have the special ed. numbers, special ed. students get labeled, it isn't fair. Because what we're doing is creating caste systems in education and we shouldn't be doing that. The other problem is that they base it on attendance. Your test scores were down, not necessarily because of the score but because of the fact that the students didn't have the attendance rate that they needed to have at that time, too. It's all tied into all of these factors and so the federal government thinks they're coming in for the kill for you, to tell you, "Oh well, we're going to hold you accountable and we're going to make your teachers better." That's not what makes anybody better. What makes you better is if you become a more compassionate teacher. If you become a more compassionate human being, then you see the differences in the students and that if the student is a bad test taker you can help them through it. And that you're not held to such a strict timeline. The curriculum is held to a strict timeline, too. When my oldest was in fifth grade at ____, they had a math test and they had given them something that they hadn't even been taught at the end of the year. The kids did just abominable. He came home and said, "I did pretty good—I got an F+." I said, "Wait a minute, how can you get an F+?" He said "Well, yeah, 'cause some kids got F−!" I got to get in there—I got to see this teacher. I went in there and said, "Wait a minute, what's going on here? How can you have these students talking like this and getting these kinds of grades and then you're going to move on to the next year and these students aren't going to know it? They're going to be behind the eight ball that year." She sent me to the teacher and she said the excuse was, hey, the curriculum has to go on, it can't stop, it just keeps rolling. I said, "If the student doesn't learn the concept then you have done a disservice." What they did actually the next year, I really have to give them credit, in that sixth grade at the time, they actually reviewed for nine weeks and got the students caught up. That was an anomaly. As far as that state test goes, it's a test and the way it's scored even I fight about that, 'cause the quartiles and they said no, they adjusted the norm scoring—you know what? It's ridiculous, because if you have 50 percent being proficient and advanced and the other 50 percent being below or just basic then you set up for failure.

SH4 I had a problem with my oldest child—her eleventh grade honors English—stopped a month and a half before the state tests. All they did for two months was teach them how to take the state tests. It's an honors English class, but the entire learning curriculum came to a grinding halt. All they do is teach them to take these tests. Just to make the district look better or raise the scores or whatever, so they've lost all that time. Her English teacher got very resentful and got to the point that just before the state tests he would do nothing—we're not doing class, sit in his chair with his feet up, he got his paycheck and held it up for all the kids and said, "See, I get paid for doing nothing." In an honors junior English class—he's next on my list.

MH   That happened in my daughter's algebra class, but at the same time the kids are getting ready for SATs [Scholastic Achievement Test]. The teacher taught to the state tests in the class but then offered any student who wanted to stay after to work on what they needed to know for the SATs. But held over their heads was that if you don't do good this year, then you have to take remedial classes next year. She stressed about SATs, state tests, and what she's going to have to take next year—close to a nervous breakdown, truly.

CH1 The idea of the remedial class—the problem is that the students aren't doing what they should be doing on the state tests and they do need to be brought up. Personally, I don't want to use that as a threat over someone's head; I want them to be able to catch up. But by the same token people thought that if there were consequences, because the students aren't taking the test seriously either. They weren't in the beginning. By the flip side, by the administrators saying, "Well, we're not going to get any money"—you can't do that either. It isn't learning for learning's sake. When we went to school you gained knowledge because you wanted to have a career someday, you knew it was going to be your responsibility—it was a whole different atmosphere and now it's just a pressure cooker.

KH   My son is in special ed. and he has been in that since second grade and his reading ability, no matter how much tutoring or whatever, he's where he's at. But he takes the test with every other student, yet when that test comes back if it shows he's not proficient, which they know he's not going to, there's no way that he can do that work. Rather than allow him to take a class next year that he really is interested in—computer—they're taking it away so that he's got this English class. What a waste of time.

CH2 Is that according to state guidelines or district guidelines? I think everyone has to take the test, is that correct? Some school districts don't make everyone take the test. I know that.

KH No, he takes it with the regular classroom and students.

CH1 Maybe that's a good point. If the student is going to always score about the same maybe we need to look at the students who do have the capability instead. This is the first year so this is a good criticism for next year. That's part of the curriculum now to have that remedial class so that they can do better down the road.

KH To take rights away from them when they're taking this one test is very unfair—it's setting them up to fail.

CH1 The adaptations should be in place always. Why the state did not do adaptations with this is bizarre. By giving this criticism you're pointing it out to us and it's something we can talk about.

SH3 The flip side of that though for my thought is when you take those special ed. kids off of that test because they can't perform and you're only giving the test to the higher students, then you're coming back with good results and that's not a good reference of the whole school.

KH But that's not true because on his math he's always been ninety-ninth percentile. Once again, what he may drag somebody down in English taking it, he brings it up with his math.

VH I just feel that if they take my son out of that picture then they're never going to give him help. If they don't have to worry about him doing well on this test, then they'll just let him keep floundering like he's been.

CH1 If you do adaptations for other tests, why won't you adapt for this test.

Discussion

Apparently, the scores are showing that there is improvement with parent involvement. Parents believe that when they are involved, children do better. Even if it is not their own parents, just knowing someone is looking over their shoulder encourages students to perform better and behave better. Students who are the academic achievers usually have parents who are involved. It is important for parents to know about the state tests so they can encourage their children, have them eat better the night before, and get them better prepared mentally.

Parents knowing when and how the tests will be administered can prepare their children at home. The fact that the CAT is being used also may dilute some of the commitment to the state test. One parent's assessment is very telling: "Back to the question—do I think parent involvement has anything to do with the state test scores? I think if you talk to your kids and explain to them what's going on with the state tests, and I think you need to be involved to even know what the state tests are. To tell you the truth, I think there's way too much emphasis put on the state tests and that's a whole other story. Do I think it has to do with their education? Sure. Does it make my son do his homework? No. Do I make my son do his homework? No. He's fifteen and nobody makes him do anything anymore. He acts better, he acts more respectful, he's a better person because his mother is a little bit more involved and shows that she's going to be there and pay attention. Sure. And I think any kid who has a parent who cares and shows that they care in some way is going to do better than a kid who doesn't."

If parents care, then the children are going to care. Most parents understand why we have the state tests and why it's necessary to have some kind of a measure, but it almost seems like it is separated from the total student academic achievement. Student achievement should be important regardless of what's on the state test. If what's on the state test is what we should be teaching the children, then we shouldn't have to cram for it. The children should have learned the concepts over the year. If this is where we're going and this is what we're doing, we realize that certain things change with the wind: the administration, whoever happens to be the Department of Education at the time. But the kids don't see the state test as something they're doing for themselves. It should be part of the whole academic achievement.

Question #9

What do you think we should do in the school district in developing a plan to increase parent involvement in the schools?

KE You should require parents to be involved. We do this at work all the time, we always say things are "mandatory." So you tell parents we're going to have a meeting with your child and it's "mandatory." There's a lot of parents that aren't involved and I get frustrated with those kind of parents. I'm involved, so everybody should be just like me, because I care about education, how can you not care about it? They just don't. So the school has to reach out to those parents and say we're going to have a parent-teacher meeting and we expect you to be there and it's "mandatory." And maybe what we'll find is once those parents get involved, they'll say this was good and they'll look at it as a positive experience and they'll continue to be involved.

LE1 I think that it's not that they don't want to, you get a lot of people that are not expressive, they're very shy, they're afraid, they don't want conflict. Some of that is in there too, I think, and I agree with you, if they made this something where they had to attend just once, I think that would pull them in. And then they would know this isn't so bad, this teacher's all right.

KE I've managed and coached a lot of sports and a lot of coaches will say, "No parents will help me." "Did you ask them?" "Well, no." When I manage I just go up to parents and say, "Hey, John, I need you to coach first base. Joe, I need you to keep score." From a global standpoint the school district has got to go out and reach them.

JE You're saying things like mandatory, which will work on a certain level with some parents. I don't know if I can even offer any kind of an answer on some parents. Because I've seen at parent conferences, they don't even show. They'll get a phone call, a letter from a guidance counselor; you are scheduled for this time. They'll even confirm that time with that parent and then there's no show. The thing is when the district has things where they try to get parental involvement, it's always the same parents.

VE As far as that question, there has to be incentives or consequences to the parents, not the children. The parents are the ones made to be accountable.

LM   How about make us feel welcome, make us feel that our time and our involvement matters? That you welcome it, you appreciate it, that we're listened to, sometimes we have good suggestions, or we try to do things and we don't see results, so then we get frustrated and we back off again. You can lead a horse to water but you can't make it drink. When you tell somebody something over and over and over again and you can obviously see that the way you're doing it isn't right, because you're not having success, and you're offering suggestions and everybody chooses to ignore it and just keep doing it the way they're doing it, then you get frustrated and you back off, you stop being involved because you feel your valuable time is being completely wasted.

CM   I've been on numerous committees where we have made recommendation after recommendation and they're completely ignored. It's frustrating—if you're going to form a committee, actually listen to the committee.

SM   I would like to see the knowledge on both sides that we are partners in this. The teachers certainly are teaching the kids specific areas, but that we as parents have a valuable role as well. We're certainly responsible—we need to be involved and we need to be made to feel that our involvement is as important as the teacher's teaching. Another suggestion, too, is the Internet. I have no idea how to put something on a web page, am I the minority? I don't see why we don't have more information available. I have read the ____ Area School District web page, you don't really see anything until so many months pass—it we aren't going to have a calendar—couldn't each team write a fifty-word synopsis of anything that happened that week and post it on the web. Even every other week. Throw us a bone.

RM   I'd like to say ____ Area School District should go back and revisit what the elementary schools do. Start practicing some of those, evaluate your personnel—take a hard look at what you have, 'cause it sounds like we have a lot of teachers with attitudes that don't want to follow practices and procedures, and we're paying them good money to supposedly teach our children and keep us involved. And I'm actually having second thoughts about keeping my children in ____ Area School District.

CM I can honestly say that I don't know if it's necessarily even the teachers. If one more principal tells me that he just don't want to do it, and then I talk to the teachers and they say, "No, wait a minute, that's not what I said." Maybe the parents and the teachers ought to sit down and talk, because the principals who run all this stuff seem to blame everything on the teachers and I'm not buying it.

RM I think they play the parents against the teachers. Honestly, this year any call that I made to any of the teachers, I got a response. They were more than happy to help me out. It's a lack of communication—I think not really even their fault—maybe there's a paper issue. I don't know what the issue is here. I think it's a bigger issue than the teachers. I think they probably have as much control as us parents have.

CM I think the principals set the tone in the schools. If they set a tone of "You don't need to communicate with parents," then the teachers don't. That's exactly how I feel about the intermediate school—there's no communication because it's not required. They don't require the teachers to communicate with parents, they don't expect the parents to communicate with teachers, and so the teachers don't bother. It's like any other job, if it's not your job, you're not going to do it, and if it's not expected of you, a lot of times you don't. There are people that do go above and beyond, but there's a lot of people who don't—they do exactly what they have to do, and if it's something they don't have to do, then they're not going to do it.

RM They need to be directed. They need to know what they have to do. What are the rules? They need the leadership to do what they need to do. When you have a fifth grader, I've been there a while, I know the teachers, I had no problems this year. But I tell you what, sixth grade, when you go in for a team meeting, it's like playing a game that they make you feel uncomfortable. Who needs that? We're all adults. We need to communicate, speak what we feel is on our minds, if that's what you want us to do and we do it, then don't slap our hands for it. To me, you're never going to get any kind of result unless you want to hear what is bothering people. The same thing from the teachers: we want to hear, too, what are the problems on their side, on our side, everyone needs to work together and that includes the administrators. They have to listen to parents and listen to teachers. I think a lot of times they play one against the other.

CM   I don't think it just starts with the principals either. It starts with the board. I was on the board, I know the amount of respect in this district and it's pitiful. It's absolutely pitiful. I don't think they want to hear what the parents have to say. I think they feel that the parents need to go away and leave them alone.

LM   I just want to make one quick comment. The fact that all of us are saying that we are sometimes hesitant to speak up because we're not sure our voice's wanting to be heard. If we feel that way, imagine how our children feel. If we can't even address a concern, then how would we expect our children to be able to do that? That's really not a good situation. If they're feeling they can't address because either number one, the teacher's going to blow them off or don't care, whatever, or the principal, whoever, that really concerns me, that they don't have anybody to go to at school because I'm not there or other parents aren't there for them to feel comfortable.

CM   I can honestly say that they do not communicate as well with the students even in the upper grades. My son's in the intermediate school, well, was in the intermediate school; he had gym first period. They don't get the announcements in the morning. He had no clue what was going on in his school unless he asked his friends, because the gym classes don't have speakers so they got no morning announcements. Everything you need to know is on the morning announcements as far as social activities, after-school activities, anything like that. If you're not getting the morning announcements, and their answer was when I called and asked, basically, well, we send somebody down with a paper. She got there usually as the classes were changing so the kids had no time to read it, if she got there at all. How many kids are going to be able to read a paper at the same time, they're in class, so they really don't have time.

EI Definitely the website. Most families do have computers in their homes and most people spend time on them. You can go to the website any time of the day or night and get updated information. Parents need to be encouraged about it. You can never have too much communication. It's not a guarantee that people will be involved, but you have to try to make it a little easier. Definitely parent meetings scheduled for nine o'clock in the morning sending the wrong message to the majority of working parents in the district. I don't know what exactly that percentage is, but my guess is it's probably pretty darn high. You have to make it easy, you have to provide an easy way for them to be involved.

SI Maybe they could do a handbook of the activities throughout the year so the parent can know what exactly everything is. They can schedule their time around that activity so they'll be more prepared to take off those days. If they are more aware of what each activity is, they're more willing to help because they understand it and they expect it. Granted, the website's a great idea because everybody has access to it, but if you see it at the beginning of the year with all the papers coming home, you can get it in your mind what you want to do and what you don't want to do so you know what to be looking for.

EI It's hard to schedule things in September and then stick to that schedule in May. What I've found is sometimes when I get stuff at the beginning of the year I put it on my calendar and I'm planning on being somewhere on Wednesday, May 24, and like a day before, I find out that it's been changed and I never received that communication. Whether it's in my daughter's backpack or whether it's on the website and I didn't happen to go on and check—I'm not sure what the answer is to keeping people well informed and communicate with them—they have to know the changes as well.

PI I think the website—if they could put almost everything on there—because my grandson tells me nothing. I get no com-

	munication on anything, so the website probably would do a tremendous amount.
MI	Whatever it is, it has to be something very, very flexible. I remember once I tried to volunteer for lunch duty at the middle school and I wanted to be a different day every week, and I was told "No, we just need somebody Tuesday, you have to be here every Tuesday." I don't have a schedule that works that way; I work different days every week. They couldn't use me because they couldn't commit to a specific day. I think it just has to take into account that everyone's lives are hectic and different things happen different days of the week, different months, there has to be someway to mesh everybody in at different times.
MH	Just because I do use the Internet perpetually, I would say if they could add something to the website. It doesn't hurt—I was even reading about baccalaureate and I didn't even have a senior. They had posted all of the guides because I thought that this would help me for next year. Personally I do use the Internet, if they could at all possible beef that up somehow.
CH2	Start mailing. Use the U.S. postal system.
CH1	The only reason they don't mail any news is the cost.
KH	I remember when my kids were in elementary school they would have the envelopes that would go down to the office in the morning and they would fill them with a bunch of papers for the week. Or once a month—let the teachers and everyone know that if you want something to go out, get in the packets.
DH	I think it's hard no matter what the school tries to do, if you have a child that's not involved—I'm a band parent and I'm there all the time and my daughter loves it. I know all the kids and we have a great time. My son wants to be a rock star, so it's so hard to get involved with him. I don't know anything that's going on with him. I don't have an answer for you—I'm just stating it's very difficult, there needs to be some kind of way to reach out to these kids who don't want to be involved in sports or in band or in chorus or plays. What do you do?
CH2	Let's form a committee, you're on it!

SH3   I think parents do get involved in a lot of the extracurricular things like band and play and get to know the kids that way. I have a son who's very active with other activities outside of school so he doesn't do a lot of in-school things, but my main concern is the academics. I would like to see more of an atmosphere that values academic achievements and I don't mean just the top students. Have every kid do as well as they can in school and learn as much as they can, be excited about learning. Often it seems there's more emphasis on the activities, especially the sports—homecoming—my husband can't understand this thing about homecoming. He thinks homecoming is the most important thing; he doesn't have a clue why that is.

DH   I just want to touch on that. When you get involved in the extracurricular activities, you meet other parents who are so helpful and you find out what you need to know about other things as far as academics even. That helps me a lot. My daughter's going to be a senior, but when she was a freshman that's really how I learned what was going on, a lot was from other parents. Which is sad, too, and goes back to the schools just not letting you know what's going on.

CH1   I think we need support groups. I'm serious. I remember when my first son was little and we did offer a parenting course. It was really nice. One of the teachers facilitated here and it was really interesting to learn whether you were the good parent or the responsible parent. It still rings in my mind. We all want to be the good parent and make them feel good about themselves, but to be the responsible parent, to make them do it themselves. Everybody is really busy with work and stuff, but I think we lose sight of that. When I go to district parent council, you see the parents breaking off and talking to each other. I think that's something we miss in our society, and it's a shame and we're victims of the twenty-four-hour everybody's on all the time. You don't have time for your family, you don't have time to just catch up and take a breather. We have a disservice to ourselves to go with this pace that we all do. I think what people are looking to the schools for is for that connection that they

	don't have anyplace else. Our society has changed so dramatically that we're just left hanging out there.
CH2	How about a school calendar?
CH1	We used to do a community calendar, but it was cut from the budget because everybody was screaming.
CH2	Let's bring that back.
SH3	I agree with what ____ said, that I think maybe, too, if you got the kids excited about school and excited about learning, somehow maybe more respect through the teachers, that they will communicate with the kids. Even the kids that aren't doing well, that are struggling, probably need it even more. My kids hate going to school. I know they've been demeaned by teachers, by administrators, by friends 'cause they're not at the level they should be. I think that would help. It's really hard for parents when you work all day, take your kids to all their activities, and you come in the door at nine o'clock at night, well, who wants to sit down and start homework. A lot more of it, unfortunately, falls to the teachers because that's their job and they should know to teach a kid. I don't know how to teach my kid. If you could get your kids excited and want to be there and if you could get the teachers to really help them so they know what they're doing. My son is going into tenth grade; he's at a fourth grade reading level. He must walk into that school and seven hours of people handing him stuff that he can't read. People telling him to do stuff that he doesn't understand. Now you have detention because you didn't follow this or now you're suspended. He was going to be suspended for not serving detention when there wasn't even enough days to serve the detention. I said, "The kid's already behind, you cannot take him out of school; he needs to be there, he needs to be learning. Someone's got to help him."
CH1	You don't need to be punished academically for behavior. That's something I've been trying to tell them. That when a child falls down academically they need tutored and they need help. They don't need the dance taken away from them, or slapped into lunch detention. What you're then telling them is, "This is your reward—more punishment." I can't

imagine, to be that frustrated, to come in and not be able to read your material. You're constantly behind the eight ball no matter what you try, no matter what you do. As I said before, there needs to be a certain compassion level. That is something that I wanted to work on at the middle school—you don't have academic punishment for bad behavior. Those are two separate entities and you keep them separate at all times. It's convenient to do it to use it as a battering ram and it shouldn't be done.

Discussion

Some parents believed that parents should be required to be involved. Telling parents that meetings are mandatory may increase attendance. It may not be that the parents don't want to get involved; some may not be very expressive, or they're very shy, afraid, and don't want conflict. If we could pull the parents in for a meeting, they may see that it is not so bad. The school district needs to go out and reach parents. Presently, parent involvement includes most of the same parents all the time. If parents are asked to be on a committee, it is recommended that their ideas be used. Ignoring their ideas causes parents not to want to be involved again. Communication between the principals and staff is important. The principals can't be saying one thing and the staff another thing. Principals need to set the tone for the buildings. If they don't require teachers to communicate with parents or encourage teachers to get parents involved, the communication and involvement won't happen.

Administrators must listen to parents and teachers so that all can work together. Parent's voices need to be heard. The district needs to use the web page more, and each building needs to beef up their web page to communicate with parents and community. There should also be more mailings to disseminate information. A school calendar for each home would help communication. Students should not be punished academically for behavior (incentive program at the middle school). If students fall down academically, they need tutoring and they need help. We need to have more compassion for kids.

DATA PRESENTATION AND ACTION-PLAN DEVELOPMENT   213

Question #10

Do you have any questions about what we are currently doing here in regard to parent involvement in our schools?

KE   What's the purpose of this? Is the purpose of this to get more parent involvement?

LE1   It scares me, but I think 90 percent of the feedback would be negative before it's positive. And that really affects me, that nobody is backing the educators. My oldest daughter is ____ and I've loved every step of the way. Everything's always been communicated, work out, I'm not saying there aren't things that I wish would be changed or weren't different, but on the whole I think there's no black and white anymore; it's all gray.

JE   As far as questions of how the district handles parental involvement, my only question would be, "Is there a mission statement for administration?" I don't see anything that is a specific thing. Should there be some type of a goal or something—they need to look to try to improve that.

LM   What are you trying to do? What are you trying to do to make us involved?

RM   I'd like to hear the school's view on how they feel they keep us involved. I think this is a good start and I think it needs to keep going. There's a lot of positive things about. If you can't communicate no one's even going to know about them. That's the sad part.

SM   I agree with you. I'd be happy to sit in—three of my kids are still going to be here even though I'm pulling the one out. I graduated from ____, and I thought it was the greatest thing to have my kids back at this school. I loved it; I thought it was a wonderful school. The world has changed, I'm not completely naïve on that, but I hope we can have more discussions like this. This is certainly a great start.

JI   I think this is great, I think this is the first time I've ever heard of this. I don't know if they've done this in the past or not, because as was stated earlier it was drawn from a pool and maybe this is the first year I've gotten drawn into it. I think this is a great way to find out and if this is the first time they're doing it then I'm glad they're taking the initiative to try to make things better. The ultimate thing is what we can do to help our children. We're all here for the same purpose and it's for the best for each one of these children in the school district, not for ourselves, but for the kids. That's what it boils down to—the kids.

CI I think it's important to extend yourself to other children. I go to the different musicals because I like seeing the other children perform. There again with the web, it does tell you what events are taking place so you can pick and choose—the dress rehearsal for the intermediate school's musicals is open to senior citizens, free of charge, that's another wonderful way for people who know other children to come out and see. The billboard out here is wonderful, but I don't always come up and down the boulevard and when I do I go pretty fast and miss what's happening.

CH2 Yes, what are they doing?

MH What are they doing—in the high school level?

CH1 The high school PTA is there and the inception of it was to communicate more with parents, but they're working, they're not there, how are they going to do it. I feel bad as I sit here and listen to this because everyone thinks they're doing a good job.

CH2 Some are, some aren't.

Discussion

Having focus groups is a good start. There are a lot of positive things about ____. If there is no communication, then no one's going to know about activities or problems. Regarding focus-group input, one parent said, "This is the first time I've ever heard of this. I don't know if they've done this in the past or not, because as was stated earlier it was drawn from a pool and maybe this is the first year I've gotten drawn into it. I think this is a great way to find out and if this is the first time they're doing it then I'm glad they're taking the initiative to try to make things better. The ultimate thing is what we can do to help our children. We're all here for the same purpose and it's for the best for each one of these children in the school district, not for ourselves, but for the kids. That's what it boils down to—the kids."

Question #11

Can you offer any other suggestions on how we can continue to improve our efforts to involve parents in their children's education?

KE   One of the things that makes this so good is the dynamics—having ____ here so we can hear the ____ point of view.

VE   A lot of parents that I talk to say about going to school board meetings say they are intimidated by that form. With this type of informal setting I believe more people would come. That's where administration comes in and that's where the school board comes in. Because when I talk to the teachers, their hands are tied, and they have to keep their mouths shut and they can't say this and they can't do that. So it is higher up. That's why I have this petition going. Because before I go to the school board I need backing. I am perfectly willing to be the spokesperson and I have enough data. I see the change. For you moms who are just going through the middle school—good luck, good luck.

RM   I will speak up on that. When you go to a school board meeting and you speak up you should feel free to speak your mind and not get the negativity. You need to air your problems—good and bad—and there needs to be a little more respect across the board with everybody. It all starts with respect. If you're there and you're a concerned parent, you're just not coming to have people laugh at you or smear—I think there needs to be respect across the board for everybody and we all should have the same concern—doing a better job for the children. Getting a better education for our kids is all it's about. It's about the children.

LM   I know this has come up many other times throughout the meeting that having parents involved in meetings and committees sometimes is offered, again. Don't offer something and then when parents get involved and have opinions and input, they're put aside. That's consistently been the case I would say from at least the middle school up. Elementary, I think they generally want your input and utilize your input as far as my experience as an elementary parent I've always felt that. You can sit and ask questions or let the parents ask questions, but if you're not going to utilize that information, if you're just going to close your eyes and do what you want to do anyway, what's the use?

LM   I've said it on one of the other questions. If you ask for the help, there isn't one thing that any of the teachers at ____ or ____ himself asked me to do this year that I've said no to. When they said, "We need this person to do the science expo," I did it. "Open the door," I've said that so many times today. Because when you don't let us know that we're welcome, then we don't try to help. No matter what you've asked me to do, I do it for you. You just have to ask and let me know I'm welcome and then also what ____ said, you can't dismiss us. Then don't ask for us to help and don't ask for our input and then dismiss us, that's very disheartening.

CM   That's my only concern about this whole thing. We're sitting here and we're taking our time and it's not like ____ and I haven't done this before. The three of us are at every meeting, we're involved in almost every committee. We go to DPC monthly without fail and no matter what you say or what they say to you, we see it time after time after time. The parents are basically dismissed. What we say counts very little for anything that's decided and we've sat in these meetings before—the assessment committee. How long did we spend on the assessment committee and they still haven't picked a test? They don't even tell us what's going on with that anymore. I spent a year of my time on that—a little bit of information would've been nice. We get nothing, and that's basically what we get is nothing.

RM   Like I said—this year I've learned a lot more and there's a lot of good teachers. Teachers, administrators, parents they need to all be on the same page and they are not. People are not listening—administrators are not listening to parents, and they're not listening to the teachers, they're playing one against the other, not all the time, but I'm just saying just different things that they want changed, the teachers want changed. They're not really getting what they want either.

LM One thing I know I have to bring up is the fact that I've heard too many times that I'm the only parent that is complaining about this or that; therefore, it's not worth doing anything about. Number one, I may be the only parent that's willing to voice my concern, but that doesn't mean I'm the only one who feels that way.

LM Some parents do not open their mouth because they don't know what's going to happen to their child. Whether something happens or not, I do not know if you open your mouth, if your child's treated differently or not. Doesn't make a difference to me, I don't think it may necessarily happen, if it does, it does. . . .

EI I think sometimes you need to look at it as part of the bigger picture. I know maybe this doesn't relate, but a lot of people who don't have children actively in school don't feel like they belong, like it's a totally separate entity. The reality is if the kid's in school and doing well and everything's going great, your community's going to be better and your community's going to be stronger. PR—really PR. See it on the marquee and you might be interested.

CI One thing I think the school district does and that's the celebration after the homecoming parade. That's young and old who come out—from babies to senior citizens—and that's a big draw. That's very positive.

JI I agree with ____. I think being more involved in the community and getting the community as a whole involved. ____, like you were saying, parents who've had their children already go through the system are parents and they're probably the most experienced. Granted, times have changed, because often I find myself going to the meetings at the middle school where it was just a select group of parents saying, "Why aren't we doing it this way, we did it this way when I was younger and it worked fine." I have to sit back and say, "Wait a minute, times have changed tremendously." Maybe more newspapers from the school being sent out. Maybe instead of a quarterly, a monthly newspaper and each school has a section. It doesn't have to be elaborate; each function for that month could have a small little paragraph or something. It should encompass the entire community, not just the current students, because my parents and my in-laws want to see some of these things, too. I know that the sporting events do offer senior citizen passes and stuff like that, but how many of the senior citizens really know that. I don't know that too many know that, and if it wasn't for my friend to tell me about it so I could inform my in-laws about it, they wouldn't have known to come up here and get a pass for the sporting events they want to see because their grandchild is involved in some of that. It all boils down to PR naturally, but it would be nice to be community-wide. If you involve the community as a whole, more people would be behind the school system and more behind getting involved in things and wanting to. Perhaps your student's graduated and you still want to be involved, you shouldn't feel like an outcast.

SI What about sending something with the quarterly newslettter that you get. Why can't you just send a schedule in there, that way it is community-wide, it's already going out, what's another piece of paper to just throw in there, and say for this quarter this is everything that's going on in the area schools. That way you get a wide range of community people to come in.

JI That has to go to all the taxpayers I believe. If you're a taxpayer you deserve that information. Our taxes go to the township, but they also go to the school district as well. Everybody who's a taxpaying family deserves to have that information. Perhaps they do and I don't know that.

CI The township paper might have a nice little insert about what the school district is offering.

JI Granted we're trying to keep costs down, too, but a single newsletter with just a little blurb and a little calendar, something like that goes a long way. It could actually be a product of a journalism class. You can make it education.

KH	It's a two-way street. Even if a parent wants to be involved you got to have that communication come back. You can't ask for our involvement if we don't know what we're supposed to be involved in.
CH1	I think a focus group with teachers would be good.
CH2	Parents and teachers together.
CH1	I think that should be the next step from this. But that means trust.
KH	We did that one year. We met in the high school library. It was a while ago, probably eight to ten years ago. We did different break-out groups. They gave us these tiles and you had to make up nonsense words and then try to learn how to spell them and that was showing you how a teacher is trying to teach your children to spell when the words don't mean anything to them. When they're in first grade it's just like throwing a bunch of letters together. And we would get in groups and discuss different topics.
CH1	On the flip side, the middle school offered a focus group last year on school safety and hardly anybody attended.
CH2	I didn't even know about it.
CH1	There have been things that have been advertised and then people don't come. Performing arts—people like to come to the concerts here. So that's something positive where we're reaching out. There are ways to do it, I think, if it grabs the interest level of the audience. I think going on with the focus group and parents, but everybody has to be honest and the teachers can't be defensive.
KH	Then you have the good teachers who come. That's the problem with that. You've got to get the core group of teachers who have been here for however long and won't change their ways and won't adapt to anything. That's the problem. Especially if you're dealing with a child who has an IEP—to get these teachers to comply is so nerve-wracking. I have been on high blood pressure medicine and my doctor doesn't know why my blood pressure's not going down. It's frustrating and you've got to come in here really cool because if you start to show one type of emotion then they're like, "You're out of control."

CH1   Maybe something that would be less intimidating is, maybe, start with the administration. The reason I say that is because then you would have your principals and you could talk to them first. Work backward from that. I think the superintendent needs to hear this.

SH3   It seems that there are parents who want to help, they want to help their kids, they want to help the teachers, they want to help the district.

SH2   I think communication is the most important—let us know what's going on, how things are going to be done. And also the atmosphere of respect would be an improvement—both respect when people are answering the phone and are dealing with you—I don't think they should be rude to you on the phone. And again the main thing I want to be involved with is just making sure that my son gets a better education. I haven't been completely happy with the quality of education that he's getting. My job is to try to make sure that he does get a good education, part of that is knowing what he's supposed to be doing, and making sure that he's doing it. There are plenty of opportunities for parents to be involved in extracurricular activities.

SH3   Just knowing when the physicals are. . . .

CH1   They put it up on the board out there.

SH3   You almost wreck your car trying to read it!

SH2   They shouldn't rely on this board—some of us don't drive past here.

DH   There are so many good teachers in this district that we've all come across, so what do you do about that handful of really bad teachers? My daughter had one this year who lost more of her work this year—his nickname was ____. I've mentioned this to other people and they know exactly the teacher I'm talking about. Why is this man still teaching? A particular math teacher—my son went from an A to an F throughout the whole year, why is this man still teaching? When there are so many good teachers out there, why do we have to get stuck with some of these teachers that are hurting our children?

SH3   That's kind of like on the accountability of teachers. If you have a class that half or three-quarters of your children fail that class, I don't think it's the kids, you better look at that teacher. If they cannot get that information to the students in a way that they can understand, then there's a problem. I always, when my kids do fail a class or a test, how many other kids failed too? Is it they slacked off and didn't study or did they really not get the information?

DH I think, too, if your child's not in an honors class, I think the teachers feel that they don't need to try as much to teach these children. I think college prep courses are just as important as honors classes. I don't want my children in honors classes, they don't work hard enough to be in them, but I just think they're put down because they're not in honors classes.

Discussion

Some of the good things about this focus-group process are the dynamics. It's important to have all the parents together to hear the different points of view. This is a good forum which the administration could use more often to hear the parents. Most parents are too intimidated to speak at school board meetings, but they would open up in a forum like this. From the middle school on up, parent input seems to be disregarded. At the elementary levels, parent input seems to be more accepted and utilized. We need to work harder at the secondary levels. If we ask for parent input, then we should use it. It is very disheartening when input is asked for and then disregarded. We need to get the community as a whole involved, and not just parents who have children in school. PR is very important. We need to do a better job of promoting the schools. We need to send out more newsletters, bulletins, and so forth, that contain information about the schools. This can be an important source of information. A focus group with teachers was suggested, or parents and teachers together. Communication is most important. Parents need to know what is going on and how they can help.

PARENTS VIEWPOINTS: AREAS TO EXAMINE

The basis of this study was to examine the viewpoints of parents regarding communication and parent participation in our schools. I honestly say that the "silence" was broken through the focus-group discussions in this study. The population that was normally silenced (parents) in regard to this issue was quite verbal and outspoken. Focus-group participants were given the opportunity to voice their feelings and opinions about the topic under discussion.

The responses, in my opinion, were candid and contained some valuable information that had not been disclosed in discussions about communication and parent involvement in our schools. The parents who participated in this focus-group research study identified forty assertions related to communication and parent participation in our schools:

1. The reason parent involvement at the elementary level is so prominent is that the children and their parents are younger, and many parents are experiencing a child in school for the first time (therefore, they are more likely to get involved).
2. There is more time for elementary school parents to be involved because the children are not involved in as many activities as at the secondary levels. Parents at the secondary levels are sometimes attending multiple activities.
3. More elementary parents (particularly moms) do not work and have more time to devote to participation. Often, parents then go back to work once their children reach secondary school, which then prohibits as much participation.
4. Elementary children are more enthusiastic about having their parents involved than children at the secondary levels.
5. Parents expressed they feel more welcome at the elementary schools; therefore, they are more likely to get involved than at the secondary levels.
6. Elementary school students are more inclined to bring information home in their book bags, and parents are more likely to read that information than at the secondary levels.
7. School populations at the secondary levels are much higher, resulting in a teacher having many more students. This may prohibit regular parent contact. It is much more difficult to contact 120–130 sets of parents as opposed to twenty-two.
8. Elementary school work is more fun than secondary work, which promotes more parent participation at the elementary level.

9. Secondary parents may be more intimidated by the level of work in those grades and, compared to elementary parents, less likely to get involved as a result.
10. The idea was shared that children at the secondary levels need to be more responsible at their age than elementary children, which causes parents to pull back at those levels. Secondary school teachers are trying to help the students establish their independence.
11. There are ways for parents to get involved at the secondary levels as a result of the great number of activities, providing the parent takes the initiative.
12. Communication needs to improve between home and school at the secondary levels, which can provide for parents ways to get involved in their child's schooling.
13. At the secondary levels there is a "confrontation" factor, where teachers and parents are more likely to experience confrontation causing each to shy away from further communication.
14. The configuration of grade levels and structure of the buildings makes it difficult to increase communication and involve parents. The middle school, intermediate school, and the high school are very large buildings with great numbers of students. The larger the buildings, the more likely communication will break down.
15. Parents who do get involved need more support from other parents. Parents who choose not to get involved have a negative influence on parents to continue their involvement. More support is needed from all parents.
16. The expectation for involvement and communication from administrators and teachers is not as prevalent at the secondary levels.
17. The district and building web pages need to be more informative, and this will increase communication.
18. There are few provisions for involvement for people who work 8:00 a.m. to 4:00 p.m. jobs. Most meetings are scheduled during that time frame.
19. Parent involvement has an effect on student performance. The more involved the parent, the more likely the student will perform better in school.

20. Parents must be willing to get involved and help all children, not just their own child. Parents need to care just a little more.
21. Many parents are more involved in their child's education at home, but not really involved in the school buildings. This gives the impression they are not involved in their child's education, because no one sees their involvement at home. In essence, many more parents are actually involved; we just do not see it.
22. Schools need to better communicate with parents regarding the state tests so parents can help prepare their children for the assessments. Schools need to be clearer on how parents can help. This would help in increasing test scores.
23. The effect of 9/11 has caused it to be more difficult to enter schools and feel welcome because of the increased security.
24. It is important for parents to be involved, but not to "hover" over their children or be overly protective. This has an adverse effect on their children and makes it more difficult for school personnel to do their job.
25. Community people who do not have children in school should be more encouraged to come into the schools. They can be a valuable resource.
26. Parents should be more involved in the curriculum. It is good to have parents on committees.
27. The district offers a wealth of activities for the parents to become involved if they take the initiative to do so.
28. Elementary school teachers do very well in making connections with parents. The higher the grade level, the less teachers connect with parents.
29. It should be up to the parents to take the initiative to get involved. Parents need to take initiative to get to know their child's teachers and find ways to get involved.
30. Many of the PTOs are supposed to be parent-teacher organizations, but are more likely to be just the parents and no teachers.
31. Some teams at the middle school are parent-friendly, some are not.
32. Parents become frustrated when they are asked to provide input, then none of their suggestions is utilized. This often discourages

them from becoming involved as much. Also, many more parents want to get involved but the schools do not use them.
33. Principals need to be more visible at all levels. In some instances, parents indicated they did not even know who their child's principal was.
34. Principals must set the tone for parent involvement and increased communication. If the principals do not require teachers to communicate, the teachers will not take the initiative.
35. It was pointed out that certain secondary teachers reach out to parents while others do not even make an attempt.
36. Parents generally believe that when they are involved, children perform better academically and behaviorally.
37. If we could find a way to pull some parents in for a meeting, we may see them get more involved after they see that it is not so bad to be active in the schools.
38. Parents' voices need to be heard.
39. This focus-group process is a good forum for parents to be heard. Most parents are intimidated to speak at board meetings and other public meetings, but are not intimidated in a forum like this.
40. We need to do a better job promoting our schools. More newsletters and publications need to be distributed.

These forty assertions served as a basis for planning that enabled our schools to increase parent involvement, and to do a better job communicating with parents and the community.

PARENTS' VIEWPOINTS: THE SILENCE IS BROKEN

Part of the effort involved in this research was to break the silence of parents and to hear their voices in regard to communication and participation in our schools.

Based upon the responses of focus-group participants to the eleven questions, I would say that the silence was broken, and these parents' voices were heard loud and clear. It is evident, through their responses, that they were able to identify areas that we (both parents and the school district) can improve upon to increase involvement and communication in our schools.

As a result of this study, each of our principals developed action plans for their buildings that were designed to increase parent involvement and improve communication between home and school. Based upon feedback from parent surveys at the building level, the district has greatly improved in the area of parent involvement and communication. You can follow the action plan development as described in an earlier section of this chapter.

CHAPTER 11

Application of the Process: The Focus-Group Process Tool

Much of the value of focus-group research involves the process used to accomplish the purpose of hearing the voices of others. Although data are specific to the school implementing the investigation, the process can be one that is beneficial for use by any school in the world. The focus-group process can be extremely valuable in allowing all stakeholders an opportunity to share their ideas.

The increased accountability expected from schools across the nation, to perform so all students reach proficient levels, places demands on public education that have never been seen before. As a result, providing input from stakeholders can be useful to allow others in the process to share in this accountability. Most important, it allows other direct influences on the students, the opportunity to share their knowledge so that the local curriculum and other programs meet the needs of the students in that school district.

The focus-group process is one that can be beneficial for use in any other school district or any school in a district. It is important that school administrators understand the process and how it can be beneficial for their school. School leaders can explore the thoughts and ideas of other stakeholders in their organization by following this process. In order to assist in hearing the voices of others, the following tool can assist principals, other administrators, and school leaders in implementing this process. This tool was developed as a result of my experiences in conducting focus-group research. The tool is in the format of a checklist and can serve as an excellent guide as you conduct your own focus-group research.

FOCUS-GROUP PROCESS TOOL

I. Preprocess Checklist
- ❑ Determine the phenomenon under investigation (e.g., curriculum reform, parent involvement, and communication).
- ❑ Clarify and describe the phenomenon being isolated for the study.
- ❑ Identify reasons why it is important to investigate this phenomenon.
- ❑ Determine how this investigation will improve the school.
- ❑ Gather appropriate research related to this phenomenon.
- ❑ Determine who needs to be involved in this process.
- ❑ Determine who will lead this process.
- ❑ Explore the advantages and disadvantages of involving a committee.
- ❑ Determine a tentative timeline for completion of the process.
- ❑ Determine how the data gathered will be used to improve the school.
- ❑ Have the project approved by the Superintendent and School Board (if necessary).
- ❑ Begin to articulate twelve questions that will be asked of the focus-group participants.
- ❑ Develop the research design.

The preprocess timeline will take approximately thirty days (one month).

II. Process Checklist
- ❑ Continue to refine the twelve focus-group questions.
- ❑ Decide which population or populations will be included in the investigation.
- ❑ Determine the number of participants in each focus group (six to nine is preferred).
- ❑ Determine the sampling technique to be utilized (e.g., purposive sampling, random sampling, etc.)
- ❑ Set a date or dates for conducting the focus group(s).
- ❑ Select and train the focus-group moderator.
- ❑ Prepare the focus-group setting (where will you conduct the focus groups?)

- ❑ Prepare for an audio and video setup.
- ❑ Prepare consent forms and statement of participation forms.
- ❑ Select the focus-group participants.
- ❑ Determine a date by which the consent and statement of participation forms are due.
- ❑ Distribute consent and statement of participation forms.
- ❑ Collect forms and organize willing participants into groups.
- ❑ Send a reminder to participants regarding the date of their focus-group interview.
- ❑ Be sure the room is set up the day before the focus-group interviews.

The process timeline will take approximately sixty days (two months).

III. Postprocess Checklist
- ❑ Have data transcribed.
- ❑ Check with the participants to be sure the record is accurate.
- ❑ Thank the participants for their contributions.
- ❑ Group the data by question (cut and paste responses specific to each question).
- ❑ Begin to develop emergent themes from the data.
- ❑ Write a discussion section (summary) from responses for each question.
- ❑ Develop assertions from the discussion sections.
- ❑ Write up a final summary of the findings.
- ❑ Share the findings with stakeholders (committee, superintendent, participants, etc.)
- ❑ Determine how the findings can serve to improve what has been investigated.
- ❑ Develop an action plan utilizing the findings in a step-by-step improvement process.
- ❑ Involve stakeholders in the improvement process.
- ❑ Develop a timeline for evaluation of the action plan.
- ❑ Evaluate the action plan and determine if measurable improvements have been accomplished.
- ❑ Update the plan as needed.

The postprocess timeline will take approximately one year to complete the evaluative process and update the action plan.

Hopefully, this tool will assist and guide you through the process. If you follow all the segments outlined, you will have conducted a successful study that will be of benefit to you and your school organization. As you become proficient in conducting your own focus-group research, you may find that certain processes might be enlarged or amended to meet your own needs.

CHAPTER 12

Other Tools of the Trade

In order to assist you further in the process of conducting your own focus-group research, I have included some other *tools of the trade* that will be helpful. Following is a sample participation request letter and statement of participation form. Also included is a sample interview guide that the facilitator reads as he/she meets with the participants and runs the group. And finally, there are some sample focus-group questions I developed for a previous study that may give you some ideas for formulating questions for your study.

PARTICIPATION REQUEST LETTER

Date:

Name:
Address:

Dear: _____

Your participation in a research study is being requested by Name and Title . You are asked to be a participant in a focus group discussion about ___Title of Study___ . **Your participation in this study is strictly voluntary and the identity of all participants will be strictly confidential.**

The purpose of this study is to ___Explain Study___ . The responses elicited during focus-group interviews will be audio- and videotaped, transcribed, and then presented in a written report to Your Name . The identity of each participant in this study will be strictly confidential.

If you choose to participate in this study, you will be asked to participate in a focus-group discussion during the week of ___List Dates___ with six to nine participants. A facilitator will ask participants to discuss ten to twelve questions concerning ___Discuss Study___ . Your participation in this study should take between forty-five and sixty minutes. All information will be handled in a confidential manner, so that no one will be able to identify you when your responses are reported. There are no risks to you from participation in this study.

If you have any questions regarding this study, please contact ___Your Name___ at telephone number _____ .

Please see the attached statement of participation form. Read and complete the form and send to me in the enclosed self-addressed, stamped envelope by _____. Thank you for your consideration of this request.

Yours in education,
Your Name

Enclosure

Statement of Participation

I do not wish to participate in this study_____ **Date:** _____
                                                    (Signature)

(By returning this letter and indicating you would not like to participate in this study, your name will be removed from the list of potential participants and you will not receive any further correspondence.)

I would like to participate in this study_____ **Date:** _____
                                                    (Signature)

Please provide a telephone number at which you may be contacted between the weeks of _____ and_____, and between the hours of 9:00 a.m. and 5:00 p.m. to schedule your focus-group interview.

Telephone Number _____   Ask for _____
                (Day Phone #)   (Name)

(Please read and sign the Statement of Informed Consent. Then return this page in the enclosed self-addressed stamped envelope by _____. You will be contacted with the time and location of the focus-group interviews during the week of _____.)

<u>Statement of Informed Consent</u>

I understand that my participation in this study is strictly voluntary. I further understand that I may refuse to answer any or all of the questions asked by the facilitator during the focus-group interview. By choosing to participate in this study, I expect that the researcher, <u> Your Name </u>, will do everything in his power to keep my responses confidential. No one will be able to identify me when my responses are reported. I understand that the responses elicited during the focus-group interview will be audio- and videotaped and then transcribed. However, I expect the information I share with the researcher will be confidential regarding my identity. I am aware that I reserve the right to withdraw my consent and terminate my participation in this study at any time.

_____   _____
Signature of Participant   Date

SAMPLE INTERVIEW GUIDE

"Hello, my name is _Facilitator's Name_, and I am facilitating this focus-group interview for _Your Name_. Today is ___Date___, and this is focus-group interview ___Number___. All participants who are present have read and signed the following Statement of Informed Consent: "I understand that my participation in this study is strictly voluntary. I further understand that I may refuse to answer any or all of the questions asked by the facilitator during the focus-group interview. By choosing to participate in this study, I expect that the researcher, _Your Name_, will do everything in his power to keep my responses confidential. No one will be able to identify me when my responses are reported. I understand that the responses elicited during the focus-group interview will be audio- and videotaped, transcribed, and presented in a written report to _Your Name_. However, I expect the information I share with the researcher to be confidential regarding my identity. I am aware that I reserve the right to withdraw my consent and terminate my participation in this study at any time."

"Does anyone have any questions about what I have just read?"

"Would anyone like to leave this room and not participate in this study?"

"Now, I am going to give you some background on this study" (insert some background here).

"The first question that I would like to discuss is . . ." (ask first question).

When all of the questions have been asked and responses exhausted, say the following:

"Thank you for giving of your time and sharing your ideas with us. We have every hope that this information will be helpful for us in continuing to upgrade our school improvement efforts."

SAMPLE FOCUS-GROUP QUESTIONS

Following are a set of sample focus-group research questions that I used in a previous study that looked at viewpoints of teachers and parents regarding standards implementation at a suburban high school and their effect on state assessment scores. I think this can give you a guideline for developing your questions. In addition, the facilitator introduction can serve as a template for you.
Facilitator Introduction:

"Work on the development and implementation of standards at _____ High School has been under way since 1998. We have completed writing standards in the core subject areas of English language arts, mathematics, and science and technology. We are currently in the process of writing our social studies standards. Standards have also been written in music, health and physical education, library science, art, technology education, and foreign languages. Along with the standards, our students are assessed using the Pennsylvania System of School Assessment (PSSA) in reading and mathematics in grades 8 and 11. We continue to experience improved scores in reading and mathematics on the Pennsylvania System of School Assessment (PSSA) in grades 8 and 11, and are trying to determine why this has occurred. We are interested in finding out what the viewpoints of parents and teachers are in regard to the implementation of standards at _____ High School and their effect on PSSA scores in grades 8 and 11."

Question #1:

The students at _____ High School have generally scored well on the PSSA in reading and mathematics in grades 8 and 11 and have actually shown increases the past few years. What do you believe has caused these scores to increase?

Question #2:

Performance indicators, which include all test scores, student grades, percentage of students reaching proficiency, and even such things as attendance and a reduction in discipline referrals reveal improvements in performance for students at _____ High School. To what would you attribute these improvements?

Question #3:

We have been tracking students from the same classes in grades 8 through 11 and have seen increases in performance on the PSSA in reading and mathematics. In other words, the same class of students has improved its performance on the PSSA in eleventh grade over their performance when they were in eighth grade. Can you offer any insights as to why this has occurred?

Question #4:

_____ High School has received performance incentive money in the past from the State Department of Education as a result of increases in PSSA scores. This money has been used to continue to upgrade our curriculum and for remedial and tutoring programs. Do you believe that this incentive money has served to increase test scores? If so, how so?

Question #5:

How do you feel about the implementation of standards-based instruction at _____ High School, and do you see standards-based instruction as a significant factor in increasing student performance on the PSSA? Please explain.

Question #6:

The students at _____ High School have scored well in grades 8 and 11 on the PSSA in reading and mathematics. What, if any, connection do you see with the implementation of the English language arts and mathematics standards and the students' performance on the PSSA?

Question #7:

We have implemented remedial classes and tutoring programs for students in grades 8 and 11 who have scored at basic or below basic on previous PSSA assessments in an attempt to help them reach the proficient level. Do you believe these programs will help students increase their future performance on the PSSA?

Question #8:

What do you believe high-stakes testing like the PSSA has done to help or hinder curriculum reform at _____ High School?

Question #9:

How do you feel about the increasing emphasis statewide on the PSSA and what it has done to reform our curriculum and increase student performance?

Question #10:

What do you think we should do at _____ High School to develop a plan to increase student assessment scores on the PSSA in grades 8 and 11, and how can we continue to meet the needs of students through standards implementation and assessment preparation in an effort to prepare them for their post–high school aspirations?

Question #11

What questions would you have about what we are doing here at _____ High School in regard to standards implementation and assessment preparation?

Question #12

Can you offer any other suggestions on how we can continue to improve students' academic performance through standards implementation, and how we can continue to raise PSSA scores?

CHAPTER 13

Reflections

The phenomenon I referred to in previous chapters, known as *discourse of silence*, where stakeholder's voices are often not heard in discussions within educational organizations, is really an extremely prevalent shortcoming in our schools. What I have found to be the most gratifying aspect of the results of any focus-group study I have conducted is that voices were heard and some interesting ideas were shared. I reiterate, *voices were heard.* My experience as an administrator has taught me that oftentimes people just want you to listen. They often do not expect that you do as they wish; they just want someone to listen.

For example, information from the two focus-group studies I included in chapter 10 was used to develop action plans at each building in the district in which the study was conducted. Stakeholders in the district were able to see that actions were being taken to improve the transition of students from grade 3 to grade 4 as in the case of the first study, and that parent involvement and communication issues were being addressed as a result of the second study. These action plans included stakeholders on committees, which served to verify that the district was in fact listening, and that information contributed by participants to the study was being used.

What is interesting to me is the fact that focus-group participants often are able to discuss similar or related circumstances that affect them in their discussions within the group. I think that while we should evaluate and celebrate what we are doing in schools to increase student achievement, we need to continually review and revise our programs based on pertinent data that are effective in helping us make decisions.

One of the strengths of focus-group research is that it allows the researcher to gain a better perspective of thoughts and ideas that others are able to share. In addition, the process used to gain that perspective is valuable to school leaders and will provide the experience to examine other school programs in the future. A weakness that is evident is the fact that you may not be able to sample large numbers of stakeholders at any one time, therefore some voices are not heard, and some ideas are not shared.

As administrators and school leaders, our jobs are to be instructional leaders and agents for change. Changes that need to be made in any facet of the organization need to be based on current research and appropriate data. Our goal should be to hear the voices of others and to utilize ideas that could be beneficial to the academic, cocurricular, and extracurricular programs in the schools. We must listen to the voices, because in those voices we will find valuable information that can benefit school leaders as we do our jobs. Those voices will also affect the entire school community with the focus on academic achievement in the interest of continuing to increase student performance.

In many organizations outside the educational arena, focus-group research is used for a variety of initiatives to develop action plans aimed at increasing productivity or to determine what the public or organization wants in regards to marketing strategies. I have used focus-group research as a means of determining a variety of educational initiatives from curriculum reform efforts to increasing parental involvement and communication in schools. I have found it to be an extremely useful tool to determine why a particular phenomenon has occurred and to then develop an action plan on how to better serve the organization and its constituents. In addition, it allows stakeholders in the organization to provide input and to know that their voices are being heard.

In the school district in which I work, we often have issues to deal with and in many cases are not aware of what it is that causes these issues to occur. Our principals have used focus-group research in their buildings to determine what has caused certain issues to occur, and then have developed action plans to address these issues. We have also used focus groups at the central office level to address various issues that face us district-wide. When I mention using this process to colleagues in other districts, they often are not aware of the process and how it can help to improve their school organization. It is my belief that many school organizations across the country and even the world do not employ this opportunity for school improvement. On a daily basis, school organizations experience issues that often are not addressed simply because no one has the ability to get the information needed to determine why the issue has occurred and then how to improve any program or process to achieve success.

Knowing how to conduct focus-group research can be an essential element for school improvement. This is an untapped opportunity and resource in the educational arena. Districts today are so engaged in analyzing quantitative data to increase student achievement they are missing an essential element, that being the determination of why a certain phenomenon is occurring that may deter student achievement. Focus-group research is the answer.

In the introduction section of this book, I discussed the circumstances surrounding the Pittsburgh Steelers draft of 2007. They did not draft one running back even though it seemed this was an area of need. The entire city seemed to be asking, "What were they thinking?"

As it turned out, they were justified in what they did, as the running backs they already had on their roster stepped in and did an admirable job. Once again, the Steelers organization obviously did their research, and it paid off. What was at stake for them was millions of dollars in salaries, as well as the pressure to put a championship-caliber team on the field. What is at stake for educators is the challenge of determining a means to provide the best education possible for the millions of children in our schools. It is through focus groups that the once-silenced voices will finally have a shareholder's stake in decisions that need their support to assure successful innovations for the future of our schools.

References

Freire, P. (2000). *Pedagogy of the oppressed*. New York: The Continuum International Publishing Group.

Kowalski, T. J. (1995). *Case studies on educational administration*. White Plains, NY: Longman Publishers USA.

Lasswell, H. D., & Kaplan, A. (1950). *Power and society: A framework for political inquiry*. New Haven: Yale University Press.

Weber, M. (1947). *The theory of social and economic organization*. New York: Oxford University Press.

Weber, M. (1968). *Economy and society*. Totowa, NJ: Bedminster.

Young, I. M. (1990). *Justice and the politics of difference*. Princeton: Princeton University Press.

About the Author

Joseph D. Latess has devoted twenty-nine years of his life to education as a teacher, coach, and administrator. He began his career in public education as a health and physical education teacher and coach. His love for education and desire to impact schools and communities on a larger scale led him to administration, where he has served school districts as assistant principal, principal, and assistant superintendent. He has published articles that have appeared in state and national education publications. He currently serves as assistant superintendent of the Shaler Area School District near Pittsburgh, Pennsylvania.